complete home
decorating

LOWE'S®
Home Improvement Warehouse

complete home decorating

STAFF FOR THIS BOOK

Developmental Editor: *Linda J. Selden*

Text and Research: *Christine Barnes (principal), Cynthia Bix, Marc Cassini, Robert Labelle, Rob Lutes, Neale McDevitt, Brian Parsons, Marcia Williamson.* "Elements of a Room" by *Christine Olson Gedye*

Design Consultant: *Juliana Edlund, ASID*

Copy Editor: *Barbara J. Braasch*

Photo Director/Stylist: *JoAnn Masaoka Van Atta*

Art Director: *Alice Rogers*

Page Production: *Linda M. Bouchard*

Illustrator: *Beverley Bozarth Colgan*

Color Palettes: *Christine Barnes, Joan Malter Osburn, Juliana Edlund*

Photo Researcher: *Emily Abernathy-Jones*

Production Coordinator: *Danielle Javier*

Proofreader: *Mary Roybal*

Other Contributors: *Philippe Arnoldi, Danny-Pierre Auger, Linda Bryant, Lorraine Doré, Joan Beth Erickson, Martin Francoeur, Joey Fraser, Dominique Gagné, Pascale Hueber, Denise Lafontaine, Anne-Marie Lemay, Francine Lemieux, Karl Marcuse, Allan Ostroff, Aldo Parise, Monique Riedel, Jean Angrignon Sirois.*

We'd especially like to thank DCS Decor, Dovetail Design, and Eric Stramberg of Lighting Design Lab. We would also like to acknowledge the Pasadena Showcase House of Design, the Napa Valley Designer Showcase, and the San Francisco Decorator Showcase.

COVER: *Plants and accessories set an inviting tone for this sunny dining room.*
INTERIOR DESIGN: *Trish Dietze*
PHOTOGRAPHY: *Jamie Hadley*
COVER DESIGN: *Vasken Guiragossian*
PHOTO DIRECTION: *JoAnn Masaoka Van Atta*

LOWE'S COMPANIES, INC.

Bob Tillman, *Chairman/CEO/President*

Karena Bailey, *Merchandise Manager*

Melissa S. Birdsong, *Director, Trend Forecasting and Design*

Robin Gelly, *Merchandiser*

Bob Gfeller, *Senior VP, Marketing*

Jean Melton, *VP, Merchandising*

Mike Menser, *Senior VP, General Merchandise Manager*

Gregg Plott, *Director, Marketing*

Dale Pond, *Executive VP, Merchandising*

Be sure to visit our web site at www.lowes.com

10 9 8 7 6 5 4 3 2 1

First printing November 2001
Copyright © 2001, Sunset Publishing Corporation, Menlo Park, CA 94025. First edition. All rights reserved, including the right of reproduction in whole or in part in any form.

ISBN 0-376-01253-6
Library of Congress Control Number: 2001088723
Printed in the United States.

Readers note: Almost any do-it-yourself project involves risk of some sort. Your tools, materials, and skills will vary, as will conditions at your project site. Lowe's Companies, Inc., and the editors of this book have made every effort to be complete and accurate in the instructions. We will, however, assume no responsibility or liability for injuries, damages, or losses incurred in the course of your home decorating or improvement projects. Always follow manufacturers' operating instructions in the use of tools and observe all standard safety precautions.

PREFACE

AT LOWE'S, WE'VE BEEN HELPING PEOPLE CREATE BEAUTIFULLY DECORATED HOMES FOR MORE THAN FIVE DECADES. NOW WE WANT TO HELP MAKE YOUR DECORATING PROJECTS EASIER, AND MORE ENJOYABLE, TOO. WITHIN THE PAGES OF THIS BOOK YOU'LL FIND GREAT IDEAS FOR PLANNING AS WELL AS INFORMATION TO GUIDE YOU TOWARD GREAT RESULTS—AND THE HOME YOU'VE ALWAYS WANTED.

This easy-to-use book is divided into five chapters, all designed to make you comfortable with the process of decorating. "Room-by-Room Design" provides a tantalizing look at a gallery of exciting rooms, from kitchens to family rooms. "Practical Design" and "Getting Color Right" offer fascinating short courses on the principles of design and color. Next, you'll examine the "Elements of a Room," a resource guide to everything from paint to furniture to light fixtures. And in "Home Decorating Techniques and Projects," you'll find easy instructions for all kinds of do-it-yourself projects, large and small. We invite you to read, enjoy, and ponder a thousand intriguing ideas in the pages of this book; then come back to Lowe's and choose just the right ingredients for all your decorating needs.

The talents and energies of many people went into making this book. Special thanks to Christine Barnes and Juliana Edlund who were instrumental in developing, creating, and reviewing content. We are especially grateful to the many others who assisted in the planning, and to those who generously allowed us to share their examples of beautifully designed rooms. (You will find their names and credits on pages 424–429.) So no matter what the scope of your project is, *Lowe's Complete Home Decorating* will inspire and guide you through the process of making your home a reflection of who you really are. Be fearless, be creative, and have fun!

MELISSA S. BIRDSONG
Lowe's Director, Trend Forecasting and Design

contents

How to Use This Book

"IT'S GREAT TO BE HOME!" WHO HASN'T SAID THAT AFTER A GRUELING DAY AT WORK—OR EVEN ON RETURN FROM A TERRIFIC VACATION? THINK HOW GOOD IT FEELS TO BE AT HOME CURLED UP ON THE SOFA WITH A CUP OF COFFEE, THE FAMILY CAT, AND THE SUNDAY PAPER.

Home is where we spend a large part of our time—where we experience life's joys and escape life's hassles. No wonder making our home a great place to be is such a high priority for us, whether we own a spacious house or rent the tiniest apartment.

Decorating your home to make it attractive, comfortable, and efficient is a simple goal—yet one not always easy to achieve. Not knowing where to begin, many of us never start at all, though we may keep decorating on the shortlist of projects we'd like to undertake—when we get up the nerve or find the time.

Now is the time. If you're holding this book in your hands, you're ready to search and to plan, perhaps to choose and to act. In short, if you've gotten this far, you're ready to begin decorating your home. Wouldn't it be helpful to have a guidebook that assists and reassures you every step of the way?

That's what *Lowe's Complete Home Decorating* is intended to do: to guide you, from start to finish, through the creative process of decorating. At our retail stores, we've always offered a wealth of materials, products, and services for all your home decorating needs.

Now, in this book, we'll lead you through every part of the process, no matter what the scope of your project. Perhaps you're thinking of a low-commitment project or considering one single purchase—a fresh coat of paint for your child's bedroom or new wood flooring to replace aging carpet. That's fine; you are welcome to dip into this book at whatever point you need help. But if you're plan-

ning a more involved project, such as designing a new living room from top to bottom, you may want to read the first four chapters in sequence. Then, if you're eager to do some of the projects yourself, you can turn to the last chapter for step-by-step help. Here's what you'll find in "Room-by-Room Design," "Practical Design," "Getting Color Right," "Elements of a Room," and "Home Decorating Techniques and Projects."

ROOM-BY-ROOM DESIGN To get you started with the exciting process of gathering ideas, this 200-plus photo chapter is packed with decorating inspiration for every room in

the house. Its room-by-room organization makes it easy to zero in on those spaces that interest you. A recurring special feature, "A Closer Look," provides in-depth, illustrated analysis of the decorating process for five different rooms. The last section, "Open House," shows you how designers carry a color-and-design theme throughout a single home. Whether you find a whole-house look that you'd like to interpret in your own home or a single furnishing that's just right for your room, ideas are what this chapter is all about.

PRACTICAL DESIGN What is design? Simply put, good design is about what's *appropriate* and *pleasing.* A well-designed room has appropriate furnishings and color as well as pleasing proportions and an atmosphere of well-being. If something is "off" in a room's design, you can probably sense it. Taking you beyond that intuition and teaching you how to consciously use the principles of design for a harmonious effect—or to affect a remedy for a room with a problem—is the purpose of this chapter. It's easier than you think, and examples bring the concepts to life.

GETTING COLOR RIGHT Color is integral to the design of any room. Discussions of color in decorating books and magazines usually stress how to choose colors and where to place them in a room. This chapter does that—and much more. As you delve into the magic of color, revel in the knowledge that color is free! Tile or fabric made in colors you love costs no more than its equivalent in colors you hate. An understanding of color—not a big budget—is what gives you the means to create a great scheme. In this chapter, you'll find everything you need to know to use color effectively, including 16 special ready-made color palettes from Lowe's.

ELEMENTS OF A ROOM The materials and furnishings that go into a home are the building blocks

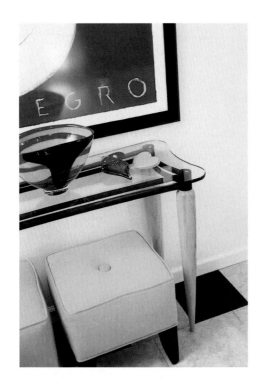

of decorating, and choosing them is both a delight and a challenge. Half the battle is knowing what you're looking for and what's available. This chapter is a resource guide that covers it all, from paint to furniture to flooring and light fixtures. You'll even see the furnishings and materials in context, providing you with yet more decorating ideas. Case studies detail the successful use of a particular design element, such as wall treatments or lighting, in one home.

HOME DECORATING TECHNIQUES AND PROJECTS

When you can take a design idea and—with your own two hands—turn it into a reality, you gain an unequaled feeling of pride and satisfaction. In this chapter, we give you an opportunity to do just that. From straightforward projects such as covering switch plates, to more complex projects like creating special paint effects on your walls and floors, you'll find plenty of practical help. Presented in easy-to-follow, fully illustrated steps, each project details all you need to know to create beautiful effects throughout your home.

As you read through this book, keep in mind that decorating is much more than just choosing a paint color, buying a chair, or hanging wallpaper. It's really about discovering who you are and how you want to live. Every decision you make, every brush stroke you paint, becomes an expression of your personal style. And remember that Lowe's will be there, every step of the way, to provide you with the materials and know-how you'll need to express that style to the fullest. Consider your options, make decisions, and implement your plan; then settle in and enjoy the rewards of your efforts. Once you've completed your decorating project, "It's great to be home!" will take on a deeper, richer meaning.

ROOM-BY-ROOM DESIGN

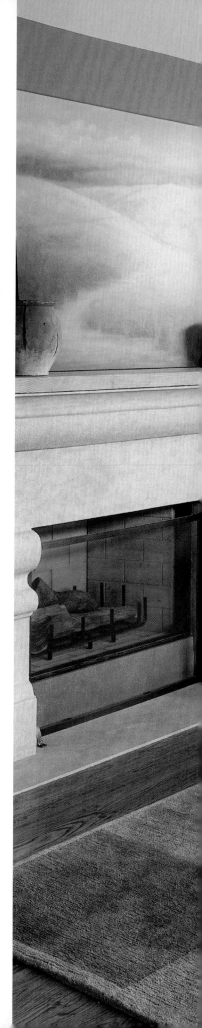

LEAFING THROUGH DECORATING MAGA-
ZINES, DO YOU WONDER HOW THOSE
BEAUTIFUL ROOMS COME TOGETHER
WITH SUCH APPARENT EASE?
Interior designers can draw on years of
experience and training to work their magic;
many of the rest of us could use, shall we say, a little help.

That help is here, in the form of visual inspiration and in-depth
captions that point out the decorating elements and detail the decisions behind the design. More than 200 photos of rooms—from
entries to kitchens to children's rooms and outdoor living spaces—
grace this chapter. You can use the examples to find a look you like,
spark your own decorating plan, or simply get acquainted with the
range of contemporary and traditional styles. Look, read, and take it
all in as this chapter wends its way through the house, room by room.

A WARM WELCOME

IF ROOMS COULD SPEAK, the entry would say "Welcome!" The space just inside the front door is usually the first part of your home visitors see, granting it a significance much greater than its size. To get off to a good start, choose one furnishing or accessory—a work of art or a focal-point table—for the entry and build on it. To achieve a smooth visual flow, use colors from adjoining rooms in the entry to hint at what's to come.

An entry has a functional role to play as well. Guests stop briefly in the entry when they first arrive. A mirror on the wall allows them the opportunity to steal a reassuring glance as they come in—and lets you check your appearance as you leave. A console table provides a convenient surface on which to lay keys and mail. If the entry has no closet, a hall tree is a useful addition.

Whether your entry is a "real room" or just a place to pause, let it greet your guests with style, and they will be delighted to come in.

There is perhaps no better way to beckon guests into your home than with fresh flowers.

More than a place to hang your hat, this painted French hall tree with marble tabletop, circa 1900, is a stunning focal-point furnishing. Such a commanding piece requires minimal accompaniment. The iron chandelier is from the same period.

FACING PAGE: A bold entry in a glamorous 1940s house is a fine example of two design principles: Matching lamps and twin doors illustrate mirror-image symmetrical balance. The bittersweet-chocolate-and-cream rug repeats the mirror motifs on a larger scale, setting up a pleasing visual rhythm. Cast-metal lamps based on Chinese cloud motifs and a fluted demilune table contribute to what designer William McWhorter calls "an exercise in squares and curves."

ABOVE: Natural materials and Asian elements set the style in this contemporary entry. Venetian plaster walls, finished with gold metallic wax, radiate warmth and reflect light. Curvilinear accessories, among them a column lamp with an Egyptian papyrus shade, repeat the circular motifs in the painting. (The antique calligraphic panel reads, "What happiness as the night rain passes and the seedlings burst forth.")

RIGHT: Light becomes an essential element in a small, windowless entry. An ottoman covered in cocoa-colored moiré slides under the marble-topped table and comes out when it's needed in the adjoining living room. (For a look at the living room, see page 203.) Architectural illustrations become art when framed and hung where a mirror might be expected.

BELOW: A wicker planter box filled with winsome flowers gives this little back-door entry its charm. Semisheer café curtains on the windows and a matching stretch panel on the door diffuse light and provide privacy.

ABOVE: An antique rug, a French bench, and a frameless painting are the only elements in this simple entry, which opens into the living room on the left and the family room on the right. Fresco-colorwashed walls and washed-wood floors add texture to the minimal look.

European country style greets visitors to this whimsical cottage. The look is decidedly vertical, from the intricately carved antique hall tree to the flanking topiaries and oversize umbrella. The bold black-and-white floor is a pleasing contrast to the curved shapes and muted hues. (To see more rooms in this home, turn to pages 60–61.)

GATHERING PLACES

DESCENDANT OF the Victorian parlor, the living room was for decades the main gathering place in the home. People actually *lived* in their living rooms.

With the advent of the family room in the early 1960s, living rooms assumed a more formal, public role: a special space for entertaining, separated from the casual clutter of daily life.

In homes with both living and family rooms that pattern continues, and the two coexist peacefully, each with its own purpose. But the function of the traditional living room has evolved slowly from a showplace for company to a tranquil space where family members congregate for quiet pursuits.

Still the dressiest room in the home, it's the perfect place to display family heirlooms or heritage pieces and more vulnerable objects. Its palette can be carried with subtle variation throughout the house, providing continuity and simplifying color and design decisions. Is it any wonder that when we decide to decorate we often start with this primary room?

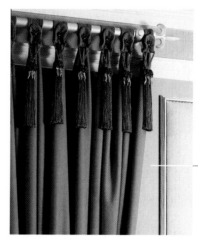

Rosettes and tassels with silver charms embellish luxuriant wool-felt panels. Technically tab-top curtains, these window treatments were never meant to move.

Shimmering neutrals pervade this formal, neoclassical-style living room. An antique Persian rug is the foundation for the smoky color palette. Re-covered in brushed aluminum, the mantel, original to the house, becomes modern. Upholstered wall panels, silver accents, and elaborate moldings everywhere make this corner an elegant retreat.

One of a pair flanking the fireplace, a large-scale mirror with an undulating gold frame brings spontaneity and sparkle to the room. The console table, itself grand and weighty, complements the mirror. (For a view of the fireplace and tables, see page 192.)

A bronze zigzag table adds a contemporary element of surprise. The patinated finish is striking against luxurious bullion fringe and the traditionally patterned rug.

The young owners of this traditional home wanted a living room that was formal yet livable. Glazed walls and millwork highlight stunning architectural features. The warmly colored, richly textured furnishings come from several different design traditions: English lounge chairs opposite a Lawson sofa, a pair of Regency chairs in chocolate leather, and a red leather barrelback chair.

A 19th-century Venetian-glass mirror hangs above a Swedish commode of similar vintage, creating a striking focal-point wall. "The goal," according to the designer, "was to create a contemporary forties look, softened by the graceful lines of antiques."

A palette of espresso brown and icy blue befits a space described by designer Kendall Wilkinson as an elegant private studio. Matte-finish paint covers the walls with warm color, while millwork painted a high-sheen silver accentuates the room's fine architectural detailing. A wide chaise upholstered in corduroy velvet, a Louis XV accent chair, and silk curtain panels topped by a "bodice" cornice impart continental sophistication.

BELOW: On the opposite side of the room, a tuxedo sofa covered in sterling blue mohair faces a pair of mocha-colored, quilted-silk chairs. The reproduction pedestal table is one of many silver accents linking the two inner rooms. Underfoot, looped wool carpet does a disappearing act in this new-neutral scheme.

ABOVE: At home, designer David Dalton exults in shapes and textures rather than colors and patterns. "Because I work with color, which goes in and out of style," he says, "I prefer to live with neutrals." A new-neutral color scheme, punctuated with black, sets the mood in his contemporary living room.

FACING PAGE, TOP: Innovative window treatments hide an unattractive view yet allow light to enter the room. David had the iron grills fabricated, then backed with rice paper and attached to the frames.

FACING PAGE, BOTTOM: Birds and branches were painted on mirror using sign-painters' paint formulated for glass surfaces; the mirror pieces were then applied to the cabinet.

a closer look

A quintessentially traditional living room designed by Elizabeth Hill exudes elegance and serenity. The light-value, new-neutral color scheme allows the furnishings and floor to blend for an airy, expansive effect. Buttercream walls bathe the room in flattering warmth; off-white accentuates the millwork and tray ceiling.

A crewel-embroidered shade trimmed with twisted cord and bead fringe tops a candle-stick base. The shade glows when the lamp is on; reflected light from the beads adds a bit of sparkle.

FACING PAGE, BOTTOM: In the adjoining dining room, the wall color shifts from creamy yellow to pale pink, yet the transition is smooth because both colors are light in value and low in intensity. The pink-toned area rug under the dining table establishes the monochromatic palette and ties the room together.

RIGHT: An open floral display contributes height and echoes the graceful lines of the piano.

a closer look

Silk taffeta is a timeless fabric for traditional schemes, adapting gracefully to many furniture styles. Striped fabrics of all kinds are classic companions to floral and other naturalistic patterns.

A Bird's-Eye View A traditional furniture plan—the sofa against one wall, facing the fireplace, with the love seat, Louis XV chair, and bergère chair placed at angles—visually widens the long, narrow room. Side chairs with open arms and exposed legs are a good choice for this room because they provide extra seating yet do not fill the space as upholstered pieces might. This arrangement serves both focal points: the fireplace flanked by French doors and the baby grand piano.

DESIGN DETAILS

1 One-way curtain panels trimmed in tassel fringe and topped by bell valances frame the French doors without interfering with the view. Mounting the top treatments at the point where the tray ceiling begins accentuates the height of the doors.

2 Gold in the Louis XV chair, art frames, and accessories serves as a glistening accent.

3 Using the same fabric on the sofa and love seat—silk shantung in this instance—links upholstered pieces of different styles and creates a sense of unity.

4 Unmatched wood pieces—a rectangular end table (in the foreground), round table (at one end of the sofa), and chest (near the dining entrance; see the bird's-eye view)—add visual weight to the pale scheme.

5 A large-scale mirror visually anchors the piano wall and reflects the dining room at the opposite end of the living room. The tall plant is an important eye-mapping element.

6 The baby grand piano adds an element of dark contrast to the light room and fills the corner beautifully with its dramatic form.

7 For occasional seating when family and guests gather, a tufted ottoman with box-pleated skirt and tassel fringe was added.

8 A marble-topped, open-frame coffee table permits a full view of the patterned rug, maximizing the sense of spaciousness.

9 The open pattern, new-neutral hues, and light-to-medium values of the rug are in keeping with the quiet sophistication of the room.

DINING IN

MORE THAN ANY OTHER ROOM in the house, the dining room has fallen victim to lifestyle changes. Few home-owners have space to spare, and what was once a room reserved for family suppers and formal dinners now doubles as a bill-paying station, a sewing studio, or homework headquarters. For some busy families, just clearing off the dining room table is a project in itself!

If you are fortunate enough to have a dedicated dining room, by all means play it up. Link it to the adjoining room (usually the living room) with related colors and patterns—a deeper version of the living room's wall color, for example, or a larger-scale plaid. When the dining area has fuzzier boundaries—a space for a two-person table in a breakfast nook or a family-size table off the kitchen, perhaps—emphasize the "room" with a freestanding piece of furniture like a hutch and define it with a distinctive area rug.

No matter where you gather to eat, make it a special spot. After all, many of life's most important conversations take place around the dining room table.

An antique lead-crystal cracker jar with a pewter top reflects light and echoes the lines of the metal grille behind it.

The view of graceful oaks through a wide bay window influenced the decorating plan for this serene yet casual dining area. A mélange of materials—metal, glass, wood, and rattan—in a range of textures and low-intensity colors sets a quiet mood. The circular table and area rug emphasize the room's gentle angles.

This contemporary dining room offers appealing simplicity of design that shows off the warmth and smooth texture of the wood walls and ceiling and the gleaming waxed-pine table. At night, dramatic lighting envelops the room in an atmosphere of intimacy.

Ivory-colored columns mark the entrance to the dining room and add a neoclassical element. Antique, hand-painted botanical engravings hanging above a single dining chair reiterate the traditional theme.

Although traditional in style, this open dining area also incorporates a number of contemporary design elements. Round-backed dining chairs upholstered in a large-scale silk plaid are a modern takeoff on the Hepplewhite chair; an antique French needlepoint rug in the same soft hues rests on mahogany floors. Buttercream yellow walls and large windows with simple curtain panels stacked back maximize light in an often cloudy climate.

A 300-year-old hutch from Ireland, complete with names carved into its surface and well-worn edges, anchors the room and houses a collection of antique English dishes. The primitive painted screen was a French flea-market find.

Loose brushstrokes and bright red color are the essence of this art fabric, discovered by the homeowner on a trip to southern France. A layer of batting under the fabric gives upholstered walls their appealing dimensional quality; same-fabric welt finishes the edges.

A hand-painted fabric depicting sprightly scenes from France is a fresh interpretation of traditional toile du Jouy. Antique furnishings, among them an African kilim rug, a French farmhouse chandelier, and a domestic colonial bench, give the room its eclectic, not-so-serious look.

Wood floors and French doors painted "country green" provide the perfect environment for casual cottage dining. A vintage tablecloth and black-and-white floor cloth inject color and pattern into the setting.

A lakefront cottage is the ideal dwelling in which to indulge a love of wicker, quilts, and a blue-and-white theme. Rough-hewn chairs pull up to a traditional trestle table. The painted mirror is playfully embellished with buttons in the shape of hands.

White takes on an entirely different feel in what designer David Dalton calls his "jewel box" dining room. David goes against conventional wisdom when it comes to small spaces: "I like to use fewer but larger objects for a sense of drama." The "flying saucer" light fixture and ballpoint-pen-inspired table are of his own design.

TAKING IT EASY

A FREEWHEELING SPACE in which members of the household read the paper, watch videos, catch the evening news, listen to CDs, or just "hang out," the family room hardly needs defining. It's the center of family recreation, the best room in which to spend that delectable downtime.

Yet for all its importance, this comfortable, casual room has in the past been the repository of mismatched, hand-me-down furnishings that even the dog was welcome to sit on. That has changed: the family room is now regarded as worthy of decorating dollars and ideally suited to a do-it-yourself approach.

Some lucky homeowners can decorate the family room from top to bottom; if you're in this category, you are free to start afresh. More typically, the family room needs sprucing up, not a complete makeover. Here's your chance to work with what you have—for instance, buying a new club chair covered in a kidproof fabric that looks good with the sofa you still like. Before you begin, however, check with the family—because that's what it's all about.

Vintage mixes with modern in this arrangement: an abstract painting rests on an antique painted chest, which stands behind a traditional chair upholstered in a contemporary checked fabric.

A matching chenille love seat and sofa "float" in this light-filled family room, making the most of the space and creating a cozy inner room. A pair of chairs facing the window forms a secondary seating area. Both groupings rest on Persian rugs placed parallel to the walls—a design trick for grounding floating arrangements.

"The clients knew exactly what they wanted," says designer Molly McGowan—
"an elegant yet relaxed look that would adapt equally well to family life and
entertaining." Warm, earthy colors and textures did the job: cinnamon chenille
sofas, a cast-form mantel, a variety of woods, and woven-grass window shades.
The painting, introduced near the end of the project, depicts the ethereal quality
of the surrounding hills. The result? A great place to gather.

RIGHT: A contemporary Tibetan wool rug makes a bold yet soft color statement in terra-cotta and new-neutral green. The square coffee table repeats the pattern of the rug.

BELOW: When situated on the wall opposite a room's entrance, a media center can easily become an unintentional focal point. Planning paid off in this family room, where the custom cabinet was positioned across a corner adjacent to the entrance. There it is easily seen from each sofa but is not the star of the room. Made of pine, with hand-pegged doors, the cabinetry features dentil detailing beneath crown molding and speaker cloth that matches the TV screen.

A breakfast table (left) overlooks the family room and shares views of the television and fireplace. Using the same granite on the countertops and the fireplace surround strengthens the connection between the two spaces. A pair of columns, a half wall, and a change in level (below) set the family room apart from the kitchen-dining space, yet the visual transition from one area to the other is smooth. Repetition of the sofa colors and twining motifs in the custom rug is a good example of the design principle of rhythm.

The gleam of copper, the grain of wood, the texture of chenille—this
warm, inviting family room is a study in good design, as well as an
example of practicality and comfort. A reading chair near a window takes
advantage of natural light; a large coffee table between seating pieces
provides ample space for snacks and books. Tying it all together in style
is a color scheme of near-complementary orange and blue-green.

The homeowners call this space in their authentic Arts and Crafts house an "outdoor retreat" because it feels like an extension of their garden. This enclosed patio functions as a family room, with a dining table that doubles as a game table and plenty of seating for family and friends.

BELOW, TOP: Crafted of intricately woven bamboo and red glass insets, an Arts and Crafts lamp becomes a focal-point accessory on a distressed, painted wood sideboard.

BELOW, BOTTOM: A conservatory-style bird cage adds height to the corner and makes a lifestyle point: pets belong in your family room, because they are a part of the family.

a closer look

A presentation urn filled with moss adds intense color, lush texture, and classic form to the contemporary scheme.

Designer Kaidon Erwin took a two-pronged approach to this spacious room: "This is a modern family that loves contemporary style but appreciates antiques and understands the depth and nuance they add to a room. At the same time, they needed durable furnishings—nothing could be precious." He delivered—a beautiful design for everyday living.

FACING PAGE, BOTTOM: Contemporary art is the focal point of this corner grouping. Accessories, including a terra-cotta sculpture of two jousters and a copy of a fifties art lamp, balance the large-scale painting. Faux-finished walls with subtle color and texture make a quiet backdrop. An oversize club chair—the seat is 45 inches deep—allows family members to curl up and tuck their feet in.

a closer look

Synthetic suede on the Art Deco sofa and mohair on the club chairs are both soft yet durable fabrics. The braided matting material—abaca, a fiber made from the stalks of banana trees—has both actual and visual texture. Linen fabrics are ideal for accent pillows.

A BIRD'S-EYE VIEW A traditional arrangement of furnishings—matching chairs flanking a sofa, with a coffee table in between—works well in a room devoted to family activities. The sense of symmetrical balance carries through to the corners, even though the antique walnut tables are different shapes. On the wall opposite the sofa, the off-center placement of the TV, art, and accessories keeps the look casual. (For a view of this wall, see page 214.) Throughout this room the scale is bold, the mood playful.

DESIGN DETAILS

1 To lighten existing dark paneling, the designer used a decorative paint technique known as faux bois ("false wood" in French). The base coat was a robin's-egg blue, brushed on thickly to mimic wood grain. Two coats of a transparent glazing compound came next, followed by an application of dark brown wax, in cake form. (The wax catches in the paint's texture, enhancing the graining effect.)

2 Loosely woven silk- and-linen panels feature a hand-printed design reminiscent of the naturalistic motifs seen on Hawaiian quilts. Dark chocolate brown, rather than black, was chosen to warm the cool palette. Matchstick shades behind the panels control light and preserve privacy.

3 Square rods and rings made of steel are in keeping with the contemporary styling. The triple pleats, tacked at the top rather than the base, are known as Paris pleats.

4 Two antique, drop-leaf dining tables, one at either end of the room, ground the light furnishings and keep the space from looking like a "period" (modern, in this case) room.

5 A large-scale coffee table features a steel frame with panels made of medium-density fiberboard that's been faux finished to resemble wood.

6 For a shot of warm color, a brilliant orange shawl is draped over one chair.

7 A contemporary twist table made of creamy white concrete is similar in visual weight and value to the chair it accompanies.

8 The designer chose a braided abaca mat for its ropelike look. Its large-scale pattern balances the oversize pieces in the room.

OPEN LIVING

A TREND TOWARD open floor plans and a preference for casual living engendered the "great" room—a combination kitchen, dining, living, family, and media room, all in one space. It might be described as "the room where everyone wants to be, and nobody wants to leave."

With its multiple functions and nonstop use, a great room presents a decorating challenge: unifying disparate activity areas. Painting the walls a single distinctive color does the job nicely. To imply inner rooms, use your palette colors in different quantities. With a green-and-yellow scheme, for example, you might emphasize green in the main seating area but yellow in the kitchen.

Hand-painted limestone tiles placed among plain ones depict the animals of the French countryside.

Continuing the same flooring throughout also yields a smooth, seamless look. If you prefer a change underfoot—such as limestone in the kitchen and carpet in the living area—choose materials of a similar value to avoid a jarring contrast.

A room where the whole family lives (except when they're sleeping)? Now that's a "great" idea.

A love of Provence and a desire for an open, airy space inspired this refreshing blue-and-yellow great room. A deep blue chenille sofa and a chair upholstered in a textured yellow fabric establish the palette. Hand-painted flowers grace the cooktop's hood; blue-and-yellow Roman shade valances link the kitchen with the main seating area.

A contemporary cottage's interior design expresses the homeowners' love of nature and their desire to venture "into the woods." The great room is awash with warm colors: integral-color plaster walls, glowing maple cabinetry, limestone floors, plush furnishings, and a new-neutral carpet.

ABOVE: Light-value, low-intensity colors from the yellow-to-red zone of the color ring are ideal for furnishings and walls, where more intense hues might overpower. The ceiling-mounted light fixtures are fabricated of acrylic plastic and copper.

RIGHT: Color-washed insets accentuate the detailing of kitchen cabinets and harmonize with less intense integral-color concrete counters.

FACING PAGE: A sofa slipcovered in summery canvas duck floats in this great room, creating a cozy inner room for television viewing. (In the fall and winter, the slipcover comes off to reveal chenille upholstery.) A jagged-edge granite slab on the island is in keeping with the natural materials and relaxed style.

BELOW: Positioned to function as a coffee table, an antique trunk adds visual weight to the setting. Plants and accessories atop the entertainment armoire fill what is sometimes a "problem" space.

A loose display of
early fall foliage
and eclectic green-
ery provides color
and texture in this
neutral scheme.

Epitomizing European country charm and style, this great room includes both antique and newly crafted furnishings and accessories. The hood, constructed of drywall and finished to resemble plaster, was hand painted with fruit images. It was then sanded to remove much of the color, leaving the impression of age. Coral-colored tumbled-marble tile makes up the backsplash; the countertops are of black granite.

ABOVE: A freestanding hutch illustrates the trend toward unfitted furniture in kitchen areas. Its distressed white finish makes it a versatile piece, should the homeowners redecorate or move. Antique French dining chairs with rattan seats become dark-value accents in the light room.

FACING PAGE, BOTTOM: "Living month to month" takes on a positive meaning with these whimsical hand-painted pieces. Arranging a group of like accessories in a grid pattern turns them into one visual unit.

FACING PAGE: Inspired by a historic, handcrafted 1930s ski lodge, this two-story great room connects to a large eat-in kitchen. The loft overlooking the living area combines a children's playroom, a study, and a reading nook (see page 127). The focal point of this impressive room? What else—the massive, 34-foot-tall, freestanding basalt fireplace.

ABOVE: The furniture arrangement facilitates conversation and allows family members and guests to enjoy the fire; a built-in window seat on the far wall becomes a secondary, perhaps solitary, seating area.

RIGHT: Warm colors, woodsy patterns, and earth-inspired textures give the furnishings their comfortable, lodgelike quality.

a closer look

Set apart from the rest of the great room, the dining area takes advantage of a view of mature oaks and native plants. The painting and furniture have earthy colors, yet their textures range from nubby to smooth. The futuristic light fixture overhead, reminiscent of a mobile, is one of three in this great room.

ABOVE: Multicolored glass tile applied to the curved bar and kitchen backsplash reiterates hues in other areas of the room, in particular the ocher-colored media center on the opposite wall. Light entering through the clerestory windows gives the tile its luminous look.

The great room in a Bauhaus-style house built in the early 1960s boasts floor-to-ceiling windows, a real plus for its light-loving owners. The designer, David Ramey, warmed to the space as soon as he saw it: "The house was strong architecturally, in a style I could appreciate. I wanted to create a design that was in keeping with the distinctive architecture, but bring it into this century." Take a look at what he did.

a closer look

Hand-dyed, handwoven chenille in shades of moss, terra-cotta, and ocher covers the chair and chaise. The cube ottomans are upholstered in leather of similar hues. Glass tiles make the light dance around the curved bar.

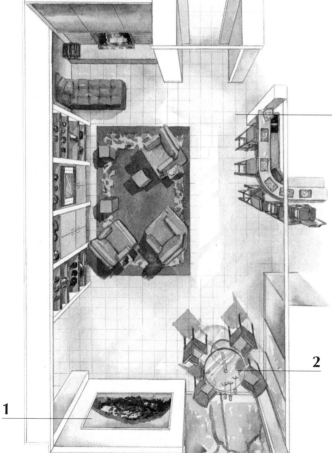

A BIRD'S-EYE VIEW   The homeowners wanted a room that was comfortable for them yet could easily accommodate family gatherings and casual parties. "A great room is just an enormous space unless you break it down into areas according to function," David says. He loosely divided the large room into inner rooms for eating (at the table and the bar), watching television, and lounging by the fire. The area rug delineates the main inner room. Traffic flows easily past the bar, around the chairs, or into the dining area.

DESIGN DETAILS

1 It all began with the "painting" (facing page), a digitally enhanced image from an acrylic painting on canvas. Blown up to twice its original size, it evokes the stippled brushwork of Pointillism and suggests a palette of nature's colors.

2 In keeping with the home's modern design and materials, the dining table is of stainless steel topped with glass. Leather chairs the color of bark show the influence of the outdoors.

3 Ceramic pieces created by the owners' son are showcased in stained shelving surrounding the focal-point media center.

4 Smooth leather ottomans contrast with the nubby textures throughout and increase the seating possibilities.

5 A wool Tibetan rug sets the stage for the rich, earth-colored furnishings. Warm, analogous colors ranging from yellow through red border its cool teal interior. (See page 185 for a detail.)

6 The stainless steel fireplace is original. Three layers of green glaze finish the adjoining wall, creating a cozy inner room.

7 Glass tiles were fabricated in three colors (lemon, tangerine, and earth) and two finishes (gloss and matte, or "sanded"). These variations in color and finish give the surface a pleasingly mottled look.

8 To minimize contrast and strengthen the color statement, the legs on the bar stools were dyed to match their leather seats.

THE HEART OF A HOME

WHO CAN STAY OUT of the kitchen? More than a place to prepare meals, the kitchen is the heart of the home, where parents share the day's news, kids eat around the clock (or so it seems), and guests congregate to chat with the cook. Everyone ends up in the kitchen, so you might as well make it look great.

"Decorating" this hardworking hub usually takes more than a new coat of paint. If you're in true remodel mode—and the kitchen is the room most often remodeled—you'll have plenty to ponder, from structural changes to surface coverings to new appliances. Happily, you'll find a mind-boggling array of efficient, innovative components and materials from which to choose.

If your goal is more modest—a new look without a major investment—choose quick decorating projects. A stenciled floor, new Roman shades, and beadboard applied to existing cabinets are examples of small changes that can make a big difference. Whether you're going all out or working with what you have, what's cookin' in the kitchen is creativity.

Cotton print fabric panels add color, pattern, and a touch of softness to pine kitchen cabinets.

Country style warms every detail of this homey kitchen, from the waxed-pine cabinetry, designed as furniture, to racks of dried flowers, display dishes, and stool cushions. The warm tones of the pine and saltillo floor pavers are enhanced by soft recessed lighting.

ABOVE: Bands at the upper and lower edges of the plaster hood feature key motifs set "on point." A pot faucet eliminates the need to tote water from sink to stove.

LEFT: Smaller metallic "keys" (accent inserts originally used to add structural strength) punctuate the backsplash tiles, reflecting light and breaking up the square-on-square tile pattern.

In this elegant yet informal kitchen, designer Molly McGowan used a range of natural materials in light but warm hues: Jerusalem limestone countertops, a tumbled-limestone backsplash, glass pendant lights, cherry cabinets, and oak flooring. The curved island, which features an antique glaze over paint, and the graceful bar stools soften the room's lines.

ABOVE: A classic Mediterranean house, built in 1927, "just needed to go French," says designer and homeowner Shirley Jensen. White walls and whitewashed birch cabinets give the room its clean-and-simple look. The fired-clay sink is French farmhouse style.

RIGHT: A "ground cover" painted on the original fir subflooring puts color and pattern underfoot. Before painting, the floor was sanded and whitewashed; after painting, it was sealed and then waxed.

Fueled by memories of Provence, Shirley designed an elevated
version of a French bread oven for her small breakfast area.
The facade is plaster, the hearth marble. Below the oven are
a display alcove and a compartment for storing firewood.

a closer look

Light dances playfully off glass tile in this art mosaic. The lyrical pattern, meant to suggest ribbonlike vines, is an essential element of the design, adding welcome curves and color to the angular room and low-key scheme. Look closely and you'll see a wide-ranging palette of hues reminiscent of decorative bottle glass, from lime green to lavender and cinnamon.

Designer Eugenia Erskine Jesberg's design goal for this elegantly proportioned kitchen and dining area was simple: "We chose to leave the tall, rectangular space virtually unchanged but to soften the angles and give it character using color and texture, in a mix of materials and finishes." The original light fixtures in the kitchen were set at the ceiling; new blown-glass bowls drop into the room to bring it down in scale.

FACING PAGE, BOTTOM: A wrought-iron, French-country chandelier over the dining table is topped by raffia shades trimmed with soft blue and green ribbons. An 18th-century mahogany Irish "wake table" coexists with an antique pine sideboard, showing that woods mix easily in casual settings.

a closer look

Design ingredients include a whimsical cotton-and-linen print with an open background for the swagged Roman shade; glass tile in shimmering, new-neutral hues for the backsplashes; and charcoal-colored granite for the kitchen countertops.

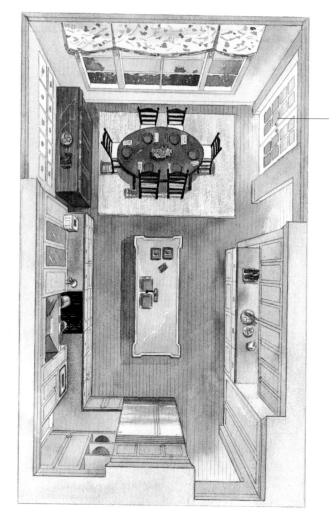

A BIRD'S-EYE VIEW Unless you choose to remodel, the kitchen is one room where you must work with existing features. When the dining area adjoins the kitchen, however, you have some options. Here, Eugenia chose a dining table that fills the space but does not crowd the island or the sideboard; in effect, the table's perimeter outlines an inner room. The shift in wall color, from a muted blue-green on the cabinets in the kitchen to a stronger yellow-green on the dining walls, also separates the areas.

DESIGN DETAILS

1 Sandblasted glass panels complement the cabinets; interior backlighting makes them glow at night.

2 Ten silk-screened oils, each 18 inches square, set 2 inches apart, make up one work of art. The designer chose this piece for its representational simplicity and contemporary style.

3 The tile backsplash visually links the countertops and cabinets; larger tiles surrounding the mosaic ease the transition.

4 An integral-color concrete island top in a hue that might be described as "artichoke" echoes the yellow-green of the dining walls. Beveled edges and corner detailing make the island unique.

5 Where crown molding meets the wall in the dining area, a subtle change in color occurs, from blue-green to yellow-green.

6 The cabinetry's subtle color began with a base coat of robin's-egg-blue paint, dulled and warmed slightly by an amber glaze. Brushed nickel pulls and knobs blend with the quiet color.

7 The yellow-green walls are of Venetian plaster, skimmed on with a trowel in a circular motion, and then waxed and polished to a faint sheen.

8 Handmade dishes in raspberry and apple green are bits of stronger color among less-intense hues. (See page 226 for a detail.)

9 Honed granite countertops in true-neutral gray play a supporting role and focus attention on the island.

10 Warm wood floors link the island, dining table, and sideboard.

REST AND RENEWAL

THE MOST PERSONAL living space in the house, the bedroom is often the most neglected—no doubt because it's seldom seen by guests. Considering its multi-purpose nature—sleep space, sanctuary, dressing area—doesn't your bedroom merit more attention?

Many of us, though we might not admit it, do a lot of living in this room that once contained only a bed and a chest of drawers. The typical bedroom is now larger and may be outfitted with a chair for reading, a chaise for stretching out, a desk for paperwork, exercise equipment for health, and an armoire or built-in unit for entertainment components. Up-to-date lighting for all of these activities is a must.

Practical functions aside, the bedroom is one place in the home where you can—and should—freely indulge your decorating whims. Choose a palette based on your very favorite color; combine patterns and textures that express your signature style, whether it's bright and breezy or quiet and contemplative. This is your oasis of privacy and serenity, and you have only yourself to please.

A piece of lace became a stencil used to embellish the walls with tone-on-tone pattern. The candlestick sconce includes an antique convex mirror.

An iron four-poster bed created by the room's designer, Amy Devault, is the focal point in this soothing bedroom of lichen green and other new-neutral hues. The behind-the-bed curtain breaks up the expanse of wall and softens the lines of the frame. The iron-and-glass light fixture etched with stars is known as a bell lantern.

FACING PAGE: A textbook example of rhythm through repetition, this small bedroom feels even cozier with its walls upholstered in yellow toile de Jouy and bed curtains fashioned from the same fabric in both yellow and blue. Even the fabric on the ottoman cushions appears again, in the bolster and as trim on the curtain panels. A matelassé coverlet lined in a simple blue print calms the profusion of color and pattern.

ABOVE: Sunshine yellow walls turn a cottage guest room into a cheery hideaway. An antique quilt and garden-style bed linens grace the hand-painted four-poster bed. The compact, rounded bouquet of roses on the nightstand is what floral designers call a pavé arrangement.

RIGHT: A light-filled yellow bedroom keeps its cool with summery, cream-colored cotton and linen bedding. White damask slipcovers on the chair, chair-and-a-half, and ottoman come off when fall arrives.

"Barely there" gray-blue pairs beautifully with buttery yellow in this serene, sophisticated bedroom; similar values (light) and intensities (low) make the colors more congenial. New neutrals in the window treatment and flooring maintain the quiet mood. A fanciful light fixture is a nod to the shell collection displayed in the niche.

RIGHT: Icy blue and yellow-green as soft as a whisper turn a guest bedroom into a cool retreat. A wool-crepe coverlet edged in white satin "melts" over a down comforter; the same white satin edges blue mohair pillows. A hand-painted Asian screen functions as an eye-mapping element and illusory headboard. Bouclé curtain panels screen the view.

BELOW: Restful blue is the color chosen most often for bedrooms; yellow, a warm hue, is often added to balance the visual temperature. In this master bedroom, a traditional floral pattern and two blue-and-cream checks carry on this time-honored palette.

ABOVE: Big, blocky accessories make a bold statement, especially when they contrast sharply with other elements in a room. A chocolate brown lamp and vase stand out against a backdrop of white walls, taupe curtain panels, and a graphic window "treatment" (see page 29 for more information).

RIGHT: A large-scale mirror, a white leather occasional chair, and an open accent table expand the perception of space in this small room.

The epitome of simplicity and sophistication, the design of this small bedroom is more about value than color itself. The bed is upholstered in medium-value natural linen; taupe cashmere pillows and a faux mink pillow function as darker accents on white bedding. The faux animal-print rug reads as medium-dark in value.

a closer look

An upholstered channel-back chair wears a whimsical cotton-viscose fabric with an avian theme. (Note that the birds have all escaped from their cages!) A tailored, slubbed-silk pillow sports braid trim and a flat ruffle.

FACING PAGE: Silk taffeta with gleaming satin stripes graces a channel-back love seat and ottoman. Using the same fabric in different colors—robin's-egg blue and coral pink here—is one way to achieve harmony in a room. This trick works best when the pattern is simple.

A fanciful print in springtime colors was the catalyst for this twins' bedroom designed by Gigi Rogers. Look closely at the comforter covers, and you will see twin girls among the flowers and ribbons. Gigi's secret to success with lots of color? "Keep the values light and choose a generous mix of patterns and textures."

a closer look

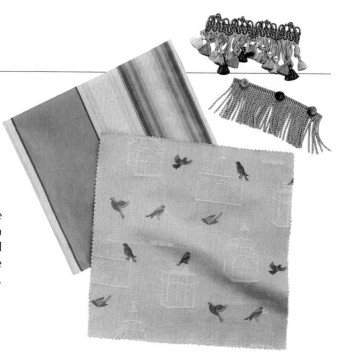

Stripes, prints, plaids, and passementerie combine with style when they share common colors yet do not "match." Another sound pattern principle applied here is to vary the scale of the designs for visual interest.

A BIRD'S-EYE VIEW Most bedroom plans begin with the bed, followed by the other furnishings, but you can still put furniture-arranging principles to work. This girls' bedroom features a number of inner rooms and activity areas: the love seat, channel-back chair, and ottoman make up a conversation area, outlined by the area rug; the desk between the beds and a secretary on the opposite wall provide study stations; the built-in window seat is the perfect place to curl up with a book or whisper with a friend.

DESIGN DETAILS

1 Simple cream-and-yellow-striped wallpaper is a good choice for a room filled with patterns and textures.

2 The silvery bedposts feature a classic Venetian finish of three washes over a base of blue.

3 Upholstered headboards make a soft yet structured backdrop for pillows. Gigi chose a unique shape that gives the beds height and provides support for reading or resting.

4 Just for fun, the French side chair with a plaid seat trimmed in contrasting welt sports a plain silk taffeta sunburst on its back.

5 Twin upholstered footstools are an elegant, old-fashioned touch—and make "springboards" for young girls when it's time for bed.

6 A print with large-scale flowers determines the room's color palette. Voluminous plaid silk-taffeta skirts in similar hues both contrast and complement.

7 Inverted pleat shades, sometimes called European or London shades, are modified versions of the Roman shade. The wide stripes echo the wallpaper and offer visual relief from the patterns.

8 New and old crystals decorate an antique Spanish chandelier, adding spots of color and a touch of whimsy to the room.

9 The bolsters and pillows in the window seat are elegantly trimmed with tassel-and-loop fringe, braid, and flat ruffles.

10 The designer chose a 1928-vintage rug for its low-intensity colors and open design.

BATHING

A SPLASH OF STYLE, a nod to efficiency—the formula for a successful bathroom is surprisingly simple.

Of all the rooms in the house, the bathroom has undergone the greatest transformation over the years. What was once a small, simple space for daily ablutions is now called upon to provide comfort in, and refuge from, a busy world.

The picture of beauty and simplicity, this beveled mirror bounces light and expands the space. For a touch of practicality, it also tilts.

New bathrooms tend to be larger; they also tend to be compartmentalized for multiple uses. And many are designed for relaxation as well as practicality, with spa-like whirlpool tubs and steam showers.

Working with the existing layout of your bathroom can be just as rewarding as new construction or a room-expanding remodel. When space is scarce, indulge in luxurious materials (you'll need less, after all, in a small area) and the latest fixtures, which come in finishes as varied as polished and brushed chrome, nickel, and brass. For the illusion of a more spacious room, install a pedestal sink or a console sink with vanity legs to reveal more of the walls and floor. Two trends especially worth noting are the introduction of freestanding furniture for storage and the conversion of vintage pieces to working sinks—proving that, even in the bathroom, what's old is new again.

A feeling of lightness and elegance characterize this small bath. Because of its open design, the mahogany vanity inhabits the space lightly; tumbled-limestone tile on walls and floors imparts a warm glow and natural texture.

ABOVE: A shallow marble-topped vanity features a large swivel mirror that also tilts up and down. Because the vanity is open and light in value, it appears to take up less space.

BELOW: Delightful touches abound in this spacious bath. Side-by-side vanities as well as cabinets are designed with the style and detail of custom furniture. Underfoot, tiles are set in a distinctive rug pattern. A door opens invitingly into a private rock garden with outdoor spa.

ABOVE: Antiqued and beveled limestone tile lines the walls and covers the floor in a spacious guest bath. Because limestone is a natural material and these tiles were handmade, they vary widely in coloration. To pay tribute to the era in which the house was built yet update the room with modern conveniences, the designer chose a reproduction 1920s Italian tub.

LEFT: A privacy half-wall is a useful feature in a one-room bath. A leather-topped reproduction stool introduces contrasting materials and shapes to the hardscape.

A marble washstand with a nickel-plated sink is both classic and up-to-date. The glass-rod towel bars and tilting mirror are simple yet functional elements. The many chrome trim pieces harken back to the home's architectural era.

The adjoining dressing room (left) is diminutive in scale and "tailored feminine" in style. A silk-upholstered chair pulls up to the built-in vanity, original to the house. Recessed lights at either side have been replaced with shallow glass shelving (below).

LEFT: A sophisticated palette of new neutrals—platinum, celadon, and oyster—was the choice for an elegant bath and dressing room in a 1940s home. Handmade ceramic tile surrounds a Greek key–trimmed mosaic on the shower wall. The dual-direction oval tub is also clad in tile; the floor is of gray-veined marble. Says designer Jean Horn, "The goal was to complement the architecture of the home, which is traditional in spirit, yet make it more glamorous."

A children's bath in a turn-of-the century house merited a remodel in keeping with post-Victorian style. The corbeled archway, medicine cabinets with crown molding, and window frame give the room its strong architectural character. The hexagonal ceramic tile on the floor was handmade, using a period fabrication process.

ABOVE: A brass wall-bracket sconce with an etched-glass shade is a reproduction of an early electric light fixture. What's that on the walls? Painted-on kelp beds and underwater creatures.

LEFT: The custom two-sink vanity with bow front—known as a bombé vanity—makes the most of the long, narrow space and adds an interesting set of curves. Its footed style suggests furniture rather than a typical built-in.

RIGHT: A striking architectural feature, this arched opening frames a spa bath appointed with colorwashed pine cabinetry, honed-marble walls, tumbled-marble floors, and integral-color plaster walls and ceiling.

BELOW: In keeping with the spirit of rejuvenation, the dressing room situated off the bath shown at right features built-in pine "lockers" and a bench topped with a box cushion. The unit frames a decorative leaded-glass window, which needs no further treatment.

FACING PAGE: Plaster walls the color of ripe papayas, colorwashed cabinetry, and integral-color concrete countertops balance a cool green slate shower and floor. The glass door leads to a private outdoor shower.

JUST FOR KIDS

"GO TO YOUR ROOM!" may no longer be such a punishment, now that kids' quarters are outfitted with fresh, fun furnishings and decorating materials. Sleeping is the least of what happens in these rooms: they've become personal environments with multiple purposes—play area, computer room, entertainment hub, study hall, and storage locker, to name a few. Flexibility is the name of the game in planning a child's room.

It's not enough to create a functional space. Kids are now more style conscious than ever, about everything from clothes to CD players. They want their rooms to look great, and that means gutsy colors and cool furnishings. Fortunately for parents, high-quality furniture that appeals to kids is plentiful and varied. Let your child pick the colors and major pieces, and resist the urge to overfurnish the room; kids need space to exercise their imaginations.

As you'll see on the following pages, some rooms are designed for a specific, limited time in a child's life, whereas others are geared for growth. Whatever your approach, make your child's room a memorable part of his or her young life.

A make-believe tea shop in the form of a gazebo is attached to the wall, as if resting in the limbs of the mural tree.

The decorating plan for this fairy-tale bedroom followed naturally from the hand-painted furniture. The patterns—none of them juvenile prints—combine for a more sophisticated look. Glazed walls, a tree mural, and a hand-painted border contribute to the charm.

FACING PAGE: Trompe l'oeil painting and vintage fabrics carry out a soft blue and yellow palette in a whimsical baby's room. Real birdhouses—one hanging, one on a stand—mingle with two-dimensional versions. A low occasional "table" next to a mini-armchair was fashioned from an old baby scale.

LEFT: Clothespins and fabric remnants turn a clothesline into a valance for white wood blinds.

BELOW: Small details make the difference in children's rooms. In the changing area, trompe l'oeil clotheslines are "strung" with tacked-on clothespins holding antique linens.

LEFT: A lighted crossing
signal incorporates
pegs for hanging hats.
The matching club
chair and ottoman are
that just-right size.

FACING PAGE, TOP: "All aboard!" is much more fun than "time for bed" when the bed looks like this. The train features beadboard strips on the upper level, a cutout (which functions as a sleep guard) at the head of the bed, a light in the smokestack, even a cowcatcher up front. Green suede-paint walls tone down the primary hues.

BELOW: Every part of this built-in window seat and storage unit—the glass-fronted cabinet, open shelving, cupboard below, and toy boxes under seat cushions—is used to stow kid stuff. Stagecoach-style valances are mounted above traditional shutters that do the real work of controlling light and maintaining privacy.

An attic nook becomes a make-believe cottage treehouse for this room's young occupant. A dormer window with its deep window seat forms a snug, crawl-in-and-curl-up space for daydreaming or reading. Through the trompe l'oeil fanlight window, the sky is always blue.

ABOVE: A profusion of fabrics speaks to a child's love of color, from exuberant florals to naturalistic prints and watery plaids. A maple dresser sports a darker-stained top to coordinate with the cherry sleigh bed. Not only the trompe l'oeil windows but even the "wallpaper" stripes are painted on.

LEFT: Handmade drawer pulls in the shape of little houses and a hand-painted lamp base keep to the cottage theme.

For a change, tone-on-tone striped wallpaper runs horizontally in this child's room, subtly altering the proportions of the square, tall space. A contemporary quilt in celery, raspberry red, and true blue balances warm and cool hues. The bed is new, crafted to look like an antique spool bed. An old, oversize wall clock serves a new purpose—as a place to set those very important belongings.

ABOVE: Everywhere this room's occupant looks—even up—there is something to delight the eye and ignite the imagination.

RIGHT: A blue-and-white check, embellished with machine stitching and trimmed with contrast piping, covers a boxed cushion. The cushion underneath is covered in a linen twill and edged with dotted chenille.

Colorwashed drawers with animal-head pulls help organize the inevitable kid clutter.

The color palette—red, blue, and yellow, with green—proves that primary colors are just as appropriate for older kids as for young ones. A bold check armchair is perfect for some serious downtime reading. Banded Roman shades are easily raised and lowered.

ABOVE: Once an unused storage area off a wide hallway, this children's study now bustles with purpose and activity. The layout makes maximum use of the space; built-in components are as efficient as they are handsome.

RIGHT: A reverse pattern on the wallpaper—light motifs on a dark background, instead of the opposite—is a nice design surprise.

LIGHT AND AIRY

YOU NEEDN'T HAVE a green thumb to long for a garden room in your home. Any room is a candidate—it might be a glass-walled sunroom filled with indoor plants and flea-market furniture, an ultra-contemporary living room adorned with white orchids, or even a mudroom with beadboard wainscoting and a wicker planter box. What these examples have in common is a special decorating style inspired by a love of plants.

Your garden room may not be elaborate—nor even situated near the garden. (But rooms bathed in natural light are ideal, because light enhances the indoor-outdoor harmony characteristic of garden rooms.) Whenever you drape greenery on a sideboard, set pots of herbs near your kitchen window, or dress a bedroom in flower-patterned fabrics, you are being true to the spirit of the garden.

Choose a room in which to celebrate the delights of the garden, and it will quickly become the next best thing to being outdoors.

Repetition of color, with slight variation, is the key to a monochromatic scheme. The low-intensity chaise fabric repeats, in a lighter value, the lattice color; even the wicker is tinged with green.

The challenge in decorating a conservatory-style garden room of this size is to introduce appropriately scaled furnishings. Here, the colorwashed lattice is a strong architectural feature that stands up to the geometry of the glass structure overhead. A visually weighty ottoman and large-scale garden urns are well suited to the generously proportioned space.

ABOVE: Garden-style decorating demands more from the floral arts than one traditional arrangement on a coffee table. This fresh look includes miniature to bold bouquets grouped in eclectic containers and juxtaposed with casual flair.

RIGHT: A picket-fence box bearing a harvest of apples makes a simple yet strong color and design statement. Decorative companions are an old-fashioned garden whirligig and a wall display of tiny birdhouses.

Crisp cotton slipcovers, pure white walls, and a sisal floor mat set the scene in this clean-and-simple garden-style living room. Three decorative elements—apples, sunflowers, and folk-art birdhouses—repeat here and there, with lots of white space in between, for a cohesive yet uncluttered look.

FACING PAGE: Lighthearted furnishings and architectural detailing in this cottage-style garden room recall old-fashioned summers. A white plate rail with decorative molding encircles the room and provides the perfect display site for accessories. Beadboard wainscoting painted gray-green establishes a muted background for the cheerful clutter of patterns in the hooked rug, settee cushions, and pillows.

RIGHT: A French bistro chair and small accent table are appropriately scaled to this tiny windowed corner. Cachepots—some filled with plants, others strictly decorative— supply instant garden ambience.

BELOW: Glazed bifold doors open to allow the garden room to merge with the patio. Continuing the Arizona flagstone underfoot and repeating furnishing styles on both sides of the glass reinforce the flow.

RECAPTURED SPACES

THE PHRASE ALONE—bonus room—has a positive ring. Yours may be a spare room awaiting its destiny, a reinvention of an existing room, or a new room carved out of wasted space. The current craze for loft living (whether the loft is the real thing or a newly constructed living area) illustrates a widespread desire to reclaim space and put it to good use.

If you think you have no space to re-capture, think—and look—again. A large laundry room could do double duty as a home office; an extra bedroom might be transformed into a dedicated play and craft room. Small recaptured spaces are just as satisfying: a captain's bed nestled between bookcases is the perfect place to catch a nap or read a few more pages of your favorite book.

By its very nature, such a space feels like a "prize," so invest the creativity, energy, and materials needed to make it special. Soon you'll wonder what you ever did without it.

A peg rack becomes a delightful decorative element when it's adorned with coats and backpacks in kid colors.

Visible from a hallway, this mudroom needed to be both functional and fun. Bead-board and rich red fabrics—one with monkeys holding parasols!—give the built-in bench its cozy charm. (The adjoining cabinet looks freestanding but is also built in.) A slate tile floor reiterates the fabric and wall colors—and withstands heavy traffic from this family on the go.

RIGHT: A section of painted trellis brought indoors and propped against the wall makes a practical as well as decorative "bulletin board," providing a handy place to tuck cards, notes, and photos.

BELOW: A long, narrow laundry room doubles as a craft and flower-arranging area. Curtained-off space under the counter keeps larger objects and clutter out of sight. At the far end of the room the counter continues, providing yet another work surface with built-in storage below.

Vintage suitcases and steamer trunks, many with their original travel stickers, store belongings in a comfy basement bedroom. More travel stickers decorate the lampshade. A black-and-white quarter canopy is attached to a 1- by 2-inch frame using hook-and-loop fastener tape; the system is screwed to the ceiling.

Wasted space adjacent to the kitchen became multipurpose with the addition of a daybed with toy storage underneath. Now it's a sunroom, play area, and occasional guest bedroom (a bathroom is just around the corner). The graceful curvature of the daybed's "headboard" helps create a subtle impression of separation between the two areas.

A captain's bed tucked between second-floor bedrooms offers a refuge for napping, reading, or simply "hiding out in plain sight." Painting the structure white, with new-neutral accents, sets the space apart from the surrounding walls.

Using space recaptured from the garage, these homeowners created a second-story guest house connected to the main house by a breezeway. A built-in bench flanked by bookcases includes plenty of storage above and below and offers lovely views through French doors to the balcony. Behind the half-door on the far wall are a microwave and small refrigerator.

WORKING QUARTERS

EVERY MORNING, more than 50 million Americans grab a cup of coffee and "commute" across the room, down the hall, or upstairs to a home office. The benefits of a home office are clear—less stress, more productive (noncommute) time, "casual Friday" every day, and a better balance between work and family life.

The need for a quiet, organized, and harmonious space in which to work is just as obvious, even if all you're doing is paying bills and e-mailing distant friends. In fact, an inverse relationship exists between the availability of new technology and the desire to create a more individual work space: the more equipment we accumulate, the more we want our home offices to look like, well, home. Who says office furniture can't be an essential part of your decorating plan—or that it can't be antique? Why can't you soften or brighten the high-tech look with color and pattern?

Start thinking of your work environment as an extension of your home, and "going to work" will become one of life's pleasures.

A streamlined adjustable lamp does the job without getting in the way.

This flexible office environment includes a consultation area with comfortable seating for both homeowner and clients and an open table as a desk. Tall storage units take best advantage of the space.

LEFT: Well-chosen materials transformed a bland basement into an efficient home office with the rustic look of a log cabin. Pine paneling covers the wall; river rocks hide the concrete foundation. A printer and scanner are stowed in an appliance garage and a drawer in the built-in pine desk.

BELOW: What was once an eating nook off the kitchen became, through the magic of remodeling, a bright home office and hub of family activity. The built-in desk features a putty-colored concrete surface and woven baskets that slide in and out of cubbies.

Combining the best features of a library and a retreat, this versatile loft office includes back-to-back computer desks, a cozy reading nook with cushioned benches, and built-in bookshelves. A glass-topped game table adds another activity to the room's repertoire. Pale green walls and a warm wood ceiling cozy up the large space.

OUTDOOR LIVING

To ALMOST EVERYONE, "the good life" includes outdoor living on a patio, porch, veranda, or deck. The trend toward spending more time outside has grown over decades, from the days of inexpensive lawn chairs randomly placed on a concrete slab patio to carefully planned environments incorporating the best of today's interior design.

Decorating an outdoor living area is really no different from decorating any room within your home—except that there are fewer walls. You begin with your givens and your goals, formulate a plan that utilizes color and design principles, and choose furnishings and accessories that meet your needs and suit your style. Every bit as important outdoors as indoors are furniture-arranging guidelines, for a significant portion of the time we spend on a patio or deck is related to entertaining.

Proceed with a plan and a purpose, and your outdoor living space will serve you well—as both a revitalizing retreat and an al fresco dining/family room. In fact, the most versatile room in your house may not be inside at all.

On a nearby wall, an assortment of jugs and vintage tin sits atop a weathered cabinet, repeating the blue-green aspect of the palette.

An elegant transitional space, a columned veranda offers the best of both worlds—
a protected open-air setting adjacent to a lush garden, with comfortable furnishings
and gloriously patterned fabrics you might also see indoors. The complementary palette
of warm red-oranges and cool blue-greens is calm, not jarring, because the values are
light to medium and the patterns varied.

ABOVE: Paradoxical as it sounds, you can create an inner room outdoors, just through furniture placement. Here, seating delineates a cozy conversation area that serves the focal-point fireplace. The space can be entered from all sides, yet it still feels intimate—the mark of a successful seating plan.

LEFT: A fountain niche is technically a secondary focal point, but no one would deny that its soothing sound and delicate mosaic pattern make it a true rest point for the eye and ear.

FACING PAGE: A space as grand as this courtyard affords the opportunity to put the principles of good design to work. A dining table and chairs set off to one side exhibit radial symmetry, echoed in the rhythmical arrangement of hand-painted Italian plates on lime-washed walls.

ABOVE: Wicker is always in style, especially on a handsome, rugged porch such as this. A dark stain on the wood flooring sets off the stark white pieces arranged for conversation (and, farther down the porch, for dining). Primary-color cushions and pillows brighten the otherwise true-neutral setting.

LEFT: Brightly painted wood chairs—flea-market finds, all—look right at home on this old-fashioned porch. Painting the floor a minty green unites the colored chairs for a more cohesive look. An antique quilt in the time-honored pattern "Grandmother's Flower Garden" adds charm to the scene and takes the chill off early mornings.

Arched arbors frame the brick path from the street to a front-yard patio that lies just beyond swinging teak privacy doors. Simple furniture is always appropriate in an outdoor living setting with strong architectural aspects. (The home's entry is to the left, past the doors.)

A trickling wall fountain makes a stunning yet tranquil focal point just off the home's living room. Whitewashed decking eases the transition from tile patio to entertaining area. Eclectic materials, furnishings, and accessories prove that "mixing it up" is a good idea when your goal is casual outdoor living.

Patinated by time, this Mediterranean-style courtyard blends terra-cotta tiles with diagonally set blue-glazed accents for a strong sense of visual rhythm through repetition. The vibrant tile fountain surrounded by bright blue chairs is a variation on radial balance.

The quiet pleasures of the patio are celebrated in this hideaway tucked beneath the eaves and covered with a blanket of star jasmine. The rustic bench blends right in with painted-on hills viewed over a crumbling "wall." Toile de Jouy curtain panels and a mélange of French-country fabrics lend a look of European style.

Gauzy panels of translucent nylon turn a wraparound patio into a serene sanctuary. Anchored to the posts top and bottom, the panels move in the breeze but remain a subtle visual barrier. Woven grass mats and zabuton-style floor cushions conjure up images of a Japanese teahouse or temple.

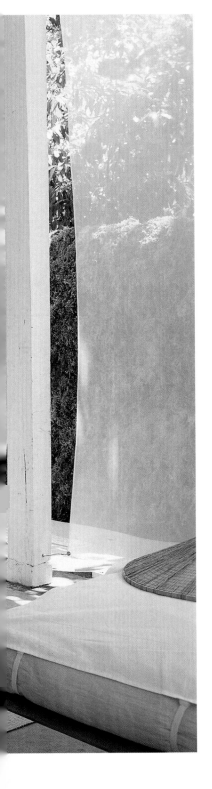

The gentle curves of a low, minimal rocker belie its material—concrete! The chair's weight is a strong counterpoint to the soft cushions and filmy fabric in this airy outdoor living space.

Aligned on a narrow shelf, white orchids are a graceful, graphic living work of art. Although there are four wood cube planters, five flower spikes illustrate the odd-number principle for grouping accessories.

OPEN HOUSE

FOR THOSE OF US who love houses and decorating, every house tour is an irresistible event, opening doors to beautifully designed, architecturally significant homes. That's what this special section offers—a kind of house tour through photos.

These homes illustrate various types of decor—updated tradition, old-world ambience, cottage charm, and city chic. You won't see every room in each house, but you'll get a strong sense of its style and perhaps discover ways to interpret its palette or adapt its overall scheme for your own home.

Hovering over another doorway, a stone cherub (actually an antique fountain ornament) looks down on his domain.

Generous room shots illustrate how the pros arrange furniture and combine colors, patterns, and textures; close-ups focus on decorating details. A number of the homes belong to artists, interior designers, and architects, who apply their signature styles to their own living spaces. All exemplify sound principles of color and design.

But why read when you can look? To "take the tour," you need not get in your car or hop on a bus—simply turn the page.

SUN-DRENCHED COLOR: Architectural fragments and ornamental objects left outdoors to weather acquire a patina that hints at their history. Salvaged pieces here include the doors, the pediment above (rescued from an old bank building), a tall stucco pedestal, and a stone finial doing duty as a doorstop.

The warm, welcoming atmosphere of the home shown here and on pages 138–139 derives from vintage architectural pieces such as the urn (now a lamp) and the old iron brackets and hinges surrounding weathered shutter doors. Furnishings vary from the distressed dining table to an elegant upholstered side chair and opulent pillows. Tuscan yellow walls bathe the space in vibrant color.

RIGHT: The owner-designer's style shows through in every detail of the decor. Here, a treasured painting of a local scene is tucked behind an old French pottery bowl.

BELOW: A shallow tile niche at the end of the kitchen counter displays earthenware pottery in all of the home's palette colors.

RETRO PANACHE:
Can there be any doubt that the occupant of this loft space loves color and design? Saturated yellow, raspberry, coral, and purple color the walls and table shown on the facing page. Pens collected during the owner's travels are grouped in mugs by country. The dining chairs come with clear backs and seats that can be unscrewed to insert colorful paper, pages torn from magazines, or photos.

A custom-built banquette (right), fabricated by a maker of restaurant components, doubles as a kitchen table and work space. Signage from the fifties and Fiesta ware on painted shelves decorate the walls. The multifunction credenza (above) was designed to hold a printer and hanging files; a laptop computer slips into the vertical yellow compartment next to the wall.

142

LAKESIDE CHARM: Summers by the lake call for bright, breezy colors, natural materials, and lots of white. Matelassé slipcovers tie together a casual mix of chairs, arranged for easy conversation. Antique quilts contribute pattern and color.

RIGHT: The mudroom, with its cottage-style casement windows, also looks out to the lake. A marble-topped counter with gingham skirt is the perfect place to set fruits and vegetables brought in from the garden or picked out at the growers' market.

RIGHT: A pure white mantel and wall showcase a collection of demitasse cups and a trio of whimsical teapot paintings.

BELOW: The blue-and-white dining area flows seamlessly from the living room, thanks in part to the seagrass mat underfoot in both areas. At the end of the room, a white wicker love seat under a wide art mirror offers another seating option—and another lovely view.

The walls in the everyday eating area began with dark yellow paint over existing paneling, followed by a lighter yellow—the same shade used in the great room—sponged and brushed on. Owner-designer Trish Dietze sanded the original wood floors, taped off the diamond pattern, and applied colored shellac. The effect is charmingly timeworn, though the finish is not very durable.

CALIFORNIA CASUAL: European travel was the catalyst for this livable decorating plan. Far from being overwhelming, the warm colors energize the space, says Trish. "When we leave for a while and come back, we're inspired all over again." Matching sofas upholstered in red silk command attention in the great room; a plaid chair and ottoman introduce geometric pattern. An antique rug in low-intensity red and gold whispers the same palette, demonstrating the principle of rhythm through repetition.

LEFT: Nowhere is it written that you can't extend your color scheme to the outdoors. Bright flowers spill over the sides of an antique cart, enlivening the loggia.

A second-floor landing becomes a cozy, comfy sitting area with the addition of a plump slipcovered sofa and a small end table with antique lamp. An original arched window adds to the ambience. (Lean over the railing, and you can just see who's come through the front door.)

FACING PAGE, TOP: Minty green walls, distressed wood, and bed linens patterned with pink roses set a sweet, romantic mood. The candy-striped lamp shades dot the scheme with morsels of bright color; a small bouquet of roses looks dyed to match. The half-shade lamp mounted at the center of the painted headboard is a nod to the styles of yesteryear.

SENTIMENTAL CHIC: Built in the 1920s, this little gem of a house radiates old-fashioned charm. White cotton duck slipcovers are meant to look rumpled; linen-and-cotton print pillows echo the leafy vista visible just beyond the patio door. In the dining room, an antique chandelier wrapped in real ivy hangs over a flea-market table and chairs.

INTIMATE SOPHISTICATION: Originally a dining room, this small space was transformed into a snug living room by designer Gigi Rogers. Focusing first on the walls, she concluded that they had to be dark: "People are afraid dark colors will make a room seem too small—but this room couldn't be anything but small." Stuccoed walls painted a deep clay color pick up light and cast tiny shadows—an example of both actual and visual texture. The ceiling, painted a metallic sage green, reflects light.

RIGHT: Loden green silk chenille club chairs complement the warmth and richness of the original oak floor. The lamp is a reproduction of an Arts and Crafts design.

BELOW: Pattern, pattern everywhere is Gigi's signature style. A maple sleigh bed is bedecked in a flurry of soft colors— coral, powder blue, willow green, and creamy yellow— and engaging patterns. A fanciful, fringed ottoman rests on a custom-made area rug. Demonstrating the effect of juxtaposed color, an icy blue tuxedo sofa looks luminous against the warm red walls.

A black-and-white chaise looks smart in a wallpapered bedroom, next to an antique fireplace surround that was rescued from a Victorian house. The old wood was scrubbed and waxed but not painted. (To see a detail of the mantel and mirror, turn to page 218.)

Club chairs situated behind the sofa make use of space just off the entrance and provide a secondary seating area for occasional use. The graceful rose topiary visually links the demilune window to the table and chairs.

CHECK IT OUT: The meadow-fresh palette for this charming cottage includes a surprise—crisp black-and-white checks, a particular favorite of the owner. The original batten-board walls are an architectural feature in themselves, but also lend subtle pattern to a room dancing with floral and geometric designs. The living room illustrates a primary pattern principle: vary the style and scale of patterns to create a pleasing visual cadence.

Owner Freddy Moran chose sunny yellow for the walls and intense violet for the trim in her quilting studio. "Yellow walls give the room a wonderful glow in the morning, a quietness in the afternoon, and serenity in the evening." Large-scale black and white floor tiles add graphic dimension to the room and provide visual relief from all the bright color.

RIGHT: "If you use enough color, you never have to worry about 'matching' anything," according to Freddy. "Everything works!" Walls painted cinnabar (a version of red-orange) in the study are warm and enveloping. Cooler hues on the wicker furniture and small side chair balance the visual temperature.

FREDDY'S HOUSE: Color, collections, and quilts are recurring elements throughout Freddy's house of surprises. "I painted one room one color, and then repeated that color in another room," Freddy explains. "I didn't want a jumble of unrelated colors, but a feeling of excitement and anticipation of what else is to be seen." A cool yet intense palette colors the living room, where guests are greeted by a daring blend of furnishings and accessories.

The children of the house have a place of their own—right in the thick of things—when they pull up their chairs to this 1950s maple school-room table. A bar stool upholstered in vintage orange mohair invites a parent to join in. Behind the table stands an old valet rack, now put to decorative use.

VINTAGE UPDATE: Designer Sasha Emerson expresses her passion for vintage fabrics and saturated colors in her own home (facing page). She used an antique yellow velvet on the sofa, a vintage orange mohair on the chaise, and blue velvet on chairs that were office furniture in a previous life. A chartreuse-and-yellow striped silk fabric covering the English lounge chairs against the far wall offers a change of pace in color and introduces pattern to the solid-color scheme. Integral-color plaster walls are waxed for a soft sheen; the Mexican pavers are original to the house.

BELOW: A single work of art when viewed as a whole, Sasha's collection of 1950s pottery (with "lovely, drippy glazes") hails from Italy, Germany, Belgium, and Czechoslovakia. A cutout in the wall between the kitchen and living room allows the cook to visit with guests.

UNDERSTATED ELEGANCE: The owner of this grand, beautifully proportioned home had in mind a dual purpose for this distinctive space, says designer Monty Collins: "Instead of a shrine to a dining table, she wanted a room that is comfortable for entertaining, as well as for dining." The mirrored cabinet is actually a bar, with linen storage below. Each wide slipper chair can accommodate two guests, the ottoman one more.

LEFT: Removing a false ceiling opened up the kitchen and allowed another row of windows to be set high in the wall. Antique schoolhouse light fixtures hang from nickel-plated poles.

BELOW: Silk curtain panels topped by scalloped valances blow in the breeze when the French doors are open. A hand-painted silk light fixture, one of two in the space, is a stunning ornament in a room with minimal pattern. New-neutral hues are everywhere—on the walls, furnishings, and floor— except for the cerulean blue Directoire-style corner cabinet.

UNCHARTED TERRITORY: "When you build a house for yourself," says homeowner and designer David Wilson, "you have a mandate to explore new territory and go in a personal design direction." In the living room, plaster walls were left unpainted, revealing bits of sand and aggregate; steel trusses, reminiscent of steel framing in old warehouses, were likewise left unfinished. The lower-grade maple floor and fir ceiling express the character of the woods. (More views of this home are shown on pages 162–163.)

LEFT: The red-violet curved wall that begins in the entry and overlaps the wall below "expresses motion that is free of the structural system of the building. It says as much about what's not there as about the wall itself," remarks David.

A fireplace surround of conglomerate granite quarried from a river bottom possesses a striking visual texture. The jagged edges, in sharp contrast to the smooth surface, reveal much about the material and how it was formed. The low table is a single sheet of sandblasted glass, ³/₄ inch thick, on a stainless steel base with ash legs.

ABOVE: A second fireplace is located in "the pod," an elliptical space that rotates out from the rest of the house. Here the palette deepens, with a dark-stained oak floor and deeper green plaster walls that announce a new room.

FACING PAGE, BOTTOM: In the kitchen, a wall of mixed slate tiles extends above the gently sloping hood and refrigerator cabinet. "I see cabinets as furniture," David says, "and I want them to have their own sculptural presence." Mini-trusses under the granite bar reiterate the full-size trusses used elsewhere in the house. Blue pendant lights make cool accents in this warm-colored space.

The fireplace hearth contains rocks picked out by David's daughter; the concrete was cast, then ground smooth to reveal the rocks' shape and color. "I wanted the mark of someone's hand on the surface," explains David. The integral-color plaster fireplace wraps around, into the pod.

LOFTY LIVING: A true loft begged for color, and designer Joan Osburn responded with a range of complex hues: "Because of the industrial nature of the space, it needed strong, warm colors to counteract the cold concrete." In the primary seating area, the wall was painted a sophisticated red with yellow undertones, forming a rich backdrop for the antique bird's-eye-maple armoire, gold-leaf folding screen, and vintage French print. Bold in shape and color, the chenille sofa and leather chairs correspond to the scale of the space. Reclaimed vintage maple flooring lightens the scheme. (More views of this home are shown on pages 166–167.)

Industrial sash windows and concrete columns are powerful architectural features. Near the windows, two pieces of sculpture from the homeowner's collection are on display. (Because lofts have few interior walls, sculpture is often more appropriate in them than two-dimensional art.)

The color shifts and the floor level changes in the kitchen and dining area, signaling a different purpose for the space. French rattan chairs and stools pull up to the table and bar, which (like the prominent column) is faced with maple veneer. Above the cabinets are metal strips inlaid with 8-inch glass tiles. In the daylight, the tiles are reflective; at night, they appear opalescent.

Steps in the marble
shower provide
a place to stow
towels and bath
accessories.
Architecturally, the
steps break up the
imposing vertical
plane and add
dimension to what
would have been
another flat wall.

ABOVE: "Living in a loft," Joan explains, "is about living in a space that's open but also private." Her choice of mango-colored walls here makes the cavernous interior seem warm and livable. Framed by the doorway, the view into the bedroom reveals an intimate yet spare room. The furnishings are harmonious, but nothing competes with the soaring ceilings and massive structures that typify a loft.

FACING PAGE, BOTTOM: Saturated yellow walls complement a honed-marble floor. Vertical chrome tubing forms the legs of the black laminate countertop; chrome shelves swivel in and out for easy access and efficient storage.

PRACTICAL DESIGN

PLANNING TO GIVE YOUR GUEST ROOM A FRESH NEW LOOK? OR THINKING ABOUT A WHOLE-HOUSE REVAMP? WHATEVER THE EXTENT OF YOUR DECORATING project, it starts here, with design. Great design doesn't just "happen" in your home. It's a conscious, highly creative process—but not necessarily a mysterious one. In fact, good design begins simply with knowing how you want your space to look and function, and with gathering the appropriate ideas and materials. In this chapter, our step-by-step decorating plan will help you with this process. You'll also get a quick course in a few simple design principles that will help you put together your chosen colors and materials with style. Principles such as "balance," "emphasis," and "harmony" may sound abstract, but they work like magic—even in a novice's hands. Practical strategies for arranging furniture, working with "problem" spaces, and incorporating accessories round out this idea-filled chapter.

STEP-BY-STEP TO A
DECORATING PLAN

DECORATING IS A LOT MORE FUN—AND A LOT LESS STRESSFUL—WITH A CLEAR PLAN OF ACTION. THIS SECTION WILL HELP YOU DEVELOP A DECORATING PLAN, FROM SETTING GOALS TO GATHERING MATERIALS TO DECIDING WHAT GOES WHERE IN YOUR ROOM.

ABOVE: Outstanding architectural features such as these call for minimal "decoration."

FACING PAGE, TOP: A breakfast room adjoining a kitchen is a great place to experiment with colors, materials, and finishes. Here, the faux-finished walls' subtle tones and the gleam of glazed floor pavers provide a foil for the lively, Provence-style colors and patterns of the banquette cushions and pillows.

FACING PAGE, BOTTOM: In this serene retreat, faux-finished walls in a color called cognac surround the furnishings with warm color and gentle texture. Hand-painted silk bed linens and an upholstered headboard set a "modern romantic" mood.

Once you've made the decision to decorate, it's only natural to want to jump in and begin. But before you pick up a paint brush or shop for furniture, take stock of your situation. The following five steps spell out a start-to-finish strategy. You need not follow the steps in this order, but take the time to read through them first, to get a feel for the process.

DETERMINING THE SCOPE OF YOUR PROJECT

It starts with a vision of what you hope to achieve; however, to pin down the realities of your plan, you need sketches and lists, lists, lists.

MAKE A WISH LIST. Do you plan to decorate a number of rooms or just add the finishing touches to a room that's almost done? A wish list can help you set priorities for your goals. If you're on a limited budget, start with changes that will make the most difference, such as new wall color or a new sofa; then add to the scheme as your resources permit.

IDENTIFY YOUR GIVENS. "Givens"—those things you can't change, must keep, or truly love—go hand in hand with a wish list. The most obvious given is the size and shape of your room; short of remodeling, you'll have to work with what you have. Architectural features—the walls, ceiling, trim, and floors—are also givens, along with furnishings that you like or can't yet afford to replace. Although they may seem like limitations, givens provide a place to begin.

ASSESS YOUR SPACE. This stage addresses functional goals: Do you want to subdivide an open room to create separate activity areas? Do you need to arrange seating so it's more conducive to conversation? Can you move furnishings to create a more efficient traffic pattern?

A bird's-eye-view sketch of your room can help you evaluate your space. A drawing done to scale on graph paper is ideal, but a rough thumbnail sketch will do. Add furnishings—both existing and proposed—to your sketch to better understand their relationship to the room and to other furnishings.

After you've made your sketch, consider a radical step: remove all of the furnishings and look at the room empty. When you take away familiar objects, you'll see possibilities that aren't apparent when the room is full.

CONSIDER EVERYONE. Do you ever look at show rooms in stores and wonder who could live in them? Decorating your own home is about pleasing the people in your life, not about re-creating the latest look. Whom do you need to consider, besides yourself?

❖ Do you have or are you planning to have a baby? Comfortable crawling surfaces, safe materials, and washable finishes are a must.

❖ Do you have school-age children? If so, forgo the silk sofa until they're out of college; for now, you'll need sturdy cottons that withstand heavy use. Washable slipcovers are ideal for families with kids.

❖ Is there an elderly or disabled person in your home? If so, think about ease of mobility and safety when you shop for flooring. Choose seating that is both comfortable and easy to get up from.

❖ Do you have pets? If your dog sneaks naps on the sofa now, he's not likely to mend his ways when you've re-covered it. You may want to buy extra yardage to place on the furniture when you're not on patrol.

Earthy colors, a creative mix of understated upholstery and rug patterns, and a comfy, intimate seating arrangement embody the casual traditional style of this welcoming sunroom.

TIPS

To see the newest colors, visit the linens department of prominent stores and check out the bath towels. New palettes debut in the fall and spring.

DEFINING YOUR STYLE

Focus on the feeling you want your room or home to convey. Open and spacious, or private and cozy? Boldly colorful, or quietly subdued? Relaxed and casual, or orderly and formal? That's a lot to think about, and achieving the desired effect begins with discovering your personal style.

AN IDEA FILE. A folder full of inspiring examples can help you identify your preferences and later serve as a guide to gathering and auditioning decorating materials. Look through decorating books, magazines, and catalogs, tearing out or flagging every picture that appeals to you—whether it shows an entire room, a wallpaper pattern, or just a chair. Are deeply colored walls inviting to you? Does a painted floor appeal? Do you prefer patterned or solid-color fabrics? Don't try to analyze why you like something; just collect images you love. Include family members in this process, because everyone's opinion counts.

A DECORATING QUESTIONNAIRE.

Next, sit down with your idea file and ask yourself the following questions:

❖ Are you traditional, country, or contemporary? Traditional and country continue to be the most popular decorating styles, with contemporary and Asian far behind. Don't worry if you can't put a name to your look—knowing what you like when you see it is enough for now.

❖ Do you enjoy basking in warm reds, yellows, and oranges? Or do you feel more relaxed in the presence of cool blues, greens, and violets? Identifying your preference for visual temperature is helpful when it's time to choose wall color.

❖ What's your least favorite color? Be willing to consider pale, muted versions of any color you dislike; in the right value, intensity, and situation, it may be just what's needed. Don't rule it out before you begin.

❖ Are you drawn to light, airy colors or dark, dramatic ones? Recognizing your preference is helpful because value, as much as the hue itself, determines the impact that colors have.

❖ Do you want a room that pulsates with visual energy, or do you long for a calm, soothing retreat? If you're after excitement, opt for vivid colors, and lots of them. For a quiet ambience, restrict your palette to neutrals, a single color in many variations, or closely related colors. See pages 232–233 for more about color combinations.

A contemporary room with glorious French doors and transom windows begs for a simple approach. Natural materials—note the table base fashioned from a tree trunk—and a clean white palette are all that's needed to set the style and link the room to the outdoors.

From the warm colors to the bold botanical patterns and rattan-and-wicker chairs, every element in this sunny breakfast room is in harmony. Painting the trim and molding a rich yellow-green plays up stunning windows; the fruit-and-leaf wallpaper border accentuates their height.

READY, SET, GATHER!

Armed with your room sketch, idea file, and a large canvas bag, you're ready to "hunt and gather." Your goal at this stage is to collect things you love, without worrying about how you'll use them. That comes later.

Where do you gather? Start with a trip to your Lowe's store, where you can visit the paint, flooring, lighting, and window-treatment departments for inspiration aplenty. To learn what you can find or order at Lowe's and how you can get help with Lowe's design services, see page 236. If you live in or near a large city that has a design center, visit there, too. Most admit the public; to take home samples or order materials, though, you'll need to work through an interior designer.

Collect the largest samples possible. Fabric stores will often cut generous swatches for you at no charge. If not, buy the smallest cut, usually a quarter of a yard; later, you may want to buy a full yard to see how the fabric looks draped over a chair or pinned to the window. Some stores allow you to check out "memo samples," swatches from 9 to 18 inches square labeled with the fabric's name, code number, color, and fiber content. You can usually borrow wallpaper books and flooring samples for several days.

If after a day or two of gathering you feel like a victim of sensory overload, remember: you aren't required to use everything you collect. Your goal is to assemble materials that inspire you. No commitments. Not yet.

TIPS

Collect freely, without agonizing over your choices. At this point, you can't make a "mistake."

A classic wing chair upholstered in a striking medallion print might easily inspire the gathering process. A tapestry fabric with free-form motifs and smoldering colors (above) can become the catalyst for a decorating plan and lead to a cast of stunning supporting materials.

DEVELOPING YOUR PALETTE

Whether you realize it or not, your personal palette naturally develops as you hunt and gather samples. One beautiful fabric leads to a harmonious paint hue; fabric and wall color together point you in the direction of tile or carpet. Bit by bit, sample by sample, your palette gradually evolves.

When you feel you've collected enough, lay your samples on a large surface, such as your dining room table, and evaluate them. Plan to leave them there as long as it takes—that could mean days or even weeks. Alternatively, pin them to a large piece of foam core board for a movable observation gallery.

As you analyze your materials, consider the following.

❖ Where do the colors on your table or board appear on the color ring (page 229)? On the warm side? The cool side? Equally spaced around the ring?

❖ As a group, do your gathered samples form a color scheme? Unless you're working with all neutrals, your combination will fit, or be similar to, one of the schemes described on page 232.

❖ Should you gather more samples to expand or fortify your palette? If your colors are all warm and analogous, such as yellow-orange, red-orange, and red, you may want to introduce a cooler color as an accent.

❖ Do you need one or more neutral colors among your samples to provide visual relief? Gather true-neutral or new-neutral materials and include them in the mix.

TIPS

Be aware that color on a paint chip or in a fabric sample will appear more intense when it's applied to walls or furnishings.

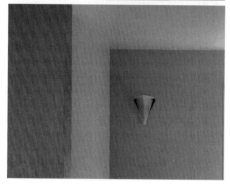

NARROWING YOUR CHOICES

At last, the time has come to make decisions. Designers call the first part of this step "editing" and the second "auditioning." Editing and auditioning are exhilarating—this is the point when it all comes together—but they're also scary. Your inclination, with a sea of samples in front of you, will be to freeze. So many beautiful materials, so many choices! Let the ideas percolate, and stay open to the possibilities. If necessary, collect more samples; hunting and gathering often continues to the very end of a project.

A few questions will arise as you begin to edit your samples:

❖ "Do I love what I see?" Keep only those things that please you, resisting the temptation to retain a material you think you need but don't really like.

❖ "Do I have too much of one thing?" If you've gathered four black-and-taupe stripes, now is the time to select one and set the others aside.

❖ "Is there too much contrast?" Very light lights and very dark darks can be jarring in combination. Strive for a range that includes medium values—unless you're going for a contemporary, high-contrast look.

❖ "Are my samples too subdued?" To play it safe, you may have unconsciously chosen all low-intensity colors. Try adding a few brighter notes.

The all-important audition comes next. You probably already have an idea of what you want to place where—it's just natural to visualize colors and materials in your room as you consider them. Now is your chance to place your samples where you anticipate using them. Lay carpet samples on the floor; prop up wallpaper books across the room; drape fabric over a chair. In other words, have your room "try on" the materials.

ABOVE, TOP: As you look from one room to another, brush-outs (page 279) give you a sense of how potential paint colors might look together.

ABOVE, BOTTOM: After painting the walls, but before the furnishings fill the room, color looks its strongest.

BELOW: Family room fabrics (left) include warm golds and greens, plus red-violet and gray. Reds and yellow-oranges (right) take their cue from the living room rug.

Here are a few placement pointers from designers:

❖ The larger the area covered, the bolder a color will appear. A blue-green that's pleasant on a pillow will look stronger on your sofa and perhaps overpowering on your walls.

❖ Reserve low-intensity colors for walls, floors, and large furnishings. As a rule of thumb, the larger the area, the less intense the color should be. (You'll want to ignore this guideline, of course, if your goal is a saturated scheme.)

❖ Remember, bold patterns look even bolder over large areas. Focus on textures, solids, or subtle patterns for large furnishings and window treatments.

❖ If you're decorating several rooms, use most or all of your palette colors in one room, and one or two of the colors in adjoining rooms. Use a color more than once in a room, or it will look like an "orphan."

Finally, when you think you're "there," ask yourself, "Do I still love these materials?" "Is the effect harmonious?" "Will I feel at home in this room?" If you've edited and auditioned thoughtfully, you'll answer "yes" to all three questions.

Gathering, editing, and auditioning samples is a process fraught with doubts and decisions, but seeing it all come together is your reward. What might have seemed a collection of disparate materials on your dining room table becomes a beautiful blend of color, pattern, and texture.

I t's essential to view your collected samples as a group, because that's how they will appear in your room.

key starting points for room design

YOU MAY ALREADY OWN A STRIKING WORK OF ART OR AN HEIRLOOM RUG—OR MAYBE YOU WANT TO FEATURE A FABRIC OR A FAVORITE COLOR IN YOUR HOME. HERE ARE FOUR EXAMPLES OF THESE POPULAR STARTING POINTS.

1 **A PAINTING** If you're fortunate enough to possess a significant painting or other work of art, it's immensely satisfying to create a palette and design a room that captures the essence of the art but does not compete with it.

In the room shown at right, the placement of the large painting firmly establishes it as the focal point. (If the painting, *Foster the Light,* looks like another opening through the shell of the wall, it may be because it's part of artist John McCormick's "portal" series.)

Using a key color from the art for paint and upholstery is a popular and reliable approach. Here, pale "flax" walls and a similarly colored silk sofa repeat the warm, new-neutral hues at the painting's center. The rug, an antique Persian Mashad colored with vegetable dyes, reiterates the blue-violet and burnt sienna in the painting, but in a different historical style.

This room boasts a secondary focal point just to the left of the mantel. A fat slipper chair covered in fine stripes of beige, black, and cream echoes starker neutrals in the painting behind it, *Café Hotel* by Impressionist M. De Gallero. A silk pillow depicting a harlequin-patterned vessel of black olives set against a tumeric-colored background ties in with the rusty golds in the primary painting and links the two areas.

Do you see the color surprise in this palette? It's the verdigris metal accent table, which is actually a Thai water drum.

2 **A KEY FABRIC** "It was love at first sight," they later confess. Many people are more powerfully attracted to fabric than to any other decorating element and will fasten on a beautiful fabric with "have-to-have-it" commitment.

A multicolored fabric provides you with a ready-made palette of harmonious hues; in effect, the fabric designer has done the creative work for you. On the practical side, beginning with fabric is a good idea if you're planning to paint, because it's easy to find paint colors that work with fabrics you've already gathered, but much more challenging to find fabrics that work with a paint color you've already chosen.

In this grouping, the whimsical fabric with stylized female figures and a creamy background is the creative catalyst. The analogous color combination of yellow-green, blue-green, and blue includes a little warmth (from the yellow-green) among the cool colors and establishes the basic palette.

Variation in scale is essential when colors come from the same side of the color ring. A boldly patterned upholstery fabric, with its free-form dots, stars, and wavy lines (lower right), provides needed contrast to the key fabric. A willow-and-cream linen fabric (upper left) in a triangle pattern is even larger in scale, whereas a deep blue silk jacquard with lime-green dots (top) is at the opposite end of the scale spectrum. An intense yellow-green linen fabric (lower left) is ideal for pillows, a cornice, or a valance. An unexpected shot of warmth comes from a bumpy cotton in a burst of bright coral.

Continued on next page >

starting points

3 **A SPECIAL RUG** Like a painting or a key fabric, a rug is a wonderful place to begin because it presents you with a well-thought-out color palette. An investment-quality Oriental rug, a contemporary ethnic rug, or even a painted floorcloth can be the start of a successful scheme.

The selection shown here evolved from a contemporary Tibetan rug in shimmering hues of cinnamon, gray, and gold. Shifting values in the checkerboard background set off paler, stylized flower motifs, which appear to float on the richly textured surface. This example of a "given" is not one that invites contrast; rather, it is reposeful, a quiet companion to the honey-toned oak flooring on which it lies.

Memo samples illustrate how each fabric might work with the rug as well as with one another. The key fabric, a wistful linen floral (lower center), repeats the rug's colors and adds low-intensity yellow-green and blue-green to the subtle mix.

A plush mohair fabric the color of bronze (far left) harmonizes with the rug without matching it. As a new neutral of medium value, this fabric would be ideal for a large upholstered piece such as a sofa or chair. A dark-value mohair fabric the color of red bark (lower right) adds depth and contrast to the grouping; a light-value silk with loosely rendered curves (bottom right) gently echoes the floral theme. Linen fabrics in (top to bottom) tangerine, sunflower yellow, and apple green provide a jolt of intense color.

TIPS

Don't struggle to match colors to your rug colors; a little dissonance is more appealing.

4 **A PAINT COLOR** What better place to begin your decorating plan than with a paint color that delights you? Start by visiting Lowe's paint department, where you can collect paint strips and chips from Lowe's house brand and from other brands. Lowe's offers ready-made palettes that group congenial colors; these are different from a paint strip, which typically shows light-to-dark values of a single color. If you choose a paint color from a palette card, you can confidently use the remaining colors for other materials.

The palette card shown here features four warm hues in light, medium, and medium-dark values. The pale yellow, which might be described as "biscotti," is the key color; it's assigned to the walls.

The photo shows a cast of materials inspired by this color. A rich tapestry displays all four of the palette-card colors, making it suitable for a sofa or generously proportioned chair. A supporting stripe (bottom left) in darker values of red-orange and yellow-green might be used for simple curtain panels. The dark-green-and-cream stripe (right) is appropriate for a smaller seat, such as an ottoman.

TIPS

If you can't find a desired hue on a standard paint chip, it may be what designers call a "rare" color. These nuanced colors—the grayish taupe of birch bark or the opalescent pink of an Oriental poppy—abound in nature but are not easily matched by paint chips (though colorwashing with three or four colors may approach their subtlety). Take your natural object to Lowe's and ask for our custom Color Matching.

TWO SUBTLETIES OF GOOD DESIGN

THE COMBINATION OF PATTERNS AND TEXTURES CAN EITHER ADD TO OR DETRACT FROM A ROOM'S DECOR. WHAT MAKES THE DIFFERENCE? IN THIS SECTION WE LOOK AT THE DESIGN SUBTLETIES OF PATTERN AND TEXTURE.

A common color, lemon yellow, is the tie that binds a delightful mix of florals, plaids, and solids in a sunny bay window. Varying pattern scale, from large and open to diminutive and dense, is essential when working with one main color.

Did you know that you should evaluate patterns from a distance to see their overall effect? Patterns that appear jarring side by side are often harmonious when separated in a room. Read on for more tips that will enable you to successfully work with patterns and textures.

PATTERN

Faced with an array of florals, checks, stripes, and plaids at a home-furnishings store, you may well experience a moment of "pattern panic." Relax. A little pattern know-how can alleviate your anxiety and help you choose and combine patterns with confidence.

PATTERN SCALE. The size of the motifs or design in a pattern is known as scale. Scale is usually described by designers as small, medium, or large.

SMALL-SCALE PATTERNS tend to read as textured or even solid from a distance. Use them with solids, or for visual relief among other patterns.

MEDIUM-SCALE PATTERNS tend to be the most versatile because they retain their design, even from a distance, yet rarely overpower other patterns. You can easily use them with small- and large-scale patterns.

LARGE-SCALE PATTERNS must be chosen with care. They can appear even bolder when covering large furnishings, such as a sofa, but may look fragmented on a small chair.

PATTERN STYLE. Patterns range from realistic depictions of natural elements—most commonly leaves and flowers—to geometric and abstract designs. Browse the samples at home-furnishings and fabric stores or look through decorating books and magazines to view the possibilities. Fabric advertisements are an excellent resource, because they often show patterns up close.

PATTERN COMBINATIONS. The principles that follow are meant to guide you as you gather, edit, and audition materials, but they are not rules. You may see designer-decorated rooms in magazines that defy these guidelines with great success.

❖ Start with one pattern as your inspiration; make it one that you absolutely love.

❖ Err on the side of caution and use only three patterns in a room. If the patterns are subtle and their colors low-key, you can probably add one or two more, but start with three.

❖ Vary the style of your chosen patterns, combining a curvy leaf pattern with a plaid, for example. Nature-inspired patterns, such as florals, marry well with stripes.

❖ Combine patterns that are different in scale. To a large-scale floral, you might add a medium-scale plaid and a smaller-scale stripe.

❖ Look for three places in a room to distribute patterns. Spreading them throughout the room creates a sense of visual equilibrium; clustering patterns can make a room look lopsided.

❖ Unite different patterns by a common color, such as a similar violet in a floral, stripe, and plaid.

ABOVE: A red-and-green pattern on the bolster and a blue-and-white patchwork design on the Roman shade are two of the many surprises in this playful children's room (see pages 108–109). The striped bench cushion with blue flange trim and the bright blue pillows bridge the color-and-pattern gap. The rose-petal velvet pillow is just for fun.

LEFT: Repetition in color and variation in pattern are a recipe for success. New-neutral colors and a blend of quiet patterns and textures set the mood in this bedroom/dressing room. Striped bed curtains echo the pattern of the stone floor; a floral coverlet makes a nice curvilinear contrast.

TEXTURE

We experience texture in two ways: with touch and with vision. Our bare feet tell us when a wood floor has been sanded so that the grain is perceptible; our fingers tell us that chenille is soft and cushy.

Actual textures—in the woven window shades, brick wall, wood-frame furnishings, and natural accessories— supply the visual interest in this monochromatic scheme and prove that color isn't everything.

Designers call this kind of texture "actual" texture.

Some patterns in fabric and wallpaper only appear textured because they *imply* light and shadow, creating the illusion of dimension. Texture in paint is perceived when its flatness is altered by faux finishes. Designers refer to these effects as "visual" texture.

Actual texture—how rough or smooth a surface is—animates a room and modulates color in powerful ways. Rough-textured materials such as tapestry have tiny peaks and valleys that absorb rather than reflect light, which lessens the intensity of the color. Smooth, shiny surfaces such as satin, on the other hand, reflect light and increase the intensity of the color.

Texture also affects the value of colors, or how light or dark a material seems: colors on shiny surfaces will look lighter; the same colors on textured surfaces, darker. Canary yellow, for instance, will seem perceptibly lighter in chintz than in wide-wale corduroy.

When it comes to paint, texture can accentuate the positive—or hide a multitude of minor sins. High-gloss paint spotlights architectural details, such as handsome moldings or window casings, but it also draws attention to defects like cracks or bumps. The matte finish of a flat paint absorbs light, and its slight texture can melt imperfections into insignificance.

LEFT: A small, angular bathroom features a mix of new-neutral colors and natural textures. Slate tiles of varying sizes and colors line the doorless shower and the adjoining wall; maple cabinets and a stained-concrete floor are in smooth contrast. The wall reflected in the mirror is integral-color plaster, a source of both actual and visual texture.

BELOW: A contemporary Tibetan rug, a leather accent ottoman, and an easy chair covered in handwoven chenille display a variety of actual textures; related colors unite the disparate materials.

TEXTURE TIPS. Combining textures, like combining patterns, is a balancing act. Too little texture gives a room a flat, dull appearance; too much is visually confusing. Here are some simple guidelines:

❖ Use a mix of textures, just as you would patterns. Toss a pebbly knit throw on a leather sofa, or juxtapose smooth silk and plush chenille.

❖ In a room with minimal or low-key color, such as a new-neutral (pages 264–265) or monochromatic (page 232) scheme, texture is the greatest source of visual interest. Play it up.

❖ Solid-colored textured materials are timeless. Use them among patterns to create places for your eye to rest.

❖ Different textures work best together if they are in the same color range. Mohair (a soft fabric) and blanket wool (a rough fabric) in a color that might be described as "cocoa" will naturally harmonize.

❖ When your palette contains several distinctly different colors, unite them with similar textures—a gleaming wood table and shimmery silk curtains in a dining room, a thick braided rug and a twill chair in a family room.

❖ The effects of texture make it nearly impossible to match colors exactly in different materials such as carpet, fabric, and paint. Strive to combine congenial, not matching, colors; it's more interesting if they vary just a little.

keeping track of your samples

INTERIOR DESIGNERS OFTEN CREATE A "PRESENTATION BOARD" TO CONVEY THEIR IDEAS TO CLIENTS. HERE YOU SEE SAN FRANCISCO DESIGNER TRES MCKINNEY'S PRESENTATION BOARD FOR A ROMANTIC RED BEDROOM, AND THE ROOM AS IT LOOKED WHEN FINISHED.

1 TRES BEGAN WITH A SKETCH of the room that showed the furnishings, window, and closet area. She included perspective drawings of the swag-and-cascade window treatment and the fanciful bed with crown canopy and upholstered headboard. Sketches of chairs and a love seat suggest furniture styles. Fabric swatches and wallpaper and carpet samples nestle among her sketches and photos.

2 THE KEY FABRIC, a large-scale cotton floral in red, cream, and beige, sets the mood. Quiet prints and a small-scale plaid echo the beige-and-cream striped wallpaper, which was chosen to imply a higher ceiling. A deep red miniprint on the tufted chair makes it a welcome visual rest point (page 87). The matelassé coverlet and sisal-weave carpet contribute actual texture and provide relief from the patterns.

3 THE WINDOW TREATMENT AND WALLPAPER illustrate an important principle: you can vary pattern style (floral, stripe, and plaid) and scale (large, medium, and small) yet still achieve harmony if you repeat key colors (red, white, and beige).

4 STERLING SILVER AND PURE WHITE ACCESSORIES convey both elegance and simplicity. Notice that they vary in both height and shape. Open-weave patterned sheers diffuse the light and provide the perfect, almost plain, backdrop.

The handwritten labels on the sample board read: Loveseat, Club Chair, KM134-L Love Note, KM135-L Lyric Opera, KM136-M Rebecca Jo, KM137-M Opera House, Ottoman and Windowseat, A Garden Guest Room in pinks + greens, Duvet Covers, Color Palette, Curtain.

Seeing fabrics, trims, and paint colors together helps you visualize how they'll look in your room; cutting the fabrics in sizes proportional to their use gives you a better feel for their impact.

MAKE YOUR OWN SAMPLE BOOK

You can easily adapt the presentation board idea on page 186 to create your own portable book of samples and materials for your room decorating project. Take this handy reference tool with you when you shop at Lowe's and other stores—it will be especially useful to salespersons who help you add compatible materials. The example above shows a homeowner's version for a garden-style bedroom that's still in progress. Here's how you can make a book to hold similar elements:

❖ You'll need a binder, photo album, or scrapbook with removable pages (shop for it at a stationery or office supply store). The pages should be heavy-weight paper or very light manila or cardboard that will support your fabric samples without buckling. Removable pages will allow you to view all the elements together. You may also want some pocket pages for holding odds and ends. Investigate your stationery store to see what kinds of creative use you can make of the various inserts available for binders, albums and scrapbooks. You'll also need fabric scissors and a glue stick or staples for attaching your samples.

❖ Draw a simple bird's-eye-view sketch of your room, roughly to scale. Locate major furniture pieces, such as the beds, love seat, chair, and ottoman in the sketch shown here. Make photocopies of your sketch; enlarge it slightly, if you like, to better show the furnishings. Trim the sketch, if necessary, to fit your book, then glue it to one of the pages. For extra protection, you can put it in a clear plastic insert.

❖ If you've collected some photos that inspired your color palette or captured the mood you hope to create, add them to your book.

❖ Cut out pieces of your fabric samples in proportion to the space they will occupy in the room or the furnishings they will cover. In our example, you see a relatively large piece of the tree fabric for the comforter covers; the small ottoman is represented by a smaller piece of solid green.

❖ Position your fabric samples in a pleasing arrangement and glue or staple them onto a page. Leave room near each sample to write in where it's intended to go; in the example above, a note was written by each piece of fabric. It will be handiest if this page faces your sketch page when the book is open.

❖ Glue samples of fringe, cord, or other embellishments to the lower edges of the appropriate fabrics; for example, the brush fringe will edge the comforter covers shown here.

❖ On another page, attach samples of wall coverings and paint chips. Add a flooring or floor covering sample (if you were able to obtain a small enough sample that's not too heavy; otherwise, tuck it into a pocket page). Label all these as you did the fabric samples.

You now have a project sample book to show family and friends. Best of all, you'll have an inspiring "sneak preview" of your room to refer to as you work toward its completion.

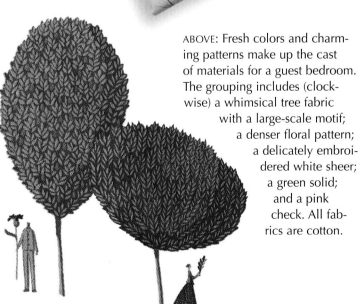

ABOVE: Fresh colors and charming patterns make up the cast of materials for a guest bedroom. The grouping includes (clockwise) a whimsical tree fabric with a large-scale motif; a denser floral pattern; a delicately embroidered white sheer; a green solid; and a pink check. All fabrics are cotton.

A PRIMER ON THE PRINCIPLES OF DESIGN

HAVE YOU EVER WONDERED WHY SOME ROOMS "WORK" AND OTHERS DON'T? COLOR IS ALWAYS A FACTOR, BUT INTELLIGENT DESIGN IS JUST AS IMPORTANT. FORTUNATELY, THE PRINCIPLES OF GOOD DESIGN ARE NOT A PROFESSIONAL SECRET.

In this section you'll get a crash course in design principles, followed by tips for arranging furniture, tying rooms together, and altering the perception of space.

BALANCE

Balance is a good place to begin, because it is relatively easy to understand. Three kinds of balance apply in decorating: symmetry, asymmetry, and radial symmetry.

ABOVE: Radial balance always emanates from a center point, exemplified by the arrangement on this round dining table and the chandelier above it.

FACING PAGE, TOP: Symmetrical balance is ideally suited to a traditional room with a strong focal point, such as the fireplace shown here. Identical chairs and wall-mounted lamps create a mirror-image effect. Lesser elements need not (and should not) match.

FACING PAGE, BOTTOM: Asymmetrical balance conveys the illusion of balance without the precision of symmetry. In this casual family room, floor-to-ceiling shelving at left is balanced by a low, wide built-in seating nook to the right.

WHAT IS VISUAL WEIGHT?

Visual weight cannot be measured; it's all about perception. Here are a few examples.

❖ *Large objects are visually heavier than small ones. An oversize club chair, for instance, visually "outweighs" a diminutive slipper chair.*

❖ *Materials that are actually weighty—limestone, for example—are visually heavier than lightweight materials, such as seagrass matting.*

❖ *Dark, warm, intense colors like black, russet, and red seem heavy. Light, cool, low-intensity colors such as straw, azure, and willow appear less weighty.*

❖ *Complex patterns are "heavier" than plain ones.*

❖ *Opaque materials are heavier than transparent ones. A stone pitcher appears heftier than a clear glass one.* ↝

SYMMETRY. Imagine an entry with a console table, a mirror hanging above it, and a matching sconce on either side. If you drew a line down the center of this picture, one half would be the mirror image of the other. That's symmetry: if it's on one side, it's on the other.

Symmetrical balance pleases us because it's orderly and predictable, demanding little effort on our part to figure it out. The effect is restful and dignified—just the look sought after in traditional and formal settings.

To achieve symmetry in your room, start by placing matching furnishings on either side of a central point. Actually, the furnishings need not be identical; the secret is to imply balance, using pieces that have the same visual weight (see "What Is Visual Weight?" on the facing page).

ASYMMETRY. In asymmetrical balance, the furnishings or pieces differ in visual weight yet appear to be balanced. More energetic and less predictable than its symmetrical counterpart, asymmetry is most typical of Asian and contemporary design.

To understand asymmetrical balance, think of a seesaw from your childhood. Do you remember? A small child at the extreme end of a seesaw could balance a larger child on the other side who was sitting closer to the center. That's how asymmetrical balance works in decorating: visually lighter objects placed farther from the center of a room, wall, or grouping of furniture balance visually heavier objects closer to the center.

If you're not sure how to achieve asymmetry, begin by arranging your furnishings symmetrically; then add or move pieces to break up the formality.

RADIAL SYMMETRY. In most decorating situations, you don't have to work at achieving radial symmetry; it occurs naturally if you have a strong center point. Still, it's helpful to recognize this kind of balance—especially if you want to accentuate it. A dropped pendant light centered over a round dining table establishes a sense of radial symmetry; seating placed around the imaginary center of a room automatically feels balanced.

ABOVE: High contrast between the dark wood and light walls makes a magnificent fireplace, original to the house, the unquestioned area of emphasis in this formal living room. Identical mirrors and tables flanking the fireplace reinforce its architecture; matching floral displays soften it.

FACING PAGE, TOP: A mirror framed in contrasting exotic woods and edged with mahogany and copper strips effectively disguises a stainless steel fireplace facade from the 1960s. Light-value, neutral walls and furnishings serve as rest points. The highlight of this Asian-style living room—its sylvan view—merits the mirror treatment.

EMPHASIS

Emphasis is really a two-part concept comprising a "focal point" and "rest points." Both are necessary to the principle; you can't have one without the other. A focal point is what we call the object or area that attracts attention; rest points are those elements that provide visual relief. Without a focal point, a room can be as monotonous as a dripping faucet; without rest points, it can feel as chaotic as rush-hour traffic. Rooms that have areas of emphasis and visual relief are the most satisfying.

FIND THE FOCAL POINT. How do you know what constitutes a focal point in your room? Whatever catches your eye first is usually the natural focal point: a fine painting, a fireplace with a carved mantel, or a bay window with a garden view may claim focal-point status. Once you've identified the focal point in your room, give it its due. Accessorize a mantel with eye-catching objects; install window treatments that enhance a beautiful window frame.

Because of its size, a sofa or an armoire is a natural object of emphasis. Similarly, entertainment or media centers often become focal points—intentionally or not—in family rooms and great rooms. If an oversize entertainment center commands unwanted attention, counterbalance it with an equally large-scale piece of furniture in a color that gives it greater visual weight.

CREATE REST POINTS. Focal points get most of the attention, naturally, but rest points are crucial to a successful decorating plan. These are more difficult to define, but when a room lacks places for your eye to pause, you know it—immediately. Think of rest points as supporting characters in a play; they are essential to the story line, but they are not the stars. Floors and walls are supportive; when you have a strong focal point, you should keep those surfaces low-key and noncompetitive. Neutral or new-neutral furnishings also provide a place for the eye to rest in a room with a prominent area of emphasis.

In the real world—your own home—you'll see varying degrees of emphasis, from a room's primary feature to its least significant accessory. Between your focal point and rest points, your scheme must have other elements of interest. In a room with a focal-point painting and understated walls, you might choose furnishings that command a little more interest than the quiet walls (such as decorative sconces) but a little less interest than the painting (such as a new-neutral sofa).

TIPS

Think about how to develop your focal point first; then think about how to support it with rest points.

A massive fireplace of native stone is the dramatic focal point in the common area of this mountain hideaway—people just naturally want to gather here. The arresting pattern and texture of the masonry attracts the eye; the warm color and earthy texture of the rock sets the indoor-outdoor tone for the entire room.

Diminutive furnishings are fitting in a small alcove (above). The lightly scaled dressing table doubles as a writing desk; a lady's armchair wears a sheer silk slipcover. In crisp counterpoint to the blue-and-cream striped wallpaper, a photo is matted in white and framed in black. The same design elements—chair, table, art, and accessories—make a dramatically different statement when the pieces are large in scale (below). Note the impact of each vase—one petite, the other massive.

SCALE AND PROPORTION

Successful design always includes appropriately scaled furnishings that are in pleasing proportion to one another. Scale and proportion go hand in hand in design, and it's well worth the time it takes to learn what each term means and to distinguish between the two.

SCALE. Simply put, scale is the size of an object or element. A tiny floral print is small-scale, a 5-inch plaid large-scale. Designers usually refer to scale as being small, medium, or large, but of course there are infinite possibilities, from very small to very large. Scale is also relative: large-scale objects look even larger in the company of small ones; small-scale objects look even smaller in the presence of large ones.

PROPORTION. Whereas scale logically refers to the size of objects, elements, furnishings, or a room itself, proportion is a subtler concept. It's about the relationships between objects or furnishings. Even the novice knows instinctively when something is "in proportion" or "out of proportion." A large ottoman is perfect with a chair-and-a-half, for example, but a Queen Anne table

looks all wrong next to an immense recliner—they are alien to one another in scale as well as style.

Scale and proportion also apply to pattern. A small-scale miniprint gets lost in a spacious dining room with a high ceiling, but it seems just right in a tiny attic bedroom. Conversely, a large-scale floral might dominate a small bedroom yet look appropriately grand in a high-ceilinged dining room.

As you shop for and arrange furnishings, ask yourself if the pieces are in pleasing proportion to each other. Is the coffee table in proportion to the sofa? Is the area rug in proportion to the seating arrangement? Is the lamp in proportion to the chair it accompanies? Proportion is just as important when choosing accessories. Arrange chunky earthenware on a large wood table, for example; on a glass-topped demilune table, group a collection of delicate porcelains.

In the end, correct scale and proportion is what is comfortable for you and your family. Much traditional furniture is comfortably scaled, which explains the enduring popularity of the style. Contemporary designers often use overscaled pieces for the sense of fun and drama they contribute; if you like this look, use fewer pieces so that space is not consumed by them. In children's rooms, you may want to deliberately scale down the furnishings to a kid-friendly size.

TIPS

A common mistake is to choose accessories that are too small in scale for the room, resulting in a spotty effect. Experiment with larger objects for a better-proportioned look.

This serene dining room is a study in appropriate scale and pleasing proportions. The scale of the mirror repeats that of the rounded chair backs; the chandelier, too, is in proportion to the mirror frame. The open structure of the marble-topped console table and the dining chairs, though not strictly a matter of scale, contributes to the impression of a well-proportioned room.

RHYTHM

Of all the design principles, rhythm is perhaps the most intriguing and fun to work with. When a room has visual rhythm, a sense of vitality carries you along, as if to a destination. Rhythm is surprisingly easy to achieve, once you're aware of how and when it occurs in a room. The following techniques set the principle in motion.

REPEAT IT. Think of this kind of rhythm as a musical beat, but with repeating patterns, textures, shapes, and lines instead of notes. In a formal living room, for example, you might put round silk bolsters on a tuxedo sofa (whose arms are slightly rounded) and a round presentation urn atop a demilune (half-circle) console table. Because of this simple repetition of round forms, the room pulses with a quiet rhythm; because the forms vary in size and material, the effect is engaging rather than monotonous.

From small-scale squares in the accent table and rug to larger ones in the plaid chairs and banded window shades, this room exemplifies progression. Art lamps, with their organic forms, soften the room's geometry.

GO FROM SMALL TO LARGE. There is something innately satisfying about similar elements that increase in size. A bathroom with a countertop of small square tiles, a stack of bath towels folded into squares, and large squares painted on the walls displays a kind of rhythm known to designers as "progression." The basic shape—

Recurring shapes in the round table, centerpiece, and three-tiered light fixture establish a pleasing visual rhythm. The harlequin-patterned upholstery fabric is itself an example of rhythm achieved through repetition, as is the grouping of identical dining chairs. Centering the table in front of a trio of atrium windows adds to the rhythmic effect.

a square in this example—repeats, but in increasing size.

This concept is especially relevant to accessories: imagine a collection of rectangular picture frames atop a piano, arranged from short to tall, front to back. A trio of nesting tables is another excellent example of progression from small to large.

MAKE IT FLOW. "It just flows" is a phrase often used to describe what designers call "transitional" rhythm, that sense of effortless visual motion within a room. Curved lines—an arched doorway, a camelback sofa, a circular area rug—lead your eye smoothly around a room, from one design element to the next.

Furniture placement is essential to creating rhythmical flow in a room; see "Furniture Arrangement" on pages 200–205. For a discussion of transitional rhythm from room to room, see "Harmonious Transitions" on pages 208–209.

INCLUDE CONTRAST. A mere repetition of shapes, lines, patterns, or colors is boring when it's not interrupted by a contrasting element. In decades past, rooms sometimes exhibited a dull sameness—all small-scale patterns on walls and upholstery, for example, with "suites" of matching wood furnishings.

Today you're freer to mix styles and scales and throw in a surprise or two for interest. You might hang an ornate carved mirror over a modern glass-topped table, contrasting the period detail of the mirror with the sleek, hard lines of the table. Contrasts in texture—bumpy tapestry, plush mohair, smooth leather—set up a lively, almost syncopated rhythm.

Two views of the same living room exhibit transitional rhythm. Once a mere corridor, the room now flows, thanks to the careful placement of furnishings. Four leather chairs surround a glass-topped cocktail table and a fireplace for a cozy "club" atmosphere (top). A view from the stairs (bottom) reveals how a contemporary striped Tibetan rug breaks up the area below the Arts and Crafts–inspired windows and draws the attention back to the seating arrangement.

RIGHT: A palette of taupe, cream, gray, and black is harmonious, the result of pattern and texture variations in the materials. Hand-painted medallion pillows contrast with solid linen canvas and a large-scale linen check. The high upholstered headboard links the grouping of antique prints to the bed.

BELOW: Subtle repetition in this sleek, simple scheme leads to a quiet sense of harmony. The curves of the bar ledge, stools, and cooktop hood convey unity; black accents are in crisp contrast. A strip of lighted glass block becomes a luminous focal point.

HARMONY

Pick up any design magazine, and you won't read long before encountering the words *harmony* and *harmonious*—they'll probably be describing a general atmosphere of well-being. What is the design principle of harmony, how does it work, and how can you realize it in your own home?

Even without a course in interior design, most of us can recognize the presence of harmony. This feeling results when two intangible and opposing qualities, unity and variety, coexist. Think of it as a kind of design equation: unity + variety = harmony. In other words, when parts of a room are *similar* enough to make the room feel unified yet *different* enough to make it interesting, the space is harmonious. Interior designers put it another way: they speak of "theme and variation." A room should have a consistent, unified theme yet enough variety to keep the look fresh.

To apply the concept of harmony, first consider its components.

UNITY. The easiest way to achieve visual unity is through repetition and similarity: use one or more colors from your palette in adjoining rooms, choose art with a related theme, or repeat geometric shapes in fabrics, for example. Repetition and continuity automatically unify a room, enabling you to make sense of the space.

Too much unity, however, can lead to monotony. Imagine a room with the same bold pattern on the upholstered pieces, the walls, and the window treatments. Without seeing the room you can feel its excess, and you sense that it may be overwhelming. In the same way, an all-beige room composed of solid-color materials with a smooth texture is likely to be predictable—or worse yet, boring.

VARIETY. That's where variety comes into play. In a harmonious room, everything seems to "belong," but one or two elements of surprise make the visual experience a little richer and less predictable. The variation can be as subtle as slight differences in color—one blue that is more grayed, another that leans toward blue-violet, for example. Or the variation can be more pronounced—a chic, two-tone leather sofa atop an antique Persian rug.

As with unity, however, too much variation can tip the scales toward chaos. Authentic Victorian design, with its profusion of color, pattern, and texture, is considered oppressive by today's design standards. You might, however, choose elements from that style and re-interpret them in a way that minimizes the visual confusion; for instance, by selecting a wallpaper pattern of simplified Victorian motifs on a more open background.

TIPS

When striving for variety, push forward, beyond what's safe; then pull back if necessary. It's all part of the process.

Harmony is the result when a decorating plan includes both theme and variation. Crackle-glazed paint, gauzy window treatments, golden-toned woods, and a new-neutral chair are similar enough to be unified (theme) yet different enough to be interesting (variation).

Walnut chairs with woven rawhide backs and seats define the inner room in a true loft and echo the dark lines and strong shapes of the industrial-style windows.

The arrangement allows easy movement from the seating area to the dining area and to the view; at the same time, each chair has access to the low table. A klismos-style chair with gilded back functions more as an accessory than as practical seating.

FURNITURE ARRANGEMENT

"Just for fun, let's rearrange the furniture." Sound familiar? Nothing gives a room a fresh look like changing the arrangement of its furnishings. But before you start moving the sofa around or swapping chairs, read the following furniture-arranging guidelines to determine which ones are relevant to your living areas. A bird's-eye-view sketch, too, can help you visualize how your furniture will look in different arrangements; see page 171.

REVIST YOUR GIVENS. You've already listed the architectural features of your room and the furnishings you plan to keep (page 170). Review those givens now, because a large media center or a bank of windows will be an automatic starting point for furniture placement. Also take the time to stand in each entrance to the room and analyze its strengths and weaknesses from that viewpoint. You may want to emphasize the most attractive part of the room with a major grouping, while downplaying a less appealing area with secondary pieces.

SERVE YOUR FOCAL POINT. Arrange seating so that your family and visitors can appreciate your room's focal point, whether it's a baby grand piano or handsome built-in bookcases. If you have more than one focal point, create seating for each one: a pair of love seats positioned to enjoy a piano, for example, and a floor lamp and chairs opposite bookcases. One disadvantage of having a single strong focal point is that it will, like a given, limit your furniture-placement options.

ENCOURAGE CONVERSATION. The number one activity in rooms where people gather is conversation, so it's important to cluster seating in a way that makes it easy for your family and guests to chat. A circular or elliptical arrangement, with a central space approximately 8 to 10 feet across, allows guests to hear and see each other clearly; any greater distance destroys the sense of intimacy. Keep in mind that most people prefer to sit across from each other rather than side by side.

CONTROL TRAFFIC. Work out a plan that guides foot traffic around, rather than through, conversation areas. One traditional arrangement consists of love seats flanking a view window, creating an inner room that you can enter but not walk through. Allow 30 to 36 inches between major furnishings for easy passage. Between a coffee table and sofa or between chairs, allow 18 inches.

ABOVE: Sofas placed at a right angle—one against the window wall, the other floating in the room—define the conversation area in an open living room. A charcoal-gray chair and a pair of matching stools increase the seating capacity without closing off the inner room. A low table unifies the seating pieces and provides a generous display surface.

LEFT: This elegant living room has a relaxed atmosphere, thanks to an inviting seating arrangement. Instead of a more formal symmetrical or aligned placement, comfy upholstered chairs and generous ottomans are arranged in intimate groupings, making the setting more conducive to easy conversation.

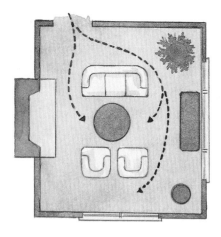 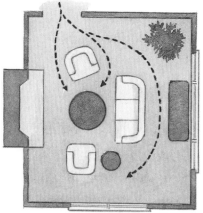 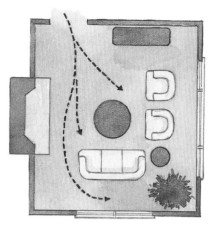

ABOVE: Consider potential traffic patterns when you arrange your furnishings. In the first example, the sofa blocks the view of the room, and guests must walk around it to be seated. In the middle scheme, guests have better access to the seating, and the back of the angled chair is less obtrusive. The arrangement in the third example welcomes guests and permits the freest circulation within the room.

START WITH THE SOFA. The sofa is often the cornerstone of a furniture plan, in part because it is large, so it's natural to determine its placement first. Taking into consideration your givens and your focal point, as well as the desire to facilitate conversation and direct foot traffic, start with the sofa and build out from it, adding chairs, tables, and lamps. (Don't feel that you must situate the sofa against a wall; see "Float Furnishings" on the facing page.)

MAKE AN ENTRANCE. Seating that faces you as you enter a room is welcoming, whereas the back of a sofa says "Stay out!" Sometimes there's no way around placing a chair or sofa with its back toward the entrance, such as when you group pieces around a fireplace opposite the room's main entrance. But even in that situation, you can try to arrange the pieces so that one or two seats face the doorway.

SUBDIVIDE FOR SUCCESS. Open floor plans and spacious great rooms are the norm in contemporary home design, but they can sometimes feel too big. To avoid the "ballroom" effect, with furniture lined up against the walls, divide a large room into several sub-areas according to activity. Designers sometimes call these sub-areas "inner rooms."

Start by creating a main conversation area; the backs of the seating can form the boundaries of this space. (As mentioned above, try to place at least one piece facing the main entrance to the room.) A secondary area might consist of two club chairs, a table, and a reading lamp near a window. The dining space is another natural sub-area with a dedicated activity.

Arrange furniture compactly to hold each sub-area together. Link the sub-areas with common flooring, such as hardwood, tile, or carpet; delineate and anchor inner rooms with area rugs. Simply changing the direction of an area rug can redefine the imaginary perimeter of an inner room.

PLAN FOR FLEXIBILITY. The easier it is to move chairs and tables to accommodate guests, the more comfortable and versatile your room will be. Occasional chairs, small benches, and ottomans are ideal for drop-in visitors; add a few of these movable pieces to make your room more livable.

FLOAT FURNISHINGS. Lining the walls with furnishings is a typical approach, but this arrangement tends to put an uncomfortable distance between people when they're seated. "Floating" furnishings in the room can make for a more convivial atmosphere; pulling furnishings away from the walls also buys valuable space for bookcases and traffic.

The typical floating arrangement consists of a sofa and chairs arranged around a focal point to create an inner room. Furnishings that float need not always be parallel to the walls: a sofa placed on the diagonal, across a corner, opens up a room. An area rug that's also on the diagonal strengthens and anchors such an arrangement. Even when an area rug is parallel to the walls, you can float the seating on it diagonally.

ABOVE: Arranging two chairs to face a sofa is a timeless plan. A Louis XV chair with a striped-silk taffeta cushion offsets the symmetry of the mantel arrangement. (The chair has a twin in the opposite corner of the room.) The slender legs of the antique leather trunk make it seem to occupy less space than it actually does.

BELOW: A different view reveals an inner room nestled in a bright but shallow bay. An antique table doubles as a desk. Matching ottomans, one stowed under the table, provide extra seating when friends and family gather.

THINK UP AND DOWN. We tend to consider first how furnishings are arranged on the floor, but it's just as important to look up and see how they relate to one another vertically. Interior designers use the term *eye-mapping* to describe the up-and-down path our eyes follow as we look around a room. If the furnishings are all about the same height and accessories are at the same level, a room is likely to appear static. But when your eye travels across the back of a sofa, goes up a lamp, then skips along the top of a window treatment and down to a painting, the effect is lively and visually satisfying.

LEAVE ROOM FOR LIGHT. Allow enough space between sofas and chairs to accommodate lighting. When light spills behind, in front of, and between pieces, it enhances the sense of space. Table and floor lamps provide additional light; they also create height between furnishings, enhancing eye-mapping.

A formal arrangement of furnishings can be surprisingly flexible. A library table subdivides this room and does double duty as a console table and desk, with lamps that serve both desk and sofa. The room's design is also an excellent example of eye-mapping: your attention is caught by the gilt chair; moves up to the desk and lamp; up again to the armoire, candelabra sconces, and art; and then back down to the central fireplace.

PLAN FOR CONVENIENCE. Be sure every seat is accompanied by some sort of surface on which to place a coffee cup or a magazine. An accent or end table should be approximately the same arm height as the chair or sofa it's partnered with.

CRITIQUE YOUR ROOM. With your furnishings in their new positions, stand back, evaluate what you've done, and ask yourself these questions:

❖ Is the room lopsided? If so, rearrange the furnishings, either symmetrically or asymmetrically, to achieve a better balance. Pay particular attention to the visual weight of each piece as you work to improve your arrangement; for example, a solid wood cube used as an end table will seem to fill more space than a slim-legged rattan table. (See "What Is Visual Weight?" on page 190.)

❖ Are there too many pieces in the room? Take out one or two to see if you like the look of less furniture and the resulting increase in floor space. Consider substituting dual-function pieces—an ottoman/coffee table or a coffee table/storage unit—if you decide you have too many furnishings. A console table situated behind a sofa can replace a pair of end tables as a surface for reading lamps.

❖ Are the furnishings all rectangular or square? Curved pieces—a round coffee table, round ottoman, or overstuffed club chair—can soften a room containing mostly square or rectangular pieces.

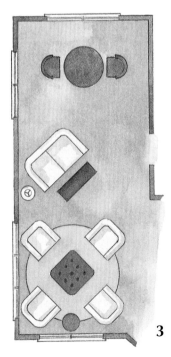

1

2

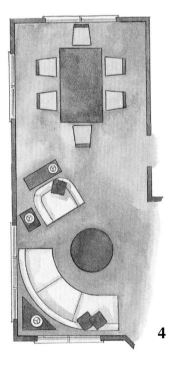

3

4

A combined living and dining room demands a flexible furniture plan for everyday living and occasional entertaining. Whatever the arrangement, ease of movement is a must. All four of these plans fit the bill.

PLAN ONE: Three inner rooms make maximum use of the space. The facing sofas facilitate conversation and take advantage of the view windows. Two comfortable chairs with a shared ottoman are positioned in front of a folding screen, creating a cozy place to read or chat.

PLAN TWO: A trio of love seats accommodates the largest number of guests in the small space; each seating piece has access to both an accent table and the coffee table. A demilune console table against the wall visually divides the two inner rooms.

PLAN THREE: In this circular plan, four chairs positioned on a round area rug share an ottoman. A separate love seat provides additional seating for larger gatherings. The bistro table is ideal when it's just dinner for two.

PLAN FOUR: A quarter-round sofa and a chair-and-a-half welcome guests into the conversation area; the circular coffee table creates a sense of rhythm through repetition of the curves. Placing the dining table lengthwise emphasizes the shape of the room.

REFLECTIVE SURFACES OPEN UP SPACE, BOUNCE LIGHT, AND PLAY WITH OUR PERCEPTION OF REALITY.

mirror and glass

1

1 MIRRORS FRAMED BY MOLDING multiply the patterns, finishes, and accessories in an exquisite bathroom and imply additional height. Diaphanous curtain panels veil the view and temper glare without blocking light. A true-neutral scheme—in this case, gray, white, and silver—is always harmonious in a room that features mirror.

2 A FACETED MIRROR SCREEN in a small sitting room complicates light and space in a magical way. The wood cornice's gentle curves contrast with the screen's straight lines and hard edges. Grass growing in simple boxes atop the screen injects fresh, natural color and texture into the scene and adds a softening element of surprise.

3 A SLEEK MIRROR reflects the simplicity and sophistication of this contemporary bedroom and visually expands the space. An accent table positioned to create a true "mirror image" unites the real room with the illusion. Placing the mirror opposite the focal-point painting also increases the impact of the art.

4 THIS INTRICATELY CARVED and gilded mirror bounces light from a graceful bow window and reflects the new-neutral hues and shimmering finishes of silk curtains and Venetian waxed walls. The mirror's elaborate design reiterates the curvilinear patterns in the architectural fragment and sconce.

5 GLASS—and lots of it—forms a strong visual link between an ultracontemporary living room and the city it overlooks. A glass table-top echoes the stark images and true-neutral colors of industry; special finishes and textures in the paint and furnishings strengthen the connection.

HARMONIOUS TRANSITIONS

It's virtually impossible to be in one room of your house without being aware of the others: an entry opens into the living room, the living room adjoins the dining room, the hallway leads to the bedrooms. Each space can have its own personality, but a home with harmonious transitions is generally more pleasing. When they're most effective, these transitions go unnoticed.

Achieving a sense of connectedness calls for a little planning. Stand in the doorways between rooms and think about how to repeat and continue colors and materials from one room to the next. Designers often start by linking the "bones" of a room—the floors and walls—followed by the window treatments.

FROM THE FLOOR UP. If you're planning to install new flooring, review your options with visual transition in mind. Tile that begins in the entry and spills into adjoining rooms welcomes guests and ushers them into the living areas. Subtly patterned carpet or hardwood flooring throughout a house imparts a sense of continuity.

If you do change flooring from one room to the next, choose closely related colors and values to ease the transition. You might lay light-value porcelain pavers in the kitchen and install similarly light-value berber carpeting in the adjoining family room, for instance.

WALL TO WALL. Carrying the same paint color or wallpaper throughout the house is a time-honored way to achieve a smooth, seamless look and expand the sense of space.

For a more complex effect that is still harmonious, use the same color in different values (a monochromatic scheme) or related colors (an analogous scheme) from room to room. When colors contrast (a complementary or complex scheme), the secret of success is to maintain similar intensity: a muted green in the living room, for example, and a muted red in the dining room.

If you've chosen dramatically different colors for adjoining rooms, keep the trim

An entry doubles as a transitional space and art gallery in this contemporary home. Pale chrome green walls extend to the first landing, where the color shifts to a light-value terra-cotta. Maple stair treads are flush with the risers for a soft, sculptural look. The sideboard with pyramid-shaped, verdigris copper "legs" is a takeoff on the traditional trestle table.

the same color throughout—a version of white is traditional—to lead the eye onward and strengthen the visual connection.

WINDOW WEAR. Identical curtains, blinds, shades, or shutters hung in neighboring rooms provide a consistent backdrop for furnishings and ease the visual transition, especially if the treatments are neutral. For a little variation, repeat the treatment style and color, such as blue swags and cascades, in adjacent rooms but use a different pattern for each space—perhaps a blue toile de Jouy in the living room but a blue stripe in the dining room.

A sweeping curved ceiling and floor in an innovative home create a smooth transition from dining area to living room, even though the wood flooring contrasts sharply in color and value. For more views of this house, see pages 160–163.

TIPS

Repeat a main color from one room in an accessory or small furnishing for an adjoining room, to subtly link the two.

A chest centered opposite two doorways becomes a focal point, guiding your attention from one room through a hallway and into another room. Although the walls vary in value from dark to light, the colors are similar in intensity—that is, muted and quiet. The distant red vase repeats the color on the near wall.

ABOVE: A chaise placed on the diagonal makes best use of the angled ceiling in an attic hideaway. Arranging furniture on an angle makes a small room more dynamic, though you do lose valuable floor space.

BELOW, RIGHT: Oversize club chairs and ottomans break the rules—and get away with it—in a small sitting room situated between the main living area and dining room. The chairs' scale and color give them visual weight and significance.

SPATIAL ILLUSIONS

When it comes to space, you probably think your rooms are too small or too large. Whether they strike you as confining or vast, there are ways to alter the sense of space and transform problem spaces into rooms that feel "just right."

"GROW" A SMALL ROOM. When small rooms feel uncomfortably close, you can make them appear roomier. Here's how:

❖ Use light values to make a room feel larger. The standard approach is to paint the walls white, but light-value colors like chamois, fawn, and celadon can be just as space enhancing.

❖ Place large furnishings against walls, so they don't break up what open space the room has.

❖ Choose sofas and chairs with open arms and exposed legs that allow light to spill around and under them, creating an airier effect. Because glass-topped tables don't interrupt your view of the floor, they can make rooms seem larger.

❖ Use smaller-scale furnishings that leave a smaller "footprint." Too many small-scale pieces, however, can make a room look like a dollhouse. Feel free to ignore conventional wisdom and include a larger furnishing or two to visually anchor the room.

❖ Maximize precious floor space with open vertical storage: a tall hutch or floor-to-ceiling bookcases.

❖ Hang a mirror to expand the sense of space and to bounce light, color, and pattern around the room. A mirror on a wall adjacent to windows will reflect the outdoors and imply another window.

TIPS

Take a hard look at your possessions and subtract what is not essential; you'll feel liberated once you're convinced that less really is more.

COZY UP A SPACIOUS ROOM.

Large rooms are a blessing—who doesn't love extra space?—yet they present their own design challenges. The following are some designer strategies for making large rooms more intimate and livable.

❖ Cover walls with warm, dark, or intense colors such as persimmon (a warm red-orange), indigo (a dark blue), or apple green (an intense yellow-green); they will visually fill a room and appear to contract space.

❖ Rather than treating the room as one gigantic conversation pit—no one wants to shout across a vast expanse of carpet—create several inner rooms with your furniture.

❖ Purchase furnishings that extend to the floor—a sofa with bun feet, a skirted chair, or a solid desk—to absorb space.

❖ Choose a complex color combination rather than a monochromatic one (see page 232). A large room that combines tangerine, violet, and lime green—three contrasting colors—will seem cozier than an all-blue one.

❖ Employ lighting to help separate smaller areas within one large room. (For more information about lighting, turn to pages 310–311.)

ABOVE: Sometimes a small room can benefit from the bold use of color. A case in point is this beach-house dining room. A wall of intense blue evokes sea and sky and forms a backdrop for a bright white sideboard; touches of white are repeated throughout this home's rooms to establish visual continuity.

LEFT: A pale, mostly monochromatic color scheme imparts that light and airy look so frequently desired in bedrooms. A large-scale bed and generous seating pieces fill the room without overwhelming it.

APPLYING THE FINISHING TOUCHES

NO SCHEME IS COMPLETE UNTIL YOU ADD THE FINISHING TOUCHES, AND ARRANGING THESE ESSENTIAL ELEMENTS SO THEY LOOK THEIR BEST IS ONE OF THE LAST, AND MOST ENJOYABLE, STEPS IN THE DECORATING PROCESS.

ABOVE: A tray can become a display shelf for collections of similar objects, like these milky white vases. Even when the objects vary in color and form, a tray can bring the grouping together.

BELOW, RIGHT: Eye-mapping can work to your advantage in a grouping of accessories, just as it does in a room. Arranged in a way that draws your attention up and around, disparate accessories coalesce into a self-contained vignette.

Finishing touches include traditional accessories such as vases and mirrors as well as tablescapes, flower arrangements, artworks, and collectibles. The options are endless, the strategies for their arrangement diverse, as you'll see on these and the following pages.

TIPS ON THE USE OF ACCESSORIES

Accessories are like jewelry for the home: without them, the best-designed room can still look "underdressed"; with them, the room looks polished.

We are drawn to certain accessories in part because they reveal our special interests and personal histories. Paintings, mirrors, vases, flowers, topiaries, candles, plates, blown glass, architectural fragments, clocks, candlesticks—anything that captures your imagination and expresses your style can be an accessory.

Some are practical as well as decorative, such as a task lamp on a desk or a folding screen dividing a room; others are strictly ornamental, like Venetian glass or porcelains. Whether they're hardworking or just for show, accessories should be objects that you love.

TIPS

Home-furnishings stores and design showrooms that display fully accessorized room settings are excellent sources of inspiration.

SHOPPING TIPS. Searching for accessories is a hunting-and-gathering process, just like choosing fabric, flooring, or paint. The most common mistake novices make is to underaccessorize a room. Unless you have a huge stash from which to choose—and few homeowners do—you'll need to buy some new decorative pieces. Designers urge you to take your time when looking. The worst approach, guaranteed to disappoint you, is to pick out all your accessories in one frenzied shopping expedition. As you did when gathering other decorating materials, cast a wide net and consider all of the possibilities.

PERFECT PLACEMENT. Where should you put accessories? The most logical places are where you naturally look: opposite the front door as you come in; wherever your eye falls when you enter a room or look from one room into another; behind a sofa or on top of an armoire; at the end of a hall. You can also position them to indicate where you want guests to look—for example, by placing a sculpture in the line of vision to a window wall.

In this scheme, the lamps are symmetrically placed in relation to the sofa and cabinet, while everything else is asymmetrical. A visually heavy vase placed closer to the center balances two tall, thin candlesticks placed farther from the center.

A small tabletop arrangement illustrates the "shiny, matte, tall, and fat" guideline (see page 214) with tall, shiny candlesticks, a chunky vase, and a matte-surface bowl.

Why hide the TV and sound system when they are, after all, essential elements in a family room? Here, a flat-screen TV hangs like a piece of art, and the stereo is front and center for all to see. A rough-hewn, "hands-on" side table is in contrast to the very modern lamp and smooth glass.

TIPS

As you evaluate an accessory, ask yourself, "Is it interesting on its own?" If it is, it will probably strengthen your room.

BEGINNER BASICS. Older, more formal rules of accessorizing have given way to a respect for individual style and fresh approaches. Conventional dictates aside, a few guidelines are still helpful.

❖ The "odd-number rule" recommends that you group an uneven number of pieces together; three or five is typical.

❖ Novices tend to use accessories that are either too small or all the same size. Include larger pieces among smaller ones to add drama to an arrangement.

❖ In general, contemporary rooms are sparsely accessorized compared with traditional or country-style rooms. Look through books and magazines that feature your chosen style, noting the number as well as the kinds of accessories in the photos.

❖ A small entry hall is the ideal spot for accessories that are best viewed at close range, such as a delicately painted chest. A grand living room, in which small accessories might go unnoticed, can accommodate pieces that make their statement from afar.

❖ Use both symmetrical and asymmetrical balance to visually organize objects. Matching lamps placed at either end of a console table visually "ground" a collection of vases arranged asymmetrically in its center.

❖ Try this designer formula: "shiny, matte, tall, and fat." When combining accessories, include items that fit these categories, such as tall, shiny candlesticks, a rotund vase, and a matte-finish plate.

- ❖ Repeat a color in at least three objects and three areas of the room for a strong visual connection. In a black, cream, and taupe living room, for example, black leather pillows, a black wrought-iron lamp, and a black lacquered bench can help tie the scheme together.

- ❖ To achieve harmony within a grouping of accessories, choose pieces of different sizes and shapes but unite them with a common color (such as verdigris) or material (such as pewter).

- ❖ Accessories offer the perfect opportunity to introduce a daring accent color that's outside your palette: envision red-violet silk pillows on a new-neutral sofa. If you simply repeat your palette colors in your accessories, the effect is likely to be boring or, as some designers shudder, "matchy-matchy."

- ❖ Leave unequal space between objects in a group—this allows each one to be seen clearly and provides needed rest points.

- ❖ To start afresh, "clear the landscape"—that is, remove all accessories—and study your room. Audition your favorite piece in different locations; then add others one by one. You'll quickly appreciate that they can be used effectively in several spots.

- ❖ Finally, get organized and dedicate specific storage space to your unused accessories. Putting them all in one place will encourage you to keep a mental inventory and remind you to rotate them more often.

Two end-of-hallway spaces illustrate different design approaches to accessorizing. Looked at as a whole, the symmetrical arrangement of Chinese figurines, artichoke planters, and an English country mirror (above) forms an imaginary circle, even though the elements are strongly vertical. An asymmetrical arrangement (left) takes a much more open, casual path. The old-world mural, the true focal point of this space, is subtly balanced by the window treatment on the opposite wall and the bronze-figured lamp with "turban" shade on the Italian bench-made cabinet.

TABLESCAPES

If there's an interior designer lurking within you, a tablescape is your chance to play with color and design principles on a small scale, usually with a small investment. The term *tablescape* typically refers to accessories, linens, and tableware on dining tables, but any solid surface—from coffee table to accent table to nightstand—can be adorned.

Tablescapes can exhibit different kinds of balance (see pages 190–191). Symmetrical centerpieces just "feel" right on a dining table, whether it's rectangular, square, or oval. When the table is round and the centerpiece is symmetrical in every direction, the balance is radial. Asymmetrical centerpieces—in which each half of the arrangement is different, yet the composition seems balanced—are elegant and artistic on a console table, accent table, or sideboard.

ABOVE: In keeping with the room's Tuscan theme is the centerpiece: a jasmine plant sitting in a majolica bowl, surrounded by lemons. Hand-painted Italian plates, French glassware, sterling silver flatware, and hand-embroidered linen placemats rest on a solid walnut tabletop.

RIGHT: When it's not on duty for a dinner party, use your dining room table as a spacious display surface. Bunches of grass growing in rough wooden boxes surround a plump bouquet of lilacs, while ceramic rabbits make off with garden vegetables. An even larger arrangement atop an antique trunk and foliage plants on the mantel carry the garden theme further.

Whatever principle of balance you follow, make your arrangement the focal point of the table. Designer tricks of the trade include the following:

❖ Think in threes or fives. Five candles are more appealing than four, three vases more graceful than two.

❖ On any large table, build your arrangement in three dimensions—height, width, and depth—by starting with the tall elements in the center and working out.

❖ In a fresh centerpiece, include materials that spill over the vase and onto the table, as if they are growing. Long, low containers are ideally suited to trailing arrangements.

❖ Cut flowers in a crystal vase, flanked by candles, are a classic for a narrow table—but use three or four different kinds of greenery to update the look.

❖ To prevent a dining table display from appearing isolated, arrange smaller elements so that they extend from the centerpiece toward the place settings.

❖ A dining table arrangement should be low enough for guests to converse without peeking around flowers or candles. Choose candles whose flames will burn well above or below eye level.

❖ Simplicity is sometimes best for formal occasions. A collection of white candles in glass candlesticks of varying heights casts an elegant glow. White flowers, such as tulips, roses, or lilies, allow gilded china to take center stage.

❖ As an inexpensive alternative to the floral centerpiece, tuck sprigs of flowers or foliage into each napkin ring or create a miniature bouquet for each place setting. A tiny potted plant serves the same purpose.

❖ A display of fresh vegetables and fruit is an earthy alternative to flowers. Underlay your arrangement with linens and dishes in garden-fresh colors.

Simplicity is often a virtue in tablescaping, especially in a minimally styled room. A trio of dish gardens on a low table is a good example of asymmetrical balance: the two small bowls situated near the edge balance the large white pot close to the center. Tall reeds become a vertical accent in a room replete with horizontal lines.

FRESH FLOWERS

Nothing delights the senses or brightens the day like fresh flowers, and today's floral displays are more creative and spontaneous-looking than ever. Bouquets are often looser and less structured, as though they were just carried in from the garden. Materials are more eclectic, from curly willow to lavender twigs to crabapples on a branch. Somewhere between ordering a standard florist's arrangement and growing your own cutting garden, there's a way to bring nature's accessories into your home.

If you opt to arrange your own bouquet, buy flowers by the stem or bunch at a florist's, flower mart, or farmer's market. To get some help at the florist's, ask for a "hand-tie"—a bunch of flowers individually chosen, arranged, and tied by the florist; you provide the vase.

WHAT'S NEW? Trends come and go in flowers, just as they do in furnishings and clothing. Although traditional displays will always have their place, current floral fashions bring back old styles and introduce new ones.

❖ The tuzzy muzzy, a small Victorian nosegay tied up with ribbon, is a "new old-fashioned" favorite. Some florists carry the long, narrow containers for them, traditionally of silver.

❖ Tall, spiky formal displays have given way to compact, rounded designs called *pavé* arrangements (after the French jewelry fashion for small, close-set gems). These may contain mixed flowers but more typically are all of a kind—such as a mass of roses cut to short stems and packed tightly in a rounded vase.

❖ Unusual filler materials, such as oregano sprigs or Chinaberry branches, add an element of surprise to contemporary displays.

Life imitates art—or is it the other way around?—with a cut-glass vase of roses arranged pavé-style against a backdrop of rose wallpaper. Petals scattered on the distressed mantel hint at the evanescence of nature's colors.

A vase of French tulips looks luminous atop a parquet-inlay armoire set against old-world faux-finished walls. European floral design emphasizes asymmetrical balance rather than more formal arrangements.

LEFT: Poised to move from potting sink to pride of place, two bouquets display very different approaches to decorating with flowers. A casual mix of color and form (left) features the green color family, from yellow-green Bells of Ireland to blue-green eucalyptus leaves. Roses and chrysanthemums bunched in a florist's bucket (right) are frothy and feminine.

BELOW: An outdoor urn's luscious bouquet of hydrangeas, garden roses, sedum, and purple sage harkens back to the "presentation urns" of the late 1800s, which were inspired by the excavation of Pompeii.

FLORAL DESIGN POINTERS. Even the novice can create artistic arrangements. Take this advice from the pros:

❖ Think of flowers as an extension of your color palette and decorating style. In a shabby-chic room with faded-linen hues, arrange a bouquet of wildflowers and herbs in a small metal florist's pail. In a formal black-and-white dining room, float red roses and gardenias in a shallow cut-glass bowl.

❖ For maximum impact, use no more than three types of flowers in your arrangement. To create a flower-market look, group generous bunches of like flowers together within it.

❖ If you're unsure of your skills, stick with a monochromatic scheme, such as all pinks, or all ivory with green accents. A one-color arrangement is guaranteed to impress, and your bouquet will appear larger than it is.

❖ If you don't have florist's foam on hand, place greenery in your container first to provide a support structure for the flowers.

❖ For a vertical arrangement, cut your tallest stems so that they're one and a half to two times the height of your vase. Fill in with medium and short stems on the sides.

❖ To fashion a dense bouquet in a wide container, gather small bunches of flowers first, using florist's wire or rubber bands to secure them. Build your arrangement bunch by bunch.

THE MOST BEAUTIFUL FLOWERS

A trio of botanical prints positioned between a painted screen and a wood-framed mirror illustrates the use of a horizontal axis in picture arranging: the midpoint of the mirror lines up with the midpoint of the second print.

DISPLAYING ARTWORKS

Arranging art is itself an art, and many a homeowner freezes at the prospect of hanging even one picture. A few simple principles and strategies can make the process less intimidating and more rewarding.

DISPLAY GUIDELINES. As with your other accessories, apply the basic design knowledge you've acquired to arranging your art, whether it's one painting over a sofa or a group of photos on a focal-point wall.

❖ Over a fireplace, hang one work or a group of several that take up roughly the same space as the opening below.

❖ Strive for a loosely circular or oval outline when grouping art; that is, if you drew a curved line around the pieces that touched their outer corners, you would see a circle or oval. Avoid a stair-stepped arrangement, which draws the eye sharply up or down rather than around.

❖ The standard guideline for spacing multiple works is to leave 1 to 2 inches between the frames. Very diverse subject matter calls for a little more space; related works, such as botanical prints, look best hung closer together. When the pieces are all the same size, a grid pattern of equal spacing unifies them.

❖ Position art at eye level. In a dining room, that means hanging it lower than usual, because its viewers will be seated; in an entry or hallway, art should be hung higher.

❖ Arrange multiple artworks on the floor first, to get a feel for how they will look as a unit. Or you can tape pieces of paper on the wall, cut to the sizes of your art, to judge potential arrangements.

❖ A single painting hung above a sofa should extend approximately two-thirds the sofa's width. If your artwork is narrower, add smaller pieces to compose a larger unit.

Identically matted and framed antique prints become one work of art in a hallway gallery. Close vertical spacing unites the pieces; a little more horizontal space between the rows allows them to breathe and creates the impression of two orderly sets of three.

When you position art on top of, or close to, furnishings, it becomes an integral part of the design. Here, two paintings rest on a sculpture whose "legs" are wood clamps. The large painting on the adjoining wall is hung so that its midpoint is aligned with the upper edge of the landscape— a variation on a horizontal axis.

HORIZONTAL AXIS

VERTICAL AXIS

PERIMETER

LAYOUT PRINCIPLES. It's generally easier to hang an odd number of pieces, such as three or five, but an even number can be just as successful. Following are three common blueprints for simple displays that start from an imaginary point of reference.

ESTABLISH A HORIZONTAL AXIS. This plan works best for three pieces of art. The horizontal axis runs from side to side through the center piece, at the midpoint. First hang the center piece where you want it; then hang the flanking pieces so that their midpoints line up along the horizontal axis.

ESTABLISH A VERTICAL AXIS. This approach is ideal for four pieces of art. Hang two pieces on one side of the vertical axis and two on the other. But offset the horizontal spacing to avoid creating a "cross" of negative space, which tends to destroy the illusion that the pieces form one unit.

ESTABLISH A PERIMETER. If you have four pieces of roughly similar size, consider creating a visual "corral." (Ideally, you would plan the matting and framing beforehand, to compensate for differences in the images.) Establish an imaginary perimeter for the space you want the grouping to occupy and hang the pieces so that their outer edges "touch" that perimeter. Again, avoid creating a cross of negative space in the center.

SHOWCASING COLLECTIONS

What you choose to collect in life, whether it's antique rolling pins, cartoon lunch boxes, or porcelain baskets, reveals much about you—your passions, your experiences, even your sense of humor. Because collections have such a personal significance for us, it's important to arrange them in ways that enhance their beauty and meaning.

Think of a collection as a visual feast, to be taken in first as a whole and then savored one piece at a time. The most successful arrangements look as though they were effortlessly composed. Here's how to achieve that effect.

❖ Color can be the tie that binds a collection of diverse objects, such as red-white-and-blue folk art or a grouping of white porcelain, mother-of-pearl, and ivory pieces.

❖ It's easy to rearrange collectibles, unlike major furnishings. Take the time to audition your collection in various locations until you find the perfect spot. Effective display always involves experimentation.

❖ For maximum impact, cluster the items in your collection. If they vary in size, layer them as you would other accessories; that is, place shorter, smaller objects in front and taller, larger objects in back for a sense of depth. You can also create subgroups within any collection, arranging some pieces in a circle, for example, offset by others in a straight line.

Rich red shelving showcases a collection of majolica plates, pitchers, candlesticks, and pewter accent pieces in a recessed corner cabinet. The focal point of the display is the second shelf, where roosters flank the largest plate. As your eye travels down, the plates increase in number, forming a wide triangle.

❖ If your prized objects are similar in size, a gridlike arrangement—or even a single row—gives equal emphasis to each one and visually organizes the grouping.

❖ Show off small objects on a wall, shelf, tabletop, or windowsill. Large objects such as urns and garden finials can go on the floor, flanking a fireplace, grouped in a corner, or marching up a flight of steps.

LEFT: "Blue and green should never be seen" is one color rule that was made to be broken! True green majolica plates on a bright blue wall emphasize the verticality of this two-story entry. Hanging your treasures on the wall, rather than arranging them on shelving, is a great way to create a three-dimensional display.

BELOW: Railed, recessed shelving in a colonial-style kitchen houses a collection of blue-patterned chargers and cups from different design traditions. Red glass and red flowers add a jolt of warm color to the cool display.

❖ Use display devices such as pedestals, plate stands, books, cubes, and miniature tabletop easels to raise your treasures. Keep these display devices inconspicuous, though, so they don't detract from the collectibles themselves.

❖ The very nature of a collection serves to unify it. Searching out and adding pieces that differ in size or material introduces a little variety.

❖ A tray can function as a "horizontal frame" or display shelf to help organize a collection of small disparate objects. Move the tray to various locations in a room to take advantage of different backdrops.

❖ Plates or other objects that you plan to hang on the wall can be arranged on the floor first to arrive at a pleasing configuration.

❖ Draw attention to three-dimensional works of art, such as a collection of bowls, by silhouetting them against a plain background. To best appreciate bowls that are decorated on the inside, display them down low—on a coffee table, for example.

GETTING COLOR RIGHT

COLOR—THAT PHENOMENON OF LIGHT THAT DELIGHTS EVERYONE, AND OCCASIONALLY CONFOUNDS THE EXPERTS—IS AN ESSENTIAL ELEMENT IN ANY ROOM. If you worry that you'll choose the "wrong" color or that certain colors won't "go together," take heart: the concepts in these pages will enable you to assemble a color palette you'll love. In this chapter, you'll learn the basics of planning great color schemes. Once you learn the special language of color and understand how color works, you'll have the confidence you need to successfully mix and match colors in every room in your home. To make it even easier, we've assembled an inspiring collection of 16 ready-made Lowe's color palettes for you to use "as is" or edit to fit your own plan. For an exact match to these palettes, see the Lowe's color chip numbers listed on pages 421–423. It's a colorful world out there—now you can bring that wonderful color into your rooms, too!

WORKING WITH COLOR

COLOR DOES MORE TO SET THE MOOD AND STYLE OF A ROOM THAN ANY OTHER DESIGN ELEMENT. WOULDN'T IT BE GREAT TO CHOOSE COLORS WITH CONFIDENCE, KNOWING YOU'LL LIKE THE RESULTS?

The warm hues of handmade stoneware and integral-color concrete balance the cool hue of the kitchen cabinetry in this example of visual temperature.

This section will teach you the language of color, introduce an updated version of the color wheel, and show you how to combine colors like a pro. The color terms used here come from traditional color theory, but they are just as applicable to home decorating as to fine art.

THE LANGUAGE OF COLOR

To develop the skill and confidence to create a great color scheme, you'll need to master a working color vocabulary. First of all, don't be intimidated by the word *hue*: it's just another name for color. Turquoise and fuchsia are hues; so are softer colors like lilac and sage. Becoming familiar with three characteristics of colors—value, temperature, and intensity—is the key to combining colors with success.

VALUE refers to the lightness or darkness of a color. Robin's-egg blue is a light value of blue; washed denim is a medium value of blue; and navy is a dark value of blue. (In reality, infinite variations in value exist, from the lightest lights to the darkest darks.) Light values appear to expand space, dark values to contract it.

TEMPERATURE is an easy term to understand, even for the novice. If you draw an imaginary line across the color ring (page 229) from yellow-green to red-violet, the colors to the left—yellows, oranges, and reds—are warm. These colors are considered "advancing," because in terms of optical psychology they seem closer to the viewer than they are; that's why warm colors on walls make a room feel cozy. Cooler hues—those to the right of your imaginary line— are considered "receding," because they appear more distant than they are, making a room feel calm and spacious.

INTENSITY, the third color characteristic, describes the brightness of a color. The 12 colors on the pure color ring are fully intense, or

TIPS

Green and violet are "bridging colors" because each one contains both a warm and a cool hue. If you're searching for another color to complete a scheme, try green or violet.

LEFT: Layered colors in and beyond a minimal bedroom display a soothing range of values, from light to medium to dark. Blues are cool and calm; warm accents—in the headboard, wall-mounted lamp, and wood floor—balance the visual temperature.

BELOW: Intense orange and yellow pulsate with visual energy in a contemporary kitchen. Black and white, true neutrals, provide welcome relief in such warm, saturated schemes.

"saturated." Low-intensity colors, on the other hand, are more muted. Turn to pages 230–231 to see less intense versions of the 12 pure colors.

To become comfortable with this distinction, try picturing two versions of your favorite color. Lime, for example, is an intense yellow-green; willow is a less intense version of yellow-green.

Designers consider intensity to be the "great unifier" of color. That is, you can combine any colors if they are similar in intensity; they just seem to belong together. Take a look at the color palette cards at your Lowe's store and you'll see that disparate colors with the same intensity are naturally harmonious. For example, bright red and soft sage might look odd, but a less intense brick would be compatible with sage.

If you have trouble distinguishing between value and intensity, try considering the two characteristics separately. When looking at a color, first ask yourself, "Is it light, medium, or dark?" That's the value. Then ask, "Is it bright or dull?" That's the intensity.

UNDERSTANDING THE COLOR RING

If you're tempted to skip these pages—after all, who hasn't seen a color wheel?—stop for a moment and reconsider. Most of us never consult a color wheel when choosing colors for our homes, and for good reason. The colors shown on the typical color wheel—neon orange, bright red, pure violet—appeal to a relatively narrow audience, and the sophisticated, nuanced colors found in home furnishings—celadon, aubergine, cinnabar—don't even appear on the wheel. No wonder we think the color wheel is useless.

It's not. In fact, the color wheel is nothing short of magical. With a basic understanding, you can use this versatile tool to build a color scheme from scratch—or fix one that doesn't work.

It helps to simplify the standard color wheel, which typically contains 36 colors, to a color ring (shown on the facing page) with only the 12 pure hues. Refer to this ring as you read about the different kinds of colors and how they are formed.

PRIMARY COLORS

SECONDARY COLORS

PRIMARY COLORS—red, blue, and yellow—are so named because they cannot be created from other colors. Instead, they make up all other colors, in different combinations and proportions. Intense primaries in large quantities can be harsh; lower-intensity versions of them—such as cranberry, navy, and gold—are easier to live with.

SECONDARY COLORS result from mixing two primaries: red mixed with yellow makes orange; blue mixed with yellow makes green; blue mixed with red makes violet (often called purple in decorating books and magazines).

INTERMEDIATE COLORS, sometimes called tertiary colors, are made by mixing a primary with an adjacent secondary. Red (a primary) and violet (a secondary) combine to make red-violet. Starting with yellow and moving clockwise around the color ring, the intermediate colors are yellow-green, blue-green, blue-violet, red-violet, red-orange, and yellow-orange. More complex than primary or secondary colors, intermediates are among the most versatile of decorating hues.

How colors are positioned on the ring in relation to one another determines their affinities and contrasts. Adjacent colors (blue, blue-violet, and violet, for example) are called analogous. These three share a common color—in this case, blue.

Opposing colors, such as blue and orange, are complements, meaning that they balance each other in visual temperature. Colors that are just approximately opposite each other are also well balanced; they're known as near complements. Lavender blue (a version of blue-violet) is the near complement of yellow.

Knowing how the color ring works is one thing; using it is another. Here's a little-known secret to success with the color ring: the pure colors on the ring shown here are the *source* of all the wonderful "real-life" colors used in decorating. (Most real-life colors also contain some black, white, or gray.) Pure orange, for example, is the source of colors such as spice, pumpkin, and peach. Put the opposite way, spice, pumpkin, and peach come from pure orange on the color ring. Being able to place real-life colors on the color ring— "olive is just a dark yellow-green; iris is really a light blue-violet"—is the first step to using the ring effectively.

To take the leap from theory to practice, turn the page and look at the four custom color rings. They show less intense versions of the 12 pure colors, in values ranging from light to dark. Just for fun, find a color you like on one of the custom rings (terra-cotta, for example, at the nine o'clock position on ring number 3); then turn back to the pure ring to identify its source (red-orange, in this example). To find a cool contrast to terra-cotta, look across the custom ring to aquamarine, a less intense version of pure blue-green. Once you realize that all colors have a place on the color ring, you'll be well on your way to making it work for you.

INTERMEDIATE COLORS

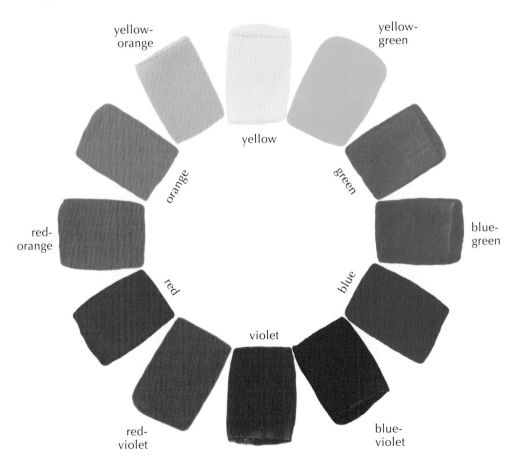

The pure color ring is fine for helping you grasp color theory, but it may not be sufficient for choosing colors for your home. Color rings that portray the colors in values and intensities that you can live with and enjoy are much more useful. Those shown on these two pages display the 12 colors in four values: light, medium-light, medium, and dark. All of the colors are less intense than the hues on the pure color ring. In reality, you will probably combine colors that vary in value and intensity: that happens naturally when you collect different materials. But the rings can help you become aware of the kinds of colors you prefer. Take a look.

COLOR RING 1

*Light-Value,
Low-Intensity Colors*

These are the colors we normally associate with the word *tint*. Light, subdued colors, such as celery, chamois, and fawn, are often chosen for walls.

COLOR RING 2

*Medium-Light-Value,
Low-Intensity Colors*

These are still low in intensity but slightly darker in value than those in ring number 1. Use them when you want quiet color with a little more body, for walls, floors, or furnishings.

COLOR RING 3

Medium-Value,
Low-Intensity Colors

These colors are versatile and easy
on the eye. Subdued colors of medium
value, such as dusty rose and lichen,
are often used for large upholstered
furnishings because they are not
visually obtrusive.

COLOR RING 4

Dark-Value,
Low-Intensity Colors

Dark, subdued colors such as burgundy
and hunter green add depth to a
scheme. They combine naturally with
rich woods, especially in rooms used
at night—a dining room, perhaps, or
a library.

TIPS

You may be asking
yourself, "Why isn't
brown on the color ring?"
It's missing because most
browns are dark-value,
low-intensity versions of
red-orange, orange, or
yellow-orange.

four strategies on combining colors

SOMETHING SPECIAL HAPPENS WHEN YOU COMBINE COLORS. YOUR LEAST FAVORITE COLOR IS "JUST RIGHT" IN THE COMPANY OF ITS COMPLEMENT, AND UNLIKELY COLORS BECOME A BEAUTIFUL BLEND.

1 MONOCHROMATIC, or one-color, combinations are among the most elegant of schemes. In this room, blue-violet is the single color; iridescent silk panels are playfully ambiguous, appearing blue-violet or blue-green depending on the light. One-color rooms demand variety, or monotony can set in. The distinctly different values of blue-violet in the paint and mohair-covered chaise provide that element in this room. Other hues can spice up a monochromatic scheme: here, bright lemons inject a shot of a near complement.

2 ANALOGOUS schemes consist of colors that lie side by side on the color ring, such as yellow, yellow-green, and green. The key to an analogous scheme is one common color—in this example, yellow is the common denominator. With its limited color range, an analogous scheme benefits from a mix of patterns, textures, and finishes (seen here in the countertop and backsplash).

3 COMPLEMENTARY schemes are based on colors opposite each other on the color ring. This living room illustrates the complements blue and orange at their most intense. Few dare to use full-strength complements like this; if you do, repeat the color throughout the room, as shown here with the orange chaise, wall, and vase. When using any complementary combination, feel free to "wander" a little around the color ring. Sometimes near complements make more interesting color schemes.

4 COMPLEX combinations combine colors that are equally spaced around the color ring. A *triad* is three colors equidistant from one another on the ring: for instance, orange, violet, and green. A four-color combination of equidistant hues is known as a *tetrad*. In the open-plan home shown here, the colors are red-orange (the terra-cotta walls), blue-green (the dining chairs), violet (the near wall), and yellow (the warm-toned wood). The pendant light fixtures are actually yellow-orange, but they prove that small amounts of "stray" colors are allowed in any combination.

1

HOW COLORS ARE AFFECTED BY THEIR SURROUNDINGS

Color doesn't exist in a vacuum; it's very much in the eye of the beholder. And certain physical variables—particularly light—dramatically affect the beholder's perception of color. In turn, color can alter our awareness of physical space in striking ways.

Daylight through the half-door and transom window bathes a minty green kitchen in natural light. Fluorescent tubes mounted under the cabinets light up the yellow tiles; rope lighting in the glass-doored cabinets adds sparkle.

COLOR AND LIGHT. Light is what enables us to see color. (At night, all flowers look white.) How the colors in your home appear to you depends on each room's exposure, and changes with the time of day and the season. North-facing rooms receive less direct sunlight year-round, and that light tends to be "cool"; south-facing rooms get more and "warmer" light. Conventional wisdom says to balance the temperature in a room by using warm colors in north-facing rooms and cool colors in south-facing ones. But you are free to ignore that advice and enhance the natural temperature of a room with colors of similar characteristics.

Most light in your home is artificial, and the color of that light varies. Warm light from standard incandescent bulbs intensifies yellows and reds but tends to dull the cooler colors. Halogen bulbs, a special category of incandescents, produce a whiter, brighter light. The cool blue light of standard fluorescent bulbs amplifies blues and greens but muddies warm yellows and reds. Newer fluorescents come closer to providing the warmth of incandescents.

Light fixtures themselves contribute color to a room. Pendant lights with brightly colored glass shades not only make effective accents but also color the light they give off. A warm-hued lamp shade will cast its own glow, influencing other colors and helping establish a mood. Be aware, however, that colorful lamp shades tend to soak up light; white or cream shades have become classics because they yield the most light.

The many new options in lighting make it only sensible to visit the lighting department of your Lowe's store as you decorate. See pages 310–311 for more information on lighting.

COLOR AND SPACE.

Using color to define or alter space is really about creating illusions. The rule of thumb is that light and cool colors visually expand space, whereas dark and warm colors make it seem smaller. Similarly, low-intensity colors are thought to make a room seem more spacious, intense ones to contract it.

In reality many factors, such as the quantity and quality of light a room receives, modify these optical effects. Painting the walls a light color will not transform a naturally dark room into an open, airy space. A rich color will not necessarily bring intimacy to a large room. Sometimes it's best to evaluate what you have and then go with it rather than against it.

But do consider putting color to use when you want to change the apparent proportions of a room. Painting the end wall of a long, narrow room a warmer, darker color than the others can create the illusion of a better-proportioned room. In a square room, painting one wall a more intense color than the others can diminish the boxy look.

Color can affect our sense of the space in adjoining rooms, as well. Carrying the same paint color and flooring from room to room makes for a smooth visual transition and opens up a small home. (See "Harmonious Transitions," pages 208–209.) If you prefer the look of layered color and distinctly separate spaces, use different colors in adjoining rooms. Or combine both techniques by choosing related colors for connecting spaces—perhaps a light, warm taupe for the entry and a darker, cooler taupe in the living room.

What a difference color makes! Yellow-orange paint illuminates and defines the space, turning a well-put-together living room (below) into a smashing one (above). Note how much more impressive the shuttered windows, crown molding, and mantel are when set off in white and surrounded by warm color.

*S*tart any decorating project with a visit to your nearby Lowe's store. There you'll find ideas galore, one-on-one professional expertise, and an inspiring array of decorative elements.

LOWE'S IN-STORE HELP WITH YOUR DECORATING PROJECT

LOWE'S DESIGN/DECOR CENTERS

Lowe's Design/Decor Centers are your design and decorating headquarters, offering hands-on assistance in creating room layouts, making product selections, and combining your elements.

DESIGN SERVICES. Make an appointment for a consultation with a knowledgeable sales associate who can help you with every phase of your project, from estimating wallpaper or flooring needs to coordinating fabric, paint, and window treatments.

Design services vary from store to store, so call or visit your nearest Lowe's to find out what is offered.

FASHION BATH & KITCHEN SHOWROOM. For free computerized kitchen and bath design services, just give us your room dimensions. A Lowe's professional will help you create a layout and select the elements for your new room. Shop right at Lowe's for everything you'll need, including bathroom fixtures, cabinets, and kitchen appliances.

HOW-TO CLINICS. Dedicated do-it-yourselfers can sign up for one of Lowe's special clinics and learn how to paint, apply faux finishes, wallpaper, set tile, and lay flooring.

INSTALLATION SERVICES. Lowe's stores offer experienced installation for most of the products we sell, including kitchen appliances, bathroom fixtures, cabinetry, flooring, carpeting, and window treatments. Ask for details when you shop.

WHAT'S AVAILABLE AT LOWE'S

You'll find a dazzling array of products to bring your decorating vision to life. In addition to hundreds of in-stock items, Lowe's offers many special-order catalogs filled with everything you'll need for rooms with truly custom looks.

PAINT & WALLPAPER. Lowe's complete paint department features a free computerized Color Matching system. Bring in anything from a seashell to a fabric swatch and our specially trained Paint Pros will help you match it. And with Lowe's Color Coordinates system, you can pair paint colors with fabrics, carpeting, and draperies. Lowe's carries paints in hundreds of colors and beautifully coordinated, ready-made palettes. Lowe's selection of wallpapers is also vast; choose in-stock papers or special-order papers from a wealth of catalog offerings.

FLOORING. Lowe's carries a full range of flooring options from hardwood to laminate and vinyl sheet to ceramic tile. We also have a huge selection of carpeting and many styles, sizes, and colors of area rugs and matting. You can choose from either in-house products or special-order selections.

LIGHTING. Popular track and recessed light is readily available at Lowe's. You can also shop from a wide selection of freestanding floor and table lamps.

WINDOW TREATMENTS. Lowe's carries curtains, draperies, blinds, shades, and shutters for all types of windows. Ready-made window treatments are always available, and Lowe's can special order custom treatments such as shutters and blinds. Buy all of the hardware you need, from curtain rods to holdbacks, from stock or by special order. ~

USING YOUR FAVORITE COLORS

Any color or combination of colors that makes you happy is the right one. If you have a keen color sense—a talent that a fortunate few possess naturally—you can forget the rules and combine colors freely and intuitively, knowing you'll enjoy the results.

But many of us suffer paralyzing hesitation when it comes to developing a palette; after all, choosing colors on a hit-or-miss basis can cost both money and time. You may know your favorite color, or know you feel more comfortable with some colors than others, yet have no clue about what to do with that information. If you fall into this much more common category, the color encyclopedia beginning here can help you visualize possibilities before committing to final choices.

Each of the 12 colors on the pure color ring (page 229) is represented on two pages. Paint dabs on the left-hand page illustrate different values and intensities of the color. The short text offers fresh ideas for using the hue, alone or in combination with others. Photos of rooms, furnishings, and accessories show the color in context. A color palette and a caption illustrating and describing the color relationships accompany one of the photos. The specific Lowe's paint colors used in the palettes are listed on pages 421–423.

Browse this section, note which colors attract you, observe how they work in real-life settings, and play designer—with a new-found sense of security—in your own home.

Clear, curved shelving displays a collection of art glass in bright colors from around the color ring. Barely noticeable supporting hardware hangs from a metal-laminate soffit.

yellow

Life-sustaining sunshine is conjured by the color yellow, which lifts the spirits and lightens the mood as it warms a room. For an airy, mono-chromatic look, try pale yellow walls with vanilla trim; paint louvered shutters the same warm white. Or enjoy the dance of outright-lively daffodil yellow and analogous apple green, perhaps with sparks of blue and red. You can spice up medium-value yellows by adding a complementary violet or a near-complementary red-violet, or you can enhance a lower-intensity yellow with rose red. Saturated mustard yellow teams handsomely with dark Chinese red; pale yellow marries well with soft versions of true green, blue, and pink. To create a springtime mix, combine yellow with mint green and analogous robin's-egg blue. If you like the high energy of chrome yellow, jazz it up with black and white; think of taxis flashing by—and, if you dare, add stoplight red.

LEFT: Low-intensity yellow and yellow-green facilitate the visual transition from dining room to living room. A more intense orange appears as an accent color; khaki is interpreted in the living room sofa.

yellow-green

Snowbound easterners cherish this hue in early spring's forsythia buds, and westerners get a comparable lift from the sight of wild willows coming into leaf along seasonal streams. In its lightest, clearest form, yellow-green is as gentle as spring air. Full strength, at its most acid intensity, it's a perfect accent color—as piping on a cushion, caterpillar fringe on a curtain, or beading on a lamp shade. You can create an analogous scheme by moving toward yellow on the color ring, including yellow-orange or orange. For a breezier look, go in the opposite direction and pair pale yellow-green with summery blue-green or blue. Small amounts of intense yellow-green combine with larger quantities of navy and titanium white for a crisp palette. To use yellow-green's near complements, work with rose for a warmer combination and violet for a cooler one.

ABOVE: A bright yellow-green wall and muted blue-green cabinetry are compatible in this kitchen because they are nearly neighbors on the color ring. New-neutral tiles in hues such as celadon, a grayed green, and "mustard seed" harmonize with the soft-colored cabinets and the more intense walls.

green

Green has a grass-pasture goodness that places it on almost everyone's list of favorite colors. It's inherent in the vitality of summer leaves, the cool refreshment of wet mint, the reprieve of conifers and ferns. Who doesn't long to see green outside a window or feel that a room is incomplete without at least a touch of this living color? Because it is made up of yellow (a warm color) and blue (a cool color), green works well with everything. In the company of warm yellow, peach, and pink, green exerts a cooling influence. With blues and blue-violets, hues on the same side of the color ring, green becomes a cool cohort in an analogous scheme. It combines just as easily with yellow-green and blue-green, its color-ring neighbors. Celadon, a very low-intensity green, wakes up with muted plum and pink or takes its repose with neutrals like taupe, gray, and white.

RIGHT: Pale green is the predominant hue in a light-filled garden room; raspberry and "petit-four pink" are complements. A dark, low-intensity yellow-green is a good addition, because it grounds the lighter-value colors.

blue-green

Blue-green brings to mind that first joyous plunge from hot sand into cool seawater. Its appeal has endured from colonial Williamsburg through the apothecary blue-green of the federal period to the peach-and-teal schemes of the 1980s. The light-value blue-green associated with aged frescoes and weathered copper suggests old-world ambience. But blue-green is equally appropriate in country homes: in Santa Fe and other southwestern decorative art, light values of it have long been used as a grain-enhancing wash or rubbed stain over natural wood. The hue makes neutrals such as gray and beige and old leather seem warmer. Blue-greens work well with analogous greens, yellow-greens, and yellows, combinations that range from casually fresh (spa blue and apple green) to handsomely formal (verdigris and gold). More often than not, blue-green begs to be balanced with warmer hues. Try it with cinnamon or with cobalt, cherry, and white.

ABOVE: Countless versions of blue-green in a range of values make up the palette for this dreamy bedroom. Located on the same side of the color ring, yellow-green is a natural accent color for blue-green.

blue

The blue family is broad, ranging from baby blue through cornflower to ultramarine. It has long connoted a spiritual quality, and a predominantly blue space is often calming and serene. But blue can be moody, even a little melancholy; it can also seem chilly and unwelcoming. Because it's the coolest of the cool hues, it must be handled with respect. Paired with white, blue comes across with invigorating freshness—visualize cumulus clouds in a summer sky with a sapphire lake flashing below, or the whitewashed stucco of a Greek island village set against the Aegean. Blue and white have been a favorite combination in the decorative arts for centuries—think of Chinese ginger jars. To bring warmth to a blue room, add low-intensity versions of orange (blue's complement) or of yellow-orange and red-orange. Blue and yellow-green, nearby but not adjacent on the color ring, are always clean and inviting with white trim.

LEFT: Cool blue and blue-green reign on the walls, but red is ideal for built-in display cabinets. Neutral black trim separates the contrasting colors.

blue-violet

Blue-violet is the color of periwinkle and grape hyacinth, the lavender blue of the nursery song, and, in its lightest form, the delicate haze on Concord

grapes. In a monochromatic scheme with neutrals or in an analogous scheme, blue-violet can expand the perception of space and make a small room's boundaries dissolve. Like its parent, violet, blue-violet absorbs light and can appear cold; energize and warm it by adding red-violet. It also pairs beautifully with its direct complement, yellow-orange. To compose a finely balanced triad, try periwinkle with lime (a light value of yellow-green) and salmon (a light value of red-orange). For a striped wall or checkered dado, consider teaming pale blue-violet with creamy white or wispy apricot. Or take your color cues from nature and check the western sky at sunset, where you might just see blue-violet barred with salmon, coral, hot pink, gold, gray, and aquamarine.

LEFT: Blue-violet curtains and yellow-orange walls are complementary. A violet band on the curtain introduces an analogous hue. A lighter, less intense blue-violet on the window frame echoes the curtain's color.

violet

At its full intensity, violet—better known in decorating circles as purple—suggests mystical depth and ancient ritual. It tends to elicit strong reactions,

both positive and negative, without much middle ground. Dark versions of violet, such as eggplant, convey formality and dignity when teamed with gray or taupe. Plum is both luscious and dramatic with complementary gold, perhaps cooled by sage green. Lighter, romantic hues like lavender and lilac combine easily with pinks of similar value and greens of similar intensity. For a monochromatic violet scheme that's light and low-key, introduce pale gray or white; warm it with a bit of creamy apricot or yellow, the complement of violet.

To see how nature mixes violet with other hues, explore the interior of an iris with a hand lens. There you'll see violet with pink, white, and sparkling yellow-orange. Or examine violets in bloom, with their lemon yellow centers and velvet green leaves.

LEFT: Dark and very dark versions of violet in the scalloped curtain are the predominant hues in this sophisticated palette. Red-violet and pink appear in the slip-cover. Grays—one a true neutral, the other a new neutral—link the colors in the patterned fabrics.

red-violet

Nestled between red and violet on the color ring, red-violet is warmer than violet but cooler than red, thanks to the blue in violet's makeup. It has a jewel-like quality—envision the sheen of a just-cut Black Mission fig—that endows a room with richness, especially in a dark-value version like wine. Orchid is a lighter value, fuchsia a more saturated form. Though intense red-violet is seldom used to cover walls, it works beautifully as an accent for the new neutrals (see pages 264–265). It's an ideal hue for silky sheer curtains—like the skin of a red onion, only airier and more transparent. Red-violet makes a dignified partner with bronze, copper, brass, brushed steel, or any other metal finish. For a tropical triad (page 232), combine teal (blue-green) and mango (yellow-orange) with fuchsia (red-violet). If you need a fresh squeeze of color, add lemon yellow.

ABOVE: Smoky red-violet walls star in this muted palette. A new-neutral yellow-green pillow makes the color combination complementary. A violet chair and dark-value hearth add deeper tones to the room.

red

Primary red is hot, eye-stopping, and somewhat risky. Because it's so visually demanding and so laden with emotional significance, intense red must be used with care. Lipstick red works with pink, even with hot pink, in contemporary schemes. Cherry red combines traditionally with cadet blue or navy and cheerfully with complementary green and yellow-green, as in summery cottage florals or 1940s print tablecloths. Red adds depth and authority as an accent to yellow-orange (apricot) or red-orange (terra-cotta). True neutrals—black, gray, and aspirin white—balance the vibrancy of reds and make them safer. New neutrals (pages 264–265) gain energy from deep reds like cranberry or Bordeaux and make calming partners for ripe tomato and chile pepper reds. Full-bodied reds look wonderful polished or glazed, such as a Chinese red–lacquered wood screen. Warm colors—and none is warmer than red—appear to advance; thus, red rooms seem more intimate.

ABOVE: A red room pulsates with visual energy, demonstrating the power of this hot color. Red and orange silk pillows add sheen and texture, the yellow-green sofa, visual relief.

red-orange

More complex than either of its parent colors, red-orange is warm and welcoming, the color of iron-rich earth and traditional clay flowerpots. Terra-cotta is a popular version of red-orange, teaming naturally with ocher (yellow-orange) and moss (yellow-green). It works beautifully with the cool greens of plants or with patio colors like awning green and Southampton blue. Red-orange also comes in lighter and brighter forms: shrimp, coral, salmon, and persimmon. In its darker values it appears as russet, burnt umber, and sienna. A natural for wherever people gather, red-orange walls envelop a room and flatter guests with their glow. Such a vivid hue accepts cooler partners with grace. Used in combination with its complement, blue-green, red-orange is the earthiest of the southwestern colors. A triad of terra-cotta (red-orange), deep periwinkle (blue-violet), and olive (yellow-green) will balance warm and cool colors.

LEFT: Red-orange appears in the fireplace facade, furniture, and rug. Even warmer yellow-orange walls are luminous. Dark-value, low-intensity blue-green and green cool things down.

orange

Mix yellow and red and you get orange—a juicy, beach-ball hue often considered too "hot" for interiors. Few dare to use it "as is" on walls or major furnishings, but less concentrated versions flatter and please almost everyone. The key to success with orange is moderation in value and intensity. Intense, light-value orange is a color we call tangerine; low-intensity, dark-value orange becomes burnt umber or brown. At full strength, orange's true complement, blue, can look harsh, but the colors that flank blue (blue-violet and blue-green) make supportive partners. Three-color schemes incorporating orange soften its impact: imagine pale peach (orange), mint (green), and lilac (violet), or maybe deep cinnamon, juniper, and eggplant.

Oranges harmonize with metallic finishes—particularly copper and bronze, of which this hue is a component. Overpowering in large quantities, orange is ideal for accents and accessories.

ABOVE: Light-value orange energizes a child's room. Raspberry and coral, versions of red-violet and red-orange, are pleasing color cohorts. Violet is calm and cooler by comparison; blue-green injects a bit of complementary color.

yellow-orange

Richer than yellow but less assertive than orange, yellow-orange has luminous qualities that make it a versatile color for the home. This cheerful hue abounds in nature, from mangoes to butternut squash to turmeric. Unpainted wicker, pine, and brass are just a few examples of natural yellow-orange materials found in the home. Lighter, creamier versions are favorites on walls, where yellow is too bright and orange too strong. Yellow-orange lends itself to elegant monochromatic schemes, but it also combines beautifully with blue-green and red-violet to form a triad (see page 232). Imagine saturated saffron (yellow-orange), jade (blue-green), and plum (red-violet)—or, for a lighter look, papaya, aquamarine, and orchid. Yellow-orange is cooled by its complement, blue-violet; picture a van Gogh landscape with ripe fields punctuated by blue-violet and yellow-green. For the home, translate these colors into a spirited palette of honey (yellow-orange), periwinkle (blue-violet), and lime (yellow-green).

SHE DIDNT KNOW W[

LEFT: A violet "boomerang" table and a blue-violet corduroy-velvet sofa cool and subdue vibrant yellow-orange walls. Intense red-orange is a perfect choice for accent pillows.

INCORPORATING NEUTRAL COLORS

The true neutrals—black, white, and gray—don't have a place on the color ring, but they play an important role in decorating. Sometimes referred to as "noncolors," true neutrals provide visual relief in a scheme without adding color or altering existing color relationships. White walls, for example, put the focus on colorful art; black metal chairs set off, but do not compete with, an intensely red table; gray granite counters balance brightly colored kitchen cabinets.

Texture always matters, but it's especially important to consider with true neutrals, whose lack of color makes the interplay of light and shadow even more significant. The bounce of sunshine off glossy white paint, the variation of light perceived in a coarsely woven black damask, the shimmer of dove gray taffeta—texture plays with neutral colors in intriguing ways. Not all materials in a neutral scheme should be the same texture, however; the hand and the eye crave variety.

A charming 1937-vintage range is the focal point in this updated kitchen. Stenciling on the fir floor reads as almost-black; on the faux-finished walls, a lighter touch yields gray. Stainless steel pendant lights serve as gray accents, while mottled granite ties the counters to the warm wall color.

WHEN WHITE IS RIGHT. White is famous for creating that sought-after light-and-airy look. Walls painted white reflect both natural and artificial light; white ceilings reflect 10 percent more light than even the palest hue. White paint is a good choice for rooms with odd or irregular features, because minor flaws nearly disappear in the absence of color—especially if the paint is matte. Used on doors, moldings, and fireplaces, white breaks up expanses of color and emphasizes the lines of a room.

If you decide to paint your walls white, you'll quickly discover that not all whites are created equal, and almost none is pure. In fact, true-neutral white, devoid of all color, is rarely used on walls because it is too cold and stark. Most white paints contain undertones of warm or cool colors: typically soft yellow, pink, or bluish gray. Undertones are easiest to see in paint brochures, where the chips are grouped for easy comparison.

BASIC BLACK. Black is everywhere in the decorating world, in both starring and supporting roles. Wrought-iron bed frames, metal floor lamps, and granite countertops are just a few examples of black furnishings, accessories, and materials. Black is graphic and sophisticated; as such, it's best used in small to moderate doses. (The classic black leather sofa and baby grand piano are notable exceptions.) Think of it as an accent, a sort of punctuation mark in a decorating scheme.

GOING GRAY. Glamorous gray, often associated with Hollywood design of the 1930s, is sometimes called "the all-purpose neutral." A mixture of black and white, gray bridges the gap between other colors without taking over. Imagine a charcoal gray suede sectional in a contemporary room with curry-toned walls and mahogany tables. In such a setting, gray creates a "neutral zone" between the intense walls and warm woods.

Gray often appears in decorating schemes in the form of metal accessories and hardware—a silver tea service, hammered-nickel drawer pulls, a polished-chrome floor lamp—or in natural materials such as slate, terrazzo, and concrete.

ABOVE: This sleek bathroom is a study in black, white, and chrome. The white element is a Carrara-marble counter. The cabinets are black lacquer and—flanking the mirror—stainless steel with frosted-glass door panels. The walls and ceiling are coated with rough-textured plaster.

LEFT: Black is the essential ingredient in this sophisticated neutral setting, even though it's limited to accent furnishings (the lamp shade and end table) and accessories (the pillows, frames, and vase). A leopard-print rug in black and beige introduces pattern to the mostly solid scheme.

New-neutral greens in a custom-designed Tibetan rug and synthetic suede bar stools contribute low-key color to a contemporary kitchen. The walls are integral-color plaster; that is, the color is mixed into the plaster, not applied to the surface. The concrete countertops and floor have been stained black and a new-neutral reddish brown. Maple cabinetry lightens and warms the scheme.

A CONTEMPORARY TAKE ON NEUTRAL COLORS

If you've ever looked at a fabric or paint chip and wondered, "What color is that, anyway? Is it green? Or is it gray?" chances are you were puzzling over a "new neutral." These versatile yet difficult-to-describe hues are very, very low-intensity (page 227) versions of the 12 colors on the color ring. Put another way, new neutrals are colors that have been "neutralized" or neutrals that have been "colorized."

Although you're not likely to mix your own paint colors, it's helpful to understand where new neutrals come from. A new-neutral color is the result of adding a bit of one color to a larger amount of its complement, thereby lowering the intensity of the latter. (Usually, black or white is added to lighten or darken the color.) For example, a small amount of red paint added to its complement, green, produces a less intense green: a new-neutral green. In the same way, a bit of green added to red creates a dull, new-neutral red.

Like any other color, new neutrals can range in value from light to dark. Ecru, linen, and pearl are examples of light-value new neutrals;

khaki, camel, and cocoa are medium; and charcoal, coffee bean, and chestnut are dark. New neutrals vary in temperature, as well: picture a warm taupe and a cool bluish gray.

These softer hues lend ambience and a hint of color to a room but never overwhelm or stand out. New-neutral walls make an excellent backdrop for art and are the perfect foil for treasured antiques, because their understated character plays up the patina on old wood finishes, antique silver and gold frames, and old brass hardware. (Many "historic" colors are in fact new neutrals.) Their quiet grace makes them a good choice for faux finishes, which rely on subtle pattern and texture for visual interest.

New neutrals marry well with major furnishings, where they agreeably adapt to changes in a room. Flooring in a new-neutral color, for example, visually anchors a room without drawing the eye downward.

The color ring is particularly invaluable when you've chosen to work with these understated hues, once you determine the source color of your new neutral. A color described as "laurel leaf," for example, is a dark-value, very low-intensity version of yellow-green. For a complementary contrast to this color, you might choose merlot, a very low-intensity red-violet that lies opposite yellow-green on the ring. To become better acquainted with new neutrals, flip through decorating magazines, picking them out and trying to determine their source colors. You'll be surprised at how often these subtle hues appear in both contemporary and traditional design.

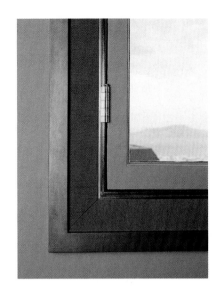

TIPS

Because they are low in intensity, new neutrals almost always "go together."

ABOVE: Disparate materials and finishes—satin paint, metallic paint, and faille, a narrowly ribbed fabric—give a vintage window frame distinction. Alternating warm and cool grays accentuates the illusion of a triple-matted painting.

LEFT: New-neutral grays, which are more colorful than true grays, and subtle textures lend sophistication to a corner seating area. Art and accessories add understated pattern.

SIXTEEN READY-MADE LOWE'S COLOR PALETTES

If you're new to working with color, creating a palette can be daunting. The palettes appearing on the next several pages are intended to inspire, whether you use one as is—pages 421–423—or edit it to fit your plan.

PALETTE 1

Peach (a light value of red-orange) and yellow-green are roughly opposite on the color ring, making them near complements. When you work with opposing colors, opt for low-intensity versions to soften the contrast. Varying the values—even a little—adds depth. A grayed white is ideal for walls.

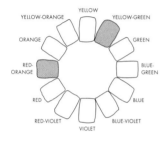

PALETTE 2

These low-intensity colors on the cool side of the color ring are related, yet different enough to intrigue. Violet, an effective bridging color (see page 226), adds a bit of warmth to cool blue and green. A new-neutral green (see pages 264–265) makes a harmonious companion color.

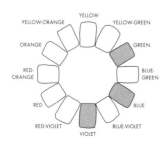

PALETTE 3

A complex combination of pale yellow-orange, red-orange (in two light values), blue, and green balances warm and cool hues. Use the lighter peach on walls for just a hint of color. To achieve a warmer, stronger effect, choose the darker peach or chamois yellow, which tends toward yellow-orange.

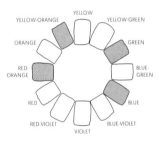

PALETTE 4

Complementary colors are most livable when their values are light and their intensity is subdued. Medium values of pink (almost mauve, a version of red-violet) and green (nearly yellow-green) strengthen their light-value counter-parts. Luminous yellow is always a welcome color in a pink-and-green scheme.

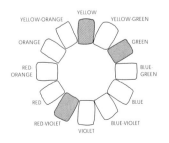

PALETTE 5

Primary red, blue, and yellow make up a triad (see page 232) that works well when the colors are dark in value and low in intensity. In this palette, brick red, cadet blue, and palomino gold set a quiet mood. Yellow-green cools the warm red and gold; light khaki is appropriate for walls or trim.

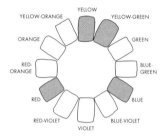

PALETTE 6

A near-complementary combination pairs glen green (a green with blue overtones) and brick red in a scheme befitting a den or library. Khaki and oatmeal, both low-intensity versions of yellow, enrich the palette. Let the warm hues predominate; punctuate them with the cool green.

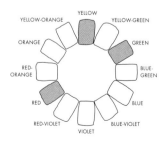

PALETTE 7

New neutrals in a mix of light, medium, and dark values make up a warm palette. Closely related values of toast and charcoal repeat the colors for a pleasing visual rhythm. Oatmeal and chamois are suited to walls or trim, browns and grays to furnishings and flooring materials.

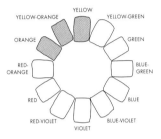

PALETTE 8

A six-color palette, loosely based on a triad of yellow-green, red-orange, and violet, is diverse and complex. Aubergine and plum temper the warm olive green (a dark value of yellow-green), gold, and russet. For walls, use either of the lightest values or seek out lighter, low-intensity versions of the darker hues.

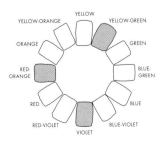

PALETTE 9

A light-value, clear violet adds an element of surprise to a classic blue and blue-green combination. Pearl gray, a true neutral, spaces out the color, while a dark-value, low-intensity blue grounds the scheme. For an airier look, consider gray walls or lighter versions of violet, green, or blue.

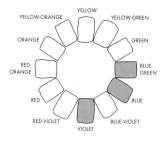

PALETTE 10

A palette of yellow, blue, and green is always fresh and summery. Slight variations in the yellow-greens take the scheme beyond the predictable. Subtly different blues (one true, the other closer to blue-green) prove that simple combinations can be intriguing when you use closely related versions of a few colors.

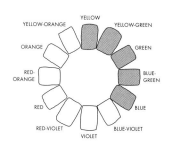

PALETTE 11

Warm and cool grays harmonize with icy blue-grays. Consider using the light gray on walls, the lightest gray on trim. A cool blue-and-gray palette benefits from the warmth of wood furniture and wood floors.

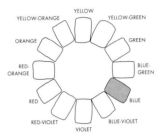

PALETTE 12

An analogous combination begs for a range of values and intensities, as in this scheme of yellow-green through blue-green. Low-intensity yellow-green warms up the cooler hues. The light and medium values are suited to walls; the darkest green is a natural for furnishings.

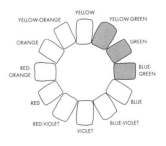

PALETTE 13

Intense, high-contrast colors are energetic and visually exciting. Two warm and two cool hues balance the visual temperature in this vibrant scheme. When you use intense colors, vary their quantities. The true neutrals black and white can be used to space out color in a high-contrast room.

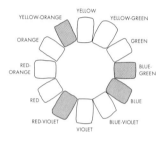

PALETTE 14

Analogous hues ranging from yellow-orange through red-orange couldn't be warmer. Varying the values and intensities just a little hushes the scheme and provides needed visual relief. Copper, a dark value of orange, tones down the brilliant hues. Use the lighter values for intensely colored walls, the darker values for furnishings.

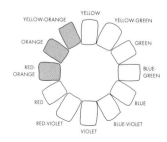

PALETTE 15

Two near complements, blue-green and red, are tempered here by a grayed yellow-green. Intense orange and yellow-orange push the scheme toward the warm side of the color ring. Consider lighter values of the warm hues for walls, darker values of the cool colors for floors, and a mix of colors for furnishings.

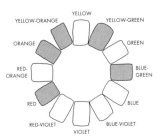

PALETTE 16

Intense red-orange, yellow-green, and blue-violet are equally spaced and perfectly balanced on the color ring, forming a triad. Shrimp, a light value of red-orange, lightens and brightens the scheme. The new neutral sage makes a quiet counterpoint to the strong hues.

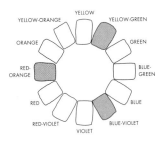

ELEMENTS OF A ROOM

WHETHER YOUR PROJECT IS CHOOSING A NEW SOFA OR REDECORATING THE WHOLE HOUSE, THE PATH TO A DECISION CROSSES THE SAME STEPPING STONES: Determine your specific needs as well as your budget; consider all of your choices from a practical as well as an aesthetic standpoint; learn where you can find what you're looking for; and draw up a shortlist of options that could work.

This chapter travels that path for each decision you're likely to face, from choosing between paint and wallpaper to finding the perfect rug, designing a lighting scheme, or rearranging a room. Use it as a resource as you narrow your selection and make your final decisions.

WALLS AND CEILINGS

WALLS AND CEILINGS MAKE UP THE LARGEST
SURFACE AREA OF ANY ROOM, CREATING A
WONDERFUL—SOMETIMES OVERWHELMING—
DESIGN OPPORTUNITY. THERE ARE ALMOST
TOO MANY DIRECTIONS TO PURSUE.

A pattern featuring oversize, umber-colored shells lends dimension to this flat wall. Note how the theme is repeated in the seashore-inspired wall sconce.

Paint options alone are myriad; add wall coverings, decorative finishes, paneling, millwork, and other treatments into the mix and making a choice becomes daunting. But—as with other design decisions—if you proceed step-by-step, your wall treatments will enhance and pull together your design scheme as no other element can.

Consider some of the options. Paint, the most inexpensive and popular treatment, can become a dramatic feature. You can choose quiet or strong colors, or use two or more contrasting colors or finishes in the same space—even on the same wall. If the room's furnishings are highly textured and patterned, walls painted a quiet color will contribute harmony and balance.

Wallpaper is making a comeback. Textured or patterned wallpaper is often used to add warmth, personality, and dimension as well as to soften living spaces. There's a trend toward more hand-painted designs and matte or even textured finishes. Also, many of the decorative paint finishes that once had to be applied by an experienced hand can now be bought "by the roll."

At the same time, the hand-sponged and marbleized paint effects that were popular in recent decades have given way to quieter decorative applications, such as combing and color washing, that add depth and texture without calling attention to themselves. Trompe l'oeil, on the other hand, is more outspoken; it can even bring the illusion of architectural detail to an otherwise plain wall.

Other wall-treatment options are numerous and as varied as the architectural styles they inhabit: panels of luxurious silk or crisp linen; terrazzo or glass-tile mosaics; vintage beadboard wainscoting; even industrial-looking concrete, brought to life with rich stains or acid etching. More will be said about these options in the following pages, but for now just leave your mind open to the possibilities.

WHERE TO BEGIN. First, take stock of what else you will be working with in the room. Furniture and fabrics seem a natural place to start, but consider more basic elements, too: the quality of the light (both natural and artificial), the proportions of the room, architectural features you may want to downplay or highlight. For example, if a room is small or dark, you may choose to go with lighter, cooler colors to lend a sense of space or an airy quality. Or you may decide not to fight these inherent qualities, instead creating a cozy, intimate room with warm, rich colors and textures.

Awkward proportions and features can be minimized with simple tricks of the trade. Vertical stripes draw the eye up and create visual height. Horizontal stripes can broaden a narrow room if used on the narrow wall. Soaring ceilings can be "lowered" with a deep, warm color, low ceilings "raised" with a color much lighter than on the walls. Similarly, if you have a long, narrow room, you can bring in the far short wall with a warm hue such as terra-cotta, painting the others a complementary cool color, such as a bluish sage.

Using the same treatment on all walls will unify a room filled with a confusion of doors, windows, sloping ceilings, and angles.

In this living room, problem walls were covered in a stucco-like embossed wall-paper, then painted sunshine yellow with a tinted glaze. The result: the foundation for a crisp black, white, and yellow color scheme, and a perfect backdrop for a beloved collection of botanical prints.

Chosen to complement the owner's collection of Bauer pottery, this shiny tile counter and backsplash brighten the cherry wood kitchen. The colorful, randomly set tiles add life and longevity: "We'll never tire of this kitchen," says the owner-designer. The gray-brown grout not only works with all the tile colors but also simplifies maintenance.

Conversely, a contrasting, eye-catching color treatment for one attractive feature, such as a fireplace wall or recessed arch, plays up its inherent visual interest and draws the eye away from less interesting areas.

PRACTICAL ASPECTS. While you continue your assessment, consider some practical issues: Are your walls in good condition, or are you prepared to fix them before you finish them? Wallpaper and certain decorative finishes can mask cracks and other irregularities, whereas a glossy or uniform paint treatment will highlight them. How will the room be used? Some paints and wallpapers are much easier to clean than others and are therefore better suited to high-use areas like kitchens, baths, and children's rooms.

Will you be doing the work yourself, or are you planning to hire professionals? Some painting, wallpapering, and simple decorative finishes are easy enough to master with a little practice, but they demand that you set aside time to learn, gather materials, complete the job, and cope with any surprises along the way.

Budget is a factor, too, of course. A few cans of paint are an inexpensive way to make a major and dramatic design change, especially if you are doing the work yourself. But the cost of some wallpapers and many professional decorative finishes can add up quickly, so wall treatments should be factored into your overall budget.

MAKING CHOICES. As you continue to gather information and ideas, scour design books and magazines and note the treatments you see in friends' homes, restaurants, and stores to get fresh, up-to-date ideas. Not all of them will translate well to your home, but by looking at them with an open mind you may find ways to incorporate certain elements successfully—a hand-stamped motif, a niche in a contrasting color, a ribbon of gold where the dining room wall meets the ceiling.

If you don't have a designer helping you, come to Lowe's; many of our stores offer one-on-one consultation with our experienced, knowledgeable sales associates. Bring in photos, fabric swatches, and any other materials you have that convey the look you are after; solicit our pros' input when making your decisions.

PAINT

Choosing the right color is probably the most time-consuming part of the painting process—mainly because judging a color on the basis of a 2-inch-square paint chip is impossible for all but the most experienced eye. The discussion of color in this book (pages 226–273) can help you decide on a fundamental color scheme. And your Lowe's store now offers ready-made "mistake-proof" palettes that allow you to mix wall, ceiling, and trim colors from room to room with confidence. Learning some basic facts about paint and how to evaluate it will be helpful, in any case.

COLOR. Assess your paint chips at home in the chosen rooms. Look carefully for the undertones, which will appear much stronger once the paint is on the walls. (Is it a pink beige or a gray beige? An orange-based yellow or a green-based yellow?) Because paint tends to look one or two values darker on walls, experts recommend sticking with the middle tones of a paint strip—if you go too light, the color will lack character.

The next crucial step is the "brush-out." Buy as small a quantity of paint as you can; usually this will be a quart, but some paint formulas can only be made in a gallon size. You can either brush a large area directly onto the wall—preferably on both walls of a corner, where you can see how the color will change on different planes—or you can paint a large piece of foam core board and move it around the room.

Examine the brush-out carefully throughout the day and at night, in both natural and artificial light. Don't forget to test the ceiling color as well, keeping in mind that it will appear darker because the ceiling gets the least light of all painted surfaces.

Intense blue walls set off this homeowner's arrangements of Majolica plates and colorful handcrafted furniture and collectibles. A fresh, cool green lightens the ceiling, and both colors come into play on the floor.

SHEEN. A paint's finish can also affect its color and determine its durability. Flat or matte paints absorb the most light, creating an opaque color, and are usually best suited for ceilings or living rooms, dining rooms, and other low-traffic areas. Eggshell, satin, and low-luster paints have a bit of sheen; because they are easier to wipe down, these are often used in kitchens, bathrooms, and high-traffic hallways. Semigloss and gloss finishes reflect a lot of light and can take vigorous scrubbing; they're especially suited to trim. (They will, however, highlight any texture, cracks, or other imperfections in walls.)

A new trend is "texture in a can." Some designer paints now have fibers in them that, when applied using standard methods and equipment, transfer denim, suede, flannel, or other feel-good textures directly onto the wall.

LATEX OR OIL? Latex is water-based paint and by far the most popular; it is nearly odorless, dries in hours rather than days, and cleans up with soap and water. It is also less likely to fade, chalk, crack, or mildew than its counterpart.

Alkyd, or oil-based, paint is a petroleum solvent. It has excellent durability, but most people find they have to vacate their house during painting due to its odor. It also takes considerably longer to dry and requires a paint-thinner cleanup. Though oil has long been favored over latex for trim and woodwork, some high-end water-based enamels now perform nearly as well as oil and are kinder to the environment and the homeowners' and painters' health.

Professionals recommend using only latex over existing latex; an oil-based paint may end up cracking. To find out what kind of paint you'll be covering, rub on some mineral spirits: an oil-based finish will dissolve, a latex base remain unaffected.

Periwinkle blue makes a soothing backdrop in this nursery, with pale yellow to deep gold highlighting the door and trim. The space between the picture rail and crown molding created a perfect home for a children's-book quote. A computer-generated banner was transferred to the wall and handpainted.

HEALTHY TRENDS IN PAINT

Although paint has come a long way since the old lead-based days, it still contains ingredients that can be harmful to both you and the environment. The most toxic ingredients are the solvents used in oil-based (or "alkyd") paints; they may be inhaled during application, drying, and curing. Toxic effects vary greatly depending on exposure (the danger is thought to be greater for babies and children), but they can affect the central nervous system. Improper disposal of leftover oil-based paints creates environmental hazards, as well.

Latex paints have fewer solvents and less odor; they are also safer and easier to dispose of.

To reduce your exposure to the harmful effects of both oil-based and latex products, always ventilate the area well with open windows and fans. Choose brushing and rolling over spraying to minimize fumes. If you're using latex paints, try to control the amount you send down the drain: brush or roll out as much paint as possible on newspaper before rinsing your applicators with soap and water. Allow paint-thinner rags to dry thoroughly before wrapping them in paper for disposal. Empty oil-based paint cans should be taken to your community's hazardous waste recycling site. Use any remaining paint in another area of the house, or give it away to neighbors or local charities. ∾

WALLPAPER

Wallpaper designs have come a long way from the heavy-handed florals and foils of earlier generations. Although traditional styles are still available (in updated hues), you will now find more coverings, such as linen look-alikes and grass cloth, that can add subtle texture while providing a muted backdrop for furnishings. Embossed wall coverings designed to look like stucco, pressed tin, or plaster fresco can add history to a more contemporary home.

Of course, wallpaper is still unsurpassed for hiding imperfect walls or providing visual interest in bathrooms and hallways where there is little furniture to do the job. It can set a theme or create detail in a house

Wavy stripes in nautical blues and sunny yellow float the sea theme through this children's bathroom. Vinyl-coated wallpaper is the best choice for such high-moisture areas.

that otherwise lacks it. The patterns in wallpaper can literally produce optical illusions, suggesting better proportions in rooms that are too long or too boxy, or whose ceilings are too low or too high. And wallpaper can be relatively simple to install—a playful border can enliven a child's room in less than an hour.

How do you decide which look is right for you? Many of the design, color, scale, and pattern principles discussed in the first chapter of this book apply to wallpaper decisions as well. By now you have probably decided what feeling you want the room to have—light and airy or rich and dark, calming or lively, clean and contemporary or arty and eclectic. You probably also have at least a basic idea of your color scheme, perhaps even some of the fabrics and floor or window coverings for the room. What common traits do your furnishings have—a style, a color palette? Wallpaper can do an excellent job of tying together disparate elements.

WALLPAPER TYPES AND TERMINOLOGY. Aside from their pattern and color, wallpapers vary significantly in their material content, which determines durability and cleanability as well as appearance, cost, installation, and ease of removal. Because technology and options are constantly changing, it is best to decide which of the following practical characteristics are most important to you and ask a Lowe's sales associate to steer you to a suitable product.

❖ Scrubbable: cleans with a brush and detergent; good for kitchens

❖ Washable: cleans with occasional soap-and-water sponging

❖ Stain resistant: stains can be thoroughly removed

❖ Abrasion resistant: withstands scraping and rubbing as well as scrubbing; excellent for hallways

❖ Colorfast: won't fade in sunlight

❖ Prepasted: only water is needed to adhere paper to the wall

❖ Peelable: decorative surface can be drypeeled but backing will remain; fine if you plan always to redecorate with wallpaper

❖ Strippable: paper can be drypeeled, leaving little paste or adhesive residue

TOP: Woven reeds lend natural color and tactile interest to a wall; the complexity of the weave also hides nail holes, a boon to those who change their wall art frequently.

MIDDLE: Textured blocks work well in contemporary, ethnic, or minimalist settings.

BOTTOM: A crackled "fresco" surface no longer requires intensive faux painting; the look is now available in wallpapers.

MATERIAL CHOICES. In general, wall coverings containing or coated with some sort of vinyl will be the sturdiest and easiest to install. But alternatives abound: grass cloth, linen, silk, and other natural fibers provide a neutral backdrop; uncoated choices such as hand-screened (rather than machine-printed) papers can be gorgeous but also very difficult to hang; foils can brighten up a dark space (some contemporary interiors are adorned with plain aluminum foil); brown craft paper provides what some consider a perfect neutral background, at once simple and sophisticated. Keep in mind that many of these alternatives must be installed by professionals.

Here, "wallpaper" takes the form of small sheets of silver leaf applied by hand to form harlequin diamonds. Soaring from floor to ceiling, these light-reflecting shapes give a small breakfast nook big personality and heighten the space visually. The silver leaf is protected with a coat of urethane.

ESTIMATING WALLPAPER QUANTITIES

Measuring correctly for your wallpaper is crucial to a successful job: rolls printed in a later run may not match your first batch, so you want to order the right amount to begin with.

Start by measuring the overall height and width of each wall with a steel tape measure. Round up to the nearest foot. Multiply the height and width of each wall, and add the figures together to get your rough square footage. Next, use the same technique to measure the openings (doors and windows), this time rounding down. Deduct these areas from the rough square footage. To allow for cutting and trimming, figure on 25 usable square feet for each single roll, as long as the pattern repeat (printed on the back of the roll) is less than 4 inches. If the repeat is more than 4 inches, you will probably get only 22 usable square feet.

To determine how many rolls you need, divide the total square footage obtained in your measurements by the usable square feet (25 or 22). If need be, round up the roll count to an even number, as rolls are now typically sold in doubles.

If you will be wallpapering for the first time, it pays to buy from Lowe's where a sales associate can verify your estimate and answer your questions. Also, ask about how-to booklets and clinics offered at Lowe's. ～

DECORATIVE PAINTING

If you are yearning for more than flat painted walls but don't want patterned wallpaper, perhaps decorative painting is the answer. Creating interest in walls by using paint effects has a long and venerable history: think Roman murals, Renaissance frescoes, and the charming Gustavian look of 18th-century Swedish interiors. Even a first-timer can apply a simple color wash or glaze to transform a wall that's in good shape into a surface with a depth of color and light that lends the room soul. More adventurous and experienced painters (and hired professionals) can take it further and create the illusion of grand paneled walls, rich wood grain, or even a Tuscan hillside.

Stenciled concentric ovals within diamonds climb the archway, providing a transition from one room to the next.

In addition to sponging and rag rolling, which have long been popular, there are subtler finishes. Colorwashing and drybrushing are widely used for good reason: they add depth and texture without calling attention to themselves. And these effects are increasingly easy for homeowners to achieve, as more and more paint and home-supply stores are offering premixed glazes with all the necessary materials and instructions for beginners.

There are plenty of ways to make a more emphatic statement. One very personal choice is to have a favorite line of poetry or other quote beautifully transcribed as a wall border, usually just below the ceiling (see photo on page 280). Many children's rooms have become fantasy environments with playful murals on the walls or dreamy clouds on the ceiling. Some talented artists can even create a wall-size replica of a homeowner's favorite Monet or van Gogh.

Knowing which technique is right for your situation involves answering a few questions:

❖ Do you want a dramatic feature or a subtle background effect? Faux finishes mimic another material—a "marble" fireplace surround, or a "wood-grained" chair rail. Quieter effects simply provide added dimension and a subtle play of colors.

❖ Do you need a treatment that will camouflage an imperfect wall? Or is the wall completely smooth?

❖ Will the finish be covering a large expanse of wall, or will it be broken up by windows, doors, and cabinets? The more features you have to work around, the more complicated it is to execute a design.

❖ What do the proportions of the room call for? Be careful not to overwhelm them. Keep in mind that some treatments, like some wallpaper patterns, can fool the eye and "correct" undesirable proportions.

❖ Will you be doing the work yourself, or hiring a professional?

Whichever technique you choose, select your colors carefully, and remember that with decorative finishes it is better to err on the side of subtlety (especially if you are new to the art). In colorwashing, the closer in tone the glaze is to the base coat the better. Practice the technique first on a large piece of foam core board until you are confident. If you are hiring a professional, have the person show you a finished sample in your chosen colors before starting on your walls.

Finally, practice restraint. Though it may be tempting to use different techniques on the crown moldings, baseboards, and everything in between, the effect will be muddled and confused and will quickly become dated.

In the gallery on page 287, we introduce a handful of paint effects and note their relative merits and drawbacks.

Reproducing part of Vermeer's "The Lacemaker" on a surreal scale (more than 11 feet square) made the dining room a focal point in this open-plan house. At the same time, the downcast eyes of the figure bring intimacy to the room. Specifying that a mural be done on canvas, as here, rather than on the wall makes your investment portable.

Once you have decided to transform an expanse of wall into a decorative

paint effects

owners to tackle; many paint stores now sell kits to make them even

backdrop, it's time to figure out which treatment best suits your space, abilities, and budget. Some techniques, such as colorwashing, are simple enough for home-

easier. Effects such as striping and dragging require a very steady hand, however, and often some assistance. Murals are best left to professionals.

1 MURALS AND TROMPE L'OEIL A mural is a scene painted directly onto the wall; it can add playfulness and whimsy or drama and high art, depending on the image chosen. Some muralists will incorporate words into their image, or they may let a beautiful text border be the sole ornamentation. Trompe l'oeil, which translates as "fool the eye," is meant to trick the viewer into believing that the scene or object is real. It can be a cost-effective means of giving a space what it lacks naturally—a wonderful view, for instance, or interesting architectural features such as millwork and windows. (Here, a trompe l'oeil door enlivens a long hall and creates a pleasing symmetry.) Murals and trompe l'oeil are best done on smooth walls (unless the artist can incorporate imperfections into the design). Be sure to inquire about maintenance, as touch-ups can be difficult. Also, consider limiting the images to one wall.

2 STENCILING This method lets you add pattern to your walls without calling for the artistic talent that murals require. Stencils are available in many designs, and it's fairly easy and very rewarding to create your own stencil. Another option, shown here, is to combine two or more stencil patterns and colors over a background paint effect for a truly unique finish. Stenciling can be done as a border at chair-rail height, just below the ceiling, or from floor to ceiling, depending on the desired effect. It can also call attention to an interesting architectural detail, like an opening or arch, or be used on wood furniture and floors. For step-by-step directions on how to stencil, turn to pages 366–367.

3 DRAGGING Also known as strié, this technique involves dragging a dry brush through wet glaze to reveal thin, irregular stripes of the background color. Its subtlety makes it a particularly good backdrop for art and antiques. Though it is typically done in straight vertical lines, an overlay of horizontal lines can give a cross-hatched look and texture. Here, wavy lines bring movement and whimsy to the walls, for a less formal effect.

4 STRIPING Though this fresh, tailored look is often achieved with wallpaper, stripes are actually easy to paint on and can be used in combination with any number of other paint effects. Vertical stripes have the effect of drawing the eye up, thereby heightening a room; horizontal stripes widen a wall. Depending on the colors, methods, and width you choose, striping is bold or subtle. Here, the stripes were achieved by removing the glaze with a sponge dipped in paint thinner. Note that stripes have a way of emphasizing out-of-plumb walls.

5 COLORWASHING Evoking the aging walls of Tuscan castles and Provençal country homes, colorwashing is achieved by layering colors—a basecoat plus one or more glaze tints—to attain a rich, warm glow. Depending on the colors chosen, the effect can be either subtle or quite dramatic. Colorwashed walls provide a rich but understated context for artwork and upholstery. The technique, which is shown in step-by-step photos and instructions on pages 360–361, is suitable for walls in less-than-perfect condition, and it can work with either formal or country decor. A more pronounced Old World look can be achieved by first skim-coating the walls with a rough layer of joint compound; this is called fresco colorwashing.

6 COMBING This all-over technique can be strong and bold or delicate and subtle, depending on the comb, colors, and pattern used. In general, combing is considered less subtle and formal than its close cousin, dragging. However, the many variations on combing make it adaptable to almost any situation. As with dragging, combing can be done vertically, horizontally, or in curves; combining directions can yield a basket-weave or moiré effect. Here, a wide-toothed comb was pulled horizontally, and, while the glaze was still wet, a different comb was pulled vertically. For step-by-step directions on how to do this painting technique, turn to pages 362–363.

architectural treatments

From the most elaborate crown molding to the simplest baseboard, millwork can introduce architectural interest to almost any home—and it's available at your nearest Lowe's. When selecting the style and scale of millwork, consider the architecture of your home as well as its proportions.

Moldings of prefinished pine or hardwoods are fine if you want a stained look, but if you plan to paint your millwork, you should buy medium-density fiberboard (MDF); it's less prone to warping and takes paint better than wood. Also consider architectural accents such as columns, pediments, fireplace mantels, decorative friezes, and ceiling medallions; new ones are stocked at home-improvement centers, originals at architectural salvage yards and specialty stores. Recycled pieces can be refinished or left as is, for an aged look.

1 CROWN AND BASEBOARD MOLDINGS are designed to conceal seams where the walls meet the ceiling and floor. They not only mask any unevenness in the joint line but, if painted in a contrasting color, frame the room. White or light-colored crown molding, in particular, draws the eye upward and visually heightens the room. Baseboard molding is usually simple, with modest trim at its top and bottom to ease the board's transition to wall and floor. For step-by-step instructions on installing crown molding, turn to pages 388–389; instructions for installing faux-plaster crown molding are on pages 410–411; and instructions for installing baseboard are on pages 380–381.

2 RAILS are strips of horizontal trim attached to a wall. **Chair rails** (pictured here) are at or below chair height (typically 3 to 4 feet from the floor). Their original purpose was to prevent chair backs from scraping the walls; they also divide walls into two design opportunities. The area below the chair rail, called the dado, is usually given a heavier, simpler treatment (perhaps beadboard or paneling) and the upper part a lighter, more decorative treatment. **Plate rails** are a wonderful way to display a china collection. They resemble a narrow shelf running high around the wall (1 to 2 feet below the ceiling); the shelf has a lip or groove in which the plates rest. Step-by-step directions for making a plate rack are given on pages 386–387. **Picture rails** make it easy to hang and rearrange art without hammering nails into the walls. They project from the wall below the ceiling; pictures hang on invisible wire or decorative cording from S-shaped hooks that grip the molding.

3 PANELING AND BEADBOARD bring architectural significance and grace to nondescript spaces. They may cover the whole wall, floor to ceiling, or only the dado, or lower half of the wall. Beadboard, shown here, adds old-fashioned charm to any room. **Frame-and-paneled walls,** either stained or painted, are usually accompanied by distinctive baseboard and cornice millwork.

4 A FIREPLACE MANTEL is a natural focal point in any room, so dressing it up can have a big impact. You may be able to find an antique or reproduction mantel that suits the room's architecture (and fits the fireplace opening). Although wood, stone, and marble are the materials traditionally associated with fireplace surrounds, inlaid tile opens limitless possibilities in terms of color, pattern, and style. Step-by-step instructions for adding tile around a fireplace are given on pages 414–416. Stained or etched concrete or resin is a more contemporary option.

5 BANISTERS, comprising the staircase handrail and supports, are worth special treatment if they're in a prominent space within the home, such as the main entry. The staircase pictured here features painted balusters topped with a scrolled, stained handrail, styles well suited to this traditional home (as well as to the stair treads). Creativity can be exercised in more eclectic or contemporary homes by using materials such as iron or choosing interesting paint treatments and colors.

6 COLUMNS AND PILASTERS sound a classical note, create visual height, and add period atmosphere. Columns are rounded and sometimes provide structural support; pilasters (shown here) are rectangular and ornamental, usually protruding from the wall on either side of an important door. Both can be made of wood, plaster, or marble.

other wall treatments

Wall-covering choices extend well beyond paint, wallpaper, and paneling. Depending on how the room will be used and maintained, and on its location within the home, any of the following materials may be appropriate. Keep in mind that many of these treatments can be used as accents in combination with simpler backdrops. Tile, for instance, can be used for just the backsplash wall of the kitchen, with the other walls painted a complementary color. Glass block might form an interior window rather than a floor-to-ceiling wall. Metal could sheathe just one wall of a room, or the upper portion of two walls, instead of all four. This accent approach is not only less expensive, but it can also be more effective.

1 TILE Typically used in bathrooms and kitchens—high-moisture, high-mess areas—tile walls are beautiful and resilient; options are myriad in tile color, material, size, pattern, style, and finish. Creating borders or inlaid designs, as in this glass-mosaic backsplash, gives tile a custom look every time. Because grout stains easily, you may want to have it tinted the same color as—or a slightly darker shade than—the tile. Step-by-step directions for installing a ceramic tile backsplash are given on pages 412–413. Directions for decorative painting on ceramic tile are given on page 417.

2 GLASS BLOCK This product both reflects light and lets it through, while offering varying degrees of privacy. It is frequently used to separate spaces in a bathroom, but is suitable for any two areas that need to share light yet be divided. Because the blocks come in square or rectangular shapes, a stair-step effect at the edge is quite common. Here, a curved wall divides the kitchen from the entry but also provides a sense of openness. Glass block is available in a wide range of textures, from clear (as in the photo) to frosted, depending on the degree of privacy or light desired.

3 CONCRETE More and more popular for lofts and contemporary houses, concrete can be formulated light enough to cover walls in slabs or tiles. A concrete-and-resin mix is light and thin, yet strong enough to be troweled onto walls. Sometimes these walls are scored and stained after installation (as here), or color may be integrated with the cement mixture beforehand. Concrete can be treated as an art surface, inlaid with anything from mosaic tiles to found objects; an acid wash or troweled-on texture gives it an aged look.

4 STONE Slate, granite, marble, limestone—all of these natural materials commonly used on floors can also cover walls, as evidenced by many bathrooms, kitchens, entries, and outdoor-dining patios. Like their ceramic cousins, stone tiles are available in many sizes and shapes. Stone is porous (some types more so than others), but new sealers are making it more stain resistant. Because it is a natural material, uniformity is rare; variation in color is usually celebrated, though, as in this slate-tile bathroom.

5 FABRIC-COVERED SCREENS The most flexible wall of all is one of screens; use them to divide a room, hide storage, or cordon off a private area. Here, a fabric-covered, wood-framed screen serves a purely decorative purpose, adding the color and texture of the damask fabric as well as architectural dimension with its chair-rail-height horizontal divider. Screens can also be covered with maps, antique prints, or wallpaper, to name a few options. If you are screening off a home office, you might cover one side of the screen with homosote, so that it can double as a bulletin board, and cover the other with a decorative treatment that ties in with the rest of the room.

6 METAL Increasingly familiar as a backsplash for commercial-style stoves, brushed stainless steel and other metals are breaking out to cover entire walls, especially in lofts (as here) and contemporary homes. Polished metal can be difficult to maintain, but brushed metal can still provide a degree of luster and light reflection while obscuring fingerprints and fine scratches. This treatment can even suggest movement and texture, if the brushstrokes are wavy or circular.

CASE STUDY

walls worth framing

HOW DO YOU DECORATE *a house that has great proportions but no specific architectural heritage? If you're Joan Osburn, of Osburn Design, you thank your lucky stars for the blank canvas. "Putting together the colors and treatments for a home is like creating a three-dimensional work of art," she says. With adventurous clients, the designer was free to mix a broad palette of shimmering colors and special effects. Throughout the house, iridescent finishes and layered glazes illuminate the colors and reflect light in a way that shifts depending on where you're standing as well as on the time of day. Every surface imparts the glow of an Impressionist masterpiece.*

TOP: Layers of ocher and melon wash texturized plaster to create an updated south-of-France look. Custom mirrors reflect light from the large windows opposite.

BOTTOM: The iridescent palette used in this entry hall staircase balances warm hues drawn from adjoining rooms with cooler colors introduced for playfulness. "These accent colors wouldn't necessarily be appropriate for a whole wall, but they are fabulous in small doses," comments Osburn.

DETAIL, LEFT: The inspiration for this whimsical powder room was a custom vanity (not shown) handpainted with a collage of fanciful motifs. The checkerboard molding around the window mirrors a black and white marble floor. On the wall, softly rendered roses provide an element of surprise, juxtaposed with the room's geometry.

Opalescent yellow walls with iridescent-glazed maple cabinets bounce light around this contemporary bathroom. The warm paint colors contrast with the cool gray-and-white marble and green-tinged glass basins. Surface-mounted square tiles of white glass give the far wall dimension, as does the "rail" near the ceiling, also of white glass tile. "Who says moldings have to be made of wood?" challenges Osburn.

FLOORING

Tumbled limestone in taupe with gold accents was a stylish but practical choice for this bathroom; the adjoining hallway's golden-hued wall-to-wall coir is durable yet soft underfoot. A wood threshold eases the transition between the two surfaces.

ALTHOUGH FLOOR COVERINGS ARE GENERALLY THOUGHT OF AS A BACKDROP, THEY DEMAND THAT YOU MAKE PLENTY OF DECISIONS IN TERMS OF THEIR DURABILITY, MAINTENANCE, FUNCTIONALITY, AND COMFORT.

Of all the design elements in a room, flooring will see the most wear. It is a working component, a structural as well as aesthetic choice. Adding even more weight to your decision is the fact that flooring comprises the second-largest surface area in the home. It therefore has a significant impact not only on the overall look of your home, but on your decorating budget as well.

The major categories of floor coverings are wood, in all manner of finishes and styles; soft flooring, in the form of rugs, carpet, and matting; resilient flooring, including laminates, vinyl, and cork; and hard flooring, including stone, tile, and concrete. The charts on the following pages describe your options within those categories. As you choose among the main flooring types, try to answer some of the following questions:

❖ What is your budget? In comparison to wall coverings, window treatments, and furniture, installed floors are a long-term investment and will take the worst beating; they should be budgeted for accordingly. But don't despair: even high-end looks can be achieved with reasonable means. For example, ceramic tiles and even vinyl can now simulate many beautiful stone materials. Old wood floors can be refinished. Whatever flooring you select, be sure to factor installation costs into your budget.

❖ How will the floor fit with the overall look of the room? Do you want the organic, natural look of slate slabs, the rustic look of aged fir, the high-tech appeal of concrete, or the sleek, formal look of polished marble? Let your home's innate style and architecture be your primary guide.

❖ How does the room relate to the rest of the floor plan? Similar floor coverings throughout the house provide a sense of continuity; conversely, a variety helps delineate different areas and allows you to suit your choice to the room's function. If you plan to mix floor coverings, it's important to harmonize tone, texture, and scale, and to think through how to make the transition from one type of flooring to another.

❖ Do you want the floors to be a feature, or a backdrop? A wood floor can be a versatile background, but an area rug placed over it might become a dramatic focal point that pulls together the room's palette. Keep in mind that even unstained wood floors have distinct coloration (anywhere from golden to reddish brown) that needs to be considered in the overall color scheme.

❖ What kind of traffic and wear will the area be subjected to? Staircases and hallway floors will see more action than those in living rooms and bedrooms, for instance. Traffic patterns show less on looped carpets than on cut pile—and, of course, not at all on hard or resilient floors.

❖ What function does the room serve? Kitchens and bathrooms suggest water-resistant coverings such as tile, whereas a formal dining room can sustain a floor high in aesthetic value, such as mahogany with an inlay border.

❖ What kind of support do you want underfoot? A cushy Saxony carpet, for instance, is an obvious choice for a bedroom. Vinyl is a practical choice in the kitchen because it cleans up readily and is easy to stand on for long periods. Slipping is an issue in bathrooms and entries, so a slightly textured finish is called for in those areas.

❖ What is the climate like where you live? Hot climates suggest cooler flooring, such as stone and tile. Carpets and rugs are better for colder regions.

❖ Is noise control an issue? For hallways and stairs (and teens' bedrooms), some people opt for a tightly looped carpet to provide sound insulation.

A homeowner-created floormat signals "eating area" in this kitchen and protects the oak floors from food as well as the scraping of chairs. The colors were borrowed from other elements in the room, rendered in acrylic paint on gessoed canvas, and then coated with urethane.

❖ Does anyone in your home have asthma, allergies, or chemical sensitivities? Carpet harbors dust mites and pesticides tracked in on shoes, and it is often treated with products that aggravate sensitivities. Some finishes on wood floors can also be toxic.

wood flooring

Wood is a classic, naturally appealing flooring that complements many styles of homes. It ages beautifully, feels good underfoot, is relatively easy to care for, and can be refinished when needed. Red and white oak are the most commonly used hardwoods, but each species has its unique color and graining. Hardwoods are less likely to dent and scratch than soft woods such as fir and pine. Environmentally sustainable timber like bamboo is increasingly available as an alternative for eco-conscious consumers. To get a rustic look, some people are seeking out recycled or reclaimed wood from old buildings and homes and refinishing it. Wood free of knots and with consistent color and grain will be more expensive. Finish treatments—from bleaching to staining to painting—both protect wood floors and offer more design options.

1 WOOD FLOORING is available in strips (1½ to 2¼ inches wide), planks (3 to 8 inches wide), and squares. It can be purchased with a factory finish or unfinished; the latter must be sanded and finished on site, after installation. All wood needs to be sealed, either with a penetrating oil followed by wax or with waterproof polyurethane. Although sealers are improving, high-moisture areas such as kitchens and bathrooms must be monitored continuously for spills.

2 PARQUET FLOORS are made up of small strips of wood arranged in intricate repeating patterns—herringbone, checkerboard, or stripes, for instance. Different woods may be used together to enhance the pattern. Usually this flooring is bought in readymade tiles. Like parquet, custom mosaic inlay uses woods of different colors to create a decorative pattern, usually around the floor's border. Parquet and mosaic inlay are expensive treatments that make the floor a feature rather than a backdrop; they may also make a room seem smaller.

3 STAINED FLOORS can change the color of the wood without obscuring its natural grain. Wood-tone stains are sometimes used to make a naturally light species look like a deeper-toned one. But wood can be stained in nearly every color of the rainbow to enliven a child's room, playroom, or entry (as here). For a stain to take, it must be applied to freshly sanded floors; after staining, the floors should be sealed and protected. See the step-by-step directions on pages 404–405 for how to stain a floor.

4 PAINTED FLOORS are a cost-effective option for surfaces that are unremarkable on their own or that are in rough condition. Paint is as versatile on floors as it is on walls: decorative finishes, a text border, bold stripes, checkerboard patterns, and trompe l'oeil "area rugs" are all options. You can buy paint specifically formulated for floors, but for the widest range of colors use a high-quality latex paint for the pattern and top it with a coat of low-luster clear floor finish. See pages 406–407 for instructions on how to paint a floor.

5 STENCILED FLOORS are another way to introduce pattern underfoot; stencils work especially well as borders or to define spaces within a room. Though stencils are typically applied with paint, in this example stains were used to suggest a contrasting wood inlay.

6 BLEACHED FLOORS give a room a lighter, more contemporary air; they allow the wood grain to show through and provide a more neutral backdrop than darker floors. However, the bleaching process is time-consuming, involving harsh chemicals, and the effect may yellow with time.

7 WOOD-LOOK LAMINATE FLOORS can be a fairly convincing alternative to real wood floors. These planks or tiles have a photograph of wood sandwiched between a top layer of melamine resin and a base of high-compression fiber core. Laminate flooring is available in a wide range of wood grains and stain colors. It is more water and scratch resistant than wood, making it an excellent choice for high-traffic, high-moisture areas. However, it lacks the texture of true wood and, because it cannot be refinished, wood's long lifespan.

8 BAMBOO FLOORING is both beautiful and an environmentally sound choice, because bamboo is a readily renewable resource. It resembles other wood floors but is even harder than oak or maple and less prone to expansion and contraction. It can be stained and finished with all of the same treatments that are available for hardwoods.

soft floor coverings

Carpets, area rugs, and matting can diguise damaged flooring, provide warmth and softness underfoot, reduce noise, conserve energy, and function as a room's focal point.

Wall-to-wall carpet usually plays a subordinate role in the decor of a room, contributing color and perhaps texture but not pattern. It is made of synthetic fibers (nylon, acrylic, Olefin, rayon), natural fibers (wool, cotton), or a blend of any of these. Its cost varies considerably depending on weave density, design complexity, and fiber used. Wool is the most expensive and durable fiber, nylon the most popular and care-free. To determine the quality of a weave, bend the carpet to see how much of the backing shows through the fibers: less is better. Also ask how many yarns per square inch were used in it: the more, the better. As with upholstery, more people are choosing commercial grades of carpeting, for durability and trim appearance.

In addition to specialty carpet and flooring shops, Lowe's is a great place to shop for a wide range of carpets, rugs, and matting. Whatever soft flooring you buy, be sure it is treated for stain resistance, either in the factory or after it is installed in your home. Also inquire about the best maintenance practices for the specific type of soft floor covering you select.

1 CUT PILE CARPET looks plush and feels soft underfoot—the longer the yarns, the more luxurious the feel. Because it shows traffic patterns, especially in less dense weaves, it's best used in lower-traffic spaces like bedrooms. Hard-twist carpets (also known as frieze) are better for high-traffic areas: they have more twists per linear inch of yarn, and their ends are heat-set to resist fraying.

2, 3 LOOP-PILE CARPETS have a more contemporary look; because they have no cut or frayed ends, they are more durable, don't show traffic patterns, and are easier to clean than pile carpets. **Berber** carpet has slightly varied loop sizes, typically available in a narrow range of neutral colors. **Sisal-weave** carpets are woven in tiny, tight loops to offer the look of sisal matting but the feel of softer fibers such as wool or synthetics. Sisal-weave carpet is easier to clean than real sisal.

4 CUT-AND-LOOP-PILE CARPETS achieve subtle pattern and texture effects by leaving some yarns looped and others cut; this style also disguises traffic patterns and wear and tear.

5 AREA RUGS can define the spaces in a room, protect high-use areas, and provide a design focal point. They may be handmade or machine made; of synthetic or natural fibers; and knotted, woven, hooked, braided, or needlepoint. Their cost can vary dramatically, so determine the size you need and then set a budget. Also think about shape: a round area rug can give an otherwise angular room soft curves. Be sure to buy a nonslip pad to fit beneath your rug, to extend its life and protect the floor.

6 MATTING is a natural material that is both neutral and sophisticated. Often, wall-to-wall matting makes a backdrop for area rugs, but it can also be woven into interesting patterns and textures to stand on its own. Although economical, most matting is less durable than hard or wood flooring and less soft underfoot than carpeting; it is also more difficult to clean. Its fresh, simple look works well in seaside or country-style homes and with Asian-inspired decor. Here, the natural look of seagrass complements a waterfront cottage.

7 TATAMI MATS are a traditional Japanese floor covering seen with Asian-inspired decor and in minimalist or very contemporary homes. Grass reeds are stitched together for a ribbed effect and bound with black cloth tape around the edges to make 6- by 3-foot mats. (These are sewn together for larger areas.) The fibers are soft and smooth to the touch, and the mats may be cleaned with a vacuum or damp cloth.

8 TIBETAN RUGS are fast gaining ground in the design world, primarily because they offer more flexibility in combination with furnishings than do the more traditional oriental rugs. In recent years, the designs have become much simpler, with soft geometric or organic patterns. The wool is handspun and hand knotted. Their colors, all derived from natural vegetable dyes, are soft on the eyes and promise aesthetic longevity. Often described as "art you walk on," Tibetans are priced accordingly. Many people, therefore, choose these rugs first and design their room around them.

resilient flooring

Resilient floors, from vinyl to cork to rubber, are softer and quieter underfoot than many other flooring surfaces, relatively easy to install and maintain, and both moisture and stain resistant. They are thus perfect candidates for kitchens, entries, bathrooms, and laundry rooms. As a category, resilient flooring is less expensive than most, though the price varies widely depending on the material. A tremendous assortment of colors, textures, patterns, and styles is available, all of which can be combined to create personalized patterns, interesting accents, and pleasing palettes. Because of its very resilience this flooring is prone to dents and tears from sharp objects or heavy appliances, but often these can be repaired. Proper installation is essential, as moisture can collect in poorly jointed seams and cause problems.

1 LINOLEUM, once relegated to hospitals, schools, and other institutions, is making a comeback. Made of ground wood, cork, linseed oil, jute, and resin, it is an environmentally sound choice; because it is so hard, it is tough and very long wearing. Linoleum is now available in a wide variety of bright and fashionable hues, almost all with a mottled appearance. It's usually sold in 12-inch-square tiles, which can be combined into classic checkerboard patterns or cut up to make more artful designs. Linoleum should be installed by experienced professionals only.

2 CORK is also enjoying a renaissance, as homeowners rediscover its desirable qualities: it is soft underfoot, retains warmth, has a luxurious look, and is an environmentally sustainable product. Once limited to shades of brown, cork is now available stained in a wide range of colors. It can be purchased in sheets, tiles, and planks (which mimic wood). Different-size granules create different surface textures, but cork is almost always filled and sealed to a completely smooth surface. Extra care must be taken to seal cork well when it is used in a high-moisture area. Note, too, that it can be dented by furniture.

3 RUBBER FLOORING, commonly found in industrial kitchens, factories, and child-care centers, is most notable for its practical advantages: it is waterproof, highly stain resistant, and the softest, quietest, and warmest type of flooring short of carpeting. As such it is best suited to kitchens, entries, laundry rooms, playrooms, and utility rooms. Studded versions are the most slip resistant, but less industrial-looking versions are available in sheets and tiles of several dimensions. Rubber flooring is produced in a range of solid colors as well as with marbled and granular effects.

4 SHEET OR TILE VINYL is generally made of solid vinyl or polyurethane and is both tough and flexible. It is available in a wide range of colors, patterns, and textures, some of which convincingly imitate stone, tile, wood, as shown in the tiles from Lowe's pictured below. Inlaid or solid designs will wear better than photographically applied patterns. Tiles are generally 12 inches square; sheets are available in widths of up to 12 feet. A polyurethane finish may eliminate the need for waxing. Check the PSI (pounds per square inch) rating to get a sense of the vinyl's vulnerability to tears and dents.

5 LEATHER is migrating from furniture to flooring, - primarily in the shape of tiles. It offers a luxurious yet laid-back look as well as warmth, softness, and sound insulation. Like leather for furniture, it comes in an array of colors and textures. It will scuff and scratch, which is fine for the person who is comfortable with natural markings.

hard flooring

Durable, beautiful, and natural—it's hard to beat clay and stone tile when it comes to these qualities. And with today's sealers, stone and clay tiles are also virtually impervious to food spills, water, and mud, making them especially practical for kitchens, bathrooms, and entries. The color range of natural stone tile is impressive, from cool white marble to black granite, with greens, browns, golds, and grays in between. Like wood, stone floors can be a neutral backdrop—perhaps topped with an area rug—or they can be a feature in themselves, accented with an inlay or a border in a contrasting stone. Glazed clay tiles come in every color and design imaginable.

Hard-flooring styles can run the gamut from country casual to grand and formal, but the luxurious look comes at a price: stone and clay tiles make up the most expensive flooring category as a whole. Seek out tiles designed specifically for flooring—they are thicker and more durable than those for walls or countertops.

All of these options share certain drawbacks. Anything that falls on hard flooring (from glassware to small children) will take a beating. They all can be tiring to stand on for very long. And unless radiant (underfloor) heating is installed, they are almost always cold. Finally, remember that most hard flooring is heavy, so it's important that the subfloor be strong enough to support it.

1 TERRA-COTTA AND QUARRY TILES are made of fired but unglazed clay; both can be either handformed or machine extruded. The major difference between the two types is that quarry tiles are fired at a higher temperature and are therefore less porous and more durable. Also, terra-cotta must be sealed to prevent staining. The French terra-cotta pavers shown here add a traditional touch to a contemporary kitchen.

2 MARBLE is an elegant metamorphosed limestone distinguished by its eye-catching mineral veining. It occurs naturally in many colors, from white and gray to sand to ocher to black with white veining. Although less porous than limestone or sandstone, marble is softer and more porous than granite: some acid- and oil-based foods will leave permanent stains. Honed marble is softer looking than polished marble. Here, tumbled-marble floor tiles are accented with glass mosaic tiles; the design is repeated in paint on the wall.

3 SLATE is an extremely dense metamorphic rock that tends to split along natural grains and fissures. Like marble, it is found in a wide range of natural colors, from buff to rust to black, but it is typically sold in blue-gray and gray-green hues. Here, a patchwork of slate colors is framed with limestone strips and tiny glass mosaics. This slate has a rough "cleft" or "riven" finish, which is nonslip and rustic looking. However, slate can be honed or even polished to achieve a smoother look.

4 CONCRETE, a lower-cost, increasingly popular surface, is no longer the drab, factory-floor gray it once was. Slab or poured floors can be stained just about any color, or the hue may be integrated with the cement when it is mixed. Postinstallation acid etching offers an appealing antique look. Concrete also comes in tiles of many textures, some mimicking marble and limestone, for instance. It does need to be sealed and properly cared for, or it will stain. Over time, it gains a patina from wear.

5 TERRAZZO is actually an agglomerate of stone and glass chips, which may include marble, granite, and onyx, in a matrix of cement or some resinous material. The aggregate is poured and then ground and polished to a smooth surface. Precast tiles and slabs are also available, however; these are less expensive and much easier to install. Originating in the 15th century, this artistic technique is gaining favor as homeowners seek ways to incorporate colorful, handwrought finishes into their surroundings.

6 ENCAUSTIC TILES are created when a shape is indented into the surface of a tile, which is then filled with "slip," or liquid clay, in a contrasting color. This process makes it one of the most durable decorative clay tiles available, as the color and pattern are more than "skin deep." Here, encaustic is used on the risers of terra-cotta stairs.

LIGHTING

A GOOD LIGHTING DESIGN CREATES THE APPRO-
PRIATE ATMOSPHERE FOR A ROOM AND HELPS
THE SPACE FULFILL ITS FUNCTION, AS WELL. THE
BEST LIGHTING DESIGNS ACCOMPLISH THESE
TASKS IN THE MOST ENERGY-EFFICIENT WAY, WITH
CAREFUL CONSIDERATION FOR THE TYPE OF
FIXTURES AND BULBS USED IN EACH SITUATION.

Ideally suited to the pleasures
of reading, this bedside lamp
can be adjusted in both
position and intensity.

Whether you're building a new home, remodeling an old
one, or simply redecorating, the following lighting
guidelines, room-by-room suggestions, and money-
saving basics will help you develop a smart plan. First, it
helps to get an overview of the four functional categories
of home lighting.

GENERAL OR AMBIENT LIGHT is what illuminates a
space as a whole: it is sufficient for watching television, entertaining,
or simply moving around in a space. A room's general light often
comes from one central ceiling fixture or from recessed ceiling lights
(ideally, one for every 20 to 25 square feet). General light can also be
provided by daylight or by indirect light sources, including uplights
(or torchères), wall fixtures, table lamps, and fluorescent-tube lighting concealed in a cove near the ceiling. Surface-mounted fluorescent
fixtures with diffusing panels provide energy-efficient, shadowless
light in workrooms, garages, and laundry rooms.

TASK OR ACTIVITY LIGHTING illuminates specific areas for activities such as reading, paperwork, cooking, and sewing. Sometimes it
comes from a built-in fixture—for example, an undercabinet light
that illuminates a countertop—but more often it comes from a movable, free-standing fixture that allows light to be directed at the task
area. It is especially important that such lights be chosen and positioned so they neither cast shadows nor introduce glare. The area
around the activity surface should be at least one-third as bright as
the focal point; any greater contrast may be hard on the eyes.

ACCENT LIGHTING can create a mood or call attention to artwork,
collections, plants, or unique architectural features—but not to itself.

In fact, accent lighting is often concealed (for instance, as strip lighting, rope lighting, or small, portable plug-in lights) or designed to blend into the background (as adjustable track lighting or recessed spotlights). Accent lighting is generally about five times brighter than the room's general light and should be positioned at an angle that minimizes glare on the feature—about a 30-degree angle between fixture and object is best. Depending on the focal point or the desired effect, one or more accent lights may be used.

DECORATIVE LIGHTING, on the other hand, calls attention to itself rather than to something else in the room. It may be a stunning, crystal-laden chandelier, an intricately cut rice-paper shade, a Tiffany glass lamp, or another eye-catching fixture designed to be enhanced by its own light. These decorative fixtures can be table or floor lamps, sconces, or ceiling-mounted pendants; their bulbs can be obscured by a shade or decorative and exposed. Decorative lights should be considered in the overall lighting scheme, as they can be a factor in planning ambient or even task lighting.

Most spaces in today's homes are host to more than one type of activity and therefore require a range of light sources. Ideally, each should have a separate control so that a variety of lighting levels can be selected. As you develop a lighting plan for each room, take into consideration any existing lights, windows, or skylights; the furniture arrangement; how the room will be used and at what times of day;

A small, open-plan remodel comprising the living room, dining room, and entry hall is lit in a cohesive, uncluttered fashion with low-voltage downlights. Extensive accent lighting is furnished by smaller, well-aimed halogen fixtures.

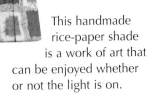

This handmade rice-paper shade is a work of art that can be enjoyed whether or not the light is on.

In a departure from the classic light fixture centered over the table, the stylish lighting in this contemporary dining area emanates from several sources. A trio of spotlights mounted on a beam bounces light off the ceiling as well as onto the table. Fluorescent lights above the cabinets silhouette a basket collection, lending a touch of drama to the scene.

and how the natural light in the room may change with the seasons. Also think about whether you want to use light to alter the appearance of a room. A small room will seem to expand if the walls are light colored and "washed" with an even distribution of light. A large room can be made cozier with less ambient light but a few pools of soft light focused on specific areas or features.

ROOM BY ROOM

Although your own home and family will have unique needs, the requirements of standard home spaces in the list that follows may suggest ways to customize each part of your home.

ENTRIES should be warmly lit, to create a welcoming atmosphere. Care should be taken to avoid too much contrast in light level, however, both between the outdoors and the foyer and between the foyer and the adjoining room inside. An attractive general overhead fixture is often sufficient; make sure its scale is in keeping with the size of the foyer and that its style sets the tone for the rest of the house. To minimize shadows, choose a style that throws light up on the ceiling rather than directing it straight down.

LIVING AREAS are by nature multipurpose spaces, and the best lighting plans take this into consideration: several layers and types of lighting, each on independent controls, are ideal. Some experts recommend having two types of general lighting: one brighter and more open, the other more subdued and intimate. Dimmer switches may be able to accomplish this without adding new fixtures. Indirect ambient light, which casts the fewest shadows and is most flattering, can be achieved with wall sconces or with cove or soffit lighting. Ceiling-mounted wall washers expand the space by directing the light onto the walls rather than down on the floors. Use accent lighting to highlight art, plants, or architectural features. Swing-arm standing or table lamps placed next to comfortable chairs direct light over reading material; a task light on or near a table facilitates games, puzzles, or writing. The living area can be enhanced further with purely decorative lighting or with a display of glowing candles.

DINING ROOMS are typically lit by a fixture that drops down over the center of the table, such as a traditional chandelier or a contemporary pendant. Chandeliers ideally measure at least 12 inches less than the dining table's width and clear its surface by at least 30 inches. A dimmer switch allows for full light while serving, lower light while dining. It is best if the central fixture does not carry the load of lighting the entire room; wall sconces help dispel glare and shadows, and a table lamp or wall fixture can illuminate a buffet. A lighted display cabinet or accent lighting focused on china collections or art can further balance the light in the room.

KITCHENS are often used not only for food preparation but also for gathering and dining, so again, several types of lighting are required. It is essential to have sufficient task lighting above all work areas, including the sink, the stove, and the countertops. The best placement for this kind of lighting is between the cook's eye level and the work surface, which is why strip lights mounted under cabinets (as far forward as possible) are so popular. Many ventilation hoods have built-in lights to brighten the cooktop; ceiling-mounted fixtures or pendants can light sink and island areas. In-kitchen dining areas often feature a decorative pendant light or chandelier—but before choosing an intricate model, consider that kitchen light fixtures will have to be cleaned more often than those in other rooms.

A central lowered "beam" of lightly pickled oak houses recessed halogen downlights focused on the work surfaces of this island. General lighting comes from track fixtures (not shown) tucked along the cross-beams overhead.

For general lighting, consider well-distributed recessed ceiling lights. Another popular choice is fluorescent tubes enclosed in ceiling-mounted boxes or lining a soffit or cove above the cabinets. It is important to have dimmer switches for these lights, especially, to make them very bright for food prep and cleanup yet warmly glowing for entertaining. Consider installing accent lighting in glass-fronted cabinets, but realize that unless the cabinet's shelves are also glass, top-mounted lights will illuminate only the top shelf.

THE DOLLARS AND SENSE OF LIGHTING

Learning the cost of various kinds of lighting is the second step in choosing fixtures that not only work for your space but are energy- and cost-efficient as well. Keep in mind that, after the initial purchase price of the fixture, 90 percent of the expense of using a light comes from the energy it consumes and only 10 percent from replacing bulbs. So choosing the most energy-efficient light will go a long way toward reducing your lighting costs. Following is some help for coming up with a plan that balances energy efficiency with your lighting needs.

There are two types of light bulbs: incandescent and fluorescent. Incandescents are the most familiar type for households; they come in hundreds of shapes and sizes and have always provided a flattering, natural-looking light. Halogen lamps are incandescents' high-tech, energy-efficient cousins, producing a whiter, brighter light. Halogen bulbs are also much smaller, making them great candidates for task and accent lighting and for the tiny, sleek, artistic fixtures being designed today. They can only be used in fixtures designed specifically for halogen bulbs. Halogen lights burn very hot and should never be used in a child's room.

Fluorescent light fixtures are making their way into homes as they shed their industrial look. They are now available in a range of color-corrected tubes, rather than the unflattering bluish tint of the past. Also, the new "compact fluorescent" bulbs are smaller than their long, tubular predecessors and can be substituted for incandescents in many traditional household fixtures as well as fitting new, specially designed built-ins and freestanding torchères. Overhead fluorescent fixtures are becoming available in a wider range of decor-friendly styles; they are lauded for the soft, shadowless general lighting they provide. But fluorescent light's strongest suit is its energy efficiency and long life: it uses only one-fifth to one-third the electricity of a standard incandescent yet lasts 10 to 20 times longer. Fluorescent lights are best used in areas where the light is on for several hours at a stretch, such as a hallway; they are less appropriate in closets and garages. ~

Banks of south-facing windows light this room during the day; at night, cove lights are directed up to and off of a curved white ceiling, providing plenty of ambient light for both the kitchen and the living area beyond. Undercabinet fluorescent tubes take care of task lighting for the countertops.

BEDROOMS demand a range of lighting effects, from quietly dim and intimate to bright enough for late-night reading. Any overhead fixtures should have shielded bulbs to minimize glare, which is hard on the eyes when reading. Wall sconces, torchères, and soffit lighting all provide soft, flattering ambient light. Directional reading lights on either side of the bed should be adjustable, in both position and brightness. Wall-mounted swing-arm lights do the job without taking up precious nightstand space; plug-in models are now available, eliminating the need for hard-wiring.

BATHROOMS must be lit brightly enough for grooming without being so harsh that unflattering shadows are cast. The best position for mirror lights is along both sides rather than centered above the top; ensure that the light will be directed at a person's face, rather than at the mirror. Incandescent lights provide the most natural color, but warm-toned fluorescents are an acceptable alternative. A bathroom larger than 100 square feet should have general overhead lighting as well, positioned close to the tub and shower; sometimes this is part of a ceiling-mounted fan vent. Finally, consider a small plug-in nightlight.

Recessed downlights and architectural cove lights provide general illumination for this understated bedroom; daylight is kept out by wood-shuttered sliding doors. Low floor lamps on each side of the bed create well-directed pools of light for reading.

This master bath features an open-fronted fir vanity with a custom marble top. The corresponding mirror cabinet is inset with flush-mounted incandescent tubes for evenly lit grooming. The backsplash and counter areas are washed by additional downlighting along the cabinet's bottom edge. Sunshine further brightens the room.

lighting

As with other design decisions, begin your search for light fixtures by assessing your needs, referring to the function-based categories described on on pages 304–305. At the same time, start noticing fixtures in restaurants, offices, and your friends' homes. Once you've acquired a sense of the effects that can be created, as well as the variety of styles available, pull together your ideas and visit the lighting department at Lowe's as well as lighting specialty stores. At Lowe's you can view the fixtures illumi-nated with the correct wattage. You can also use Lowe's special Design & Combine program to coordinate all your home light-ing needs. As you consider a fixture, notice how it directs the light—in a narrow beam, or more broadly? Does it cast shadows or create glare? Are its size and style appropriate for your home? Compare costs, in terms of both the fixtures themselves and their energy efficiency and bulb life. Consider, too, the cost and likely availability of any specialty bulbs.

1 BUILT-IN INDIRECT FIXTURES These devices are typically attached to the wall, ceiling, or underside of a cabinet and are shielded by a valance, cove, or soffit to prevent glare. The light may be directed up or down, depending on the shield. Typically these fixtures are used for general lighting, but they can also be designed for task lighting (such as over counters). Fluorescent lighting sources are ideal for indirect lighting.

2 RECESSED CEILING FIXTURES If you want gen-eral light from above without the visual intrusion of a light fixture, recessed ceiling units are the answer. (But note that these will not illuminate the ceiling.) Numer-ous trims are available to create different effects: a broad spread of light, a "wash" of light down a wall, or a beam of light focused on a work of art or architectural feature. Here, recessed accent lights are directed at the artwork behind the sofa as well as at the glass coffee table.

3 CEILING AND WALL FIXTURES For general illu-mination and the opportunity to make a style statement, you can choose from literally thousands of ceiling and wall fixtures. For hallways and smaller bedrooms, select low-profile fixtures covered by a shade or bowl to prevent glare. Larger rooms, and those with higher ceilings, can take more elaborate, decorative shades. **Track lighting** offers great flexibility. A track of any length can be wired into an existing receptacle and numerous small fixtures mounted anywhere along it.

4 SUSPENDED FIXTURES include **chandeliers,** which typically drop down on a chain, have at least four arms, and use small, low-wattage decorative bulbs. Be sure that their total light output is sufficient to illuminate any table beneath them, especially if there is no other source of ambient light. Crystal chandeliers are a tradi-tional option, but casual wrought-iron versions are more in keeping with today's less formal lifestyles. A **pendant fixture,** which hangs from a cord or stem, typically has only one or two bulbs, but they are likely to be halogen or at least of a higher wattage; generally, the shade is what makes the design statement. Here, an industrial-looking pendant is joined by track lights.

5 A SCONCE is wall mounted, pointing up or down. For general lighting, direct the light up. If sconces are illuminating stairs or a buffet, for instance, a downward cast is more appropriate. Although having sconces hard-wired into the wall is desirable, plug-in models are increasingly available. The cord extends down the wall to a socket within a metal sleeve that matches the sconce. Not only is this less expensive than bringing in an electrician, but it also allows for flexibility if your lighting needs change.

6 MOVABLE LIGHT FIXTURES, such as table lamps and floor lamps, are by far the simplest and most flex-ible lighting option. As you shop for a **table lamp,** pay close attention to the shade, as it will determine a light's effectiveness. The wider the shade's bottom diameter and the closer the bulb is to it, the greater the spread of light. The hardworking table lamp pictured here features three movable arms that illuminate the table as well as a nearby reading chair.

7 FLOOR LAMPS can serve a variety of functions: a swing-arm version is useful for reading; an uplight, or torchère, will provide general lighting; and decorative lamps, such as this striped rice-paper model, make a colorful statement or brighten a corner. Consider the lamp's stability as well as its height: if it is too short or tall for the situation, the bulb will create glare.

plan and deliver

THE BONES *of this renovated winery—foot-thick stone walls, soaring ceilings, and a 4-foot-high clerestory window running the perimeter of the roofline—presented some challenges for lighting designer Melinda Morrison. But she looked at them as inspiration rather than roadblocks. "A good lighting plan works with the architecture, not just the decorating scheme," says Morrison. "We chose the most interesting architectural features and strategized about how to emphasize them." Luckily, Morrison was brought in during the design phase of the remodel: "In too many cases, lighting is an afterthought." Here, the planning paid off.*

ABOVE, LEFT: Translucent swing panels separate this bedroom from the adjacent living area. They diffuse the light from the fixture behind and above them, creating a glare-free environment. An adjustable floor lamp craning over the daybed provides higher-intensity reading light.

TOP: The lighting in this study was designed to look "soft" to contrast with the hard stone and industrial concrete. A low-voltage cable system follows the alcove's curve. The light grazing the stone wall comes from a string of reflector lamps tucked into a light well.

BOTTOM: In this master bath, the storage niche to the right of the mirror glows with fluorescent light tempered by a diffusing panel. At the mirror, an inset fixture casts make-up light just where it's needed.

How do you provide overhead lighting when the ceilings are 20 feet high? Stylish red Italian pendants, each housing tiny but efficient halogen bulbs, solved the problem and defined the islands. White-painted electrical conduit leads from the ceiling to the fixtures, which were originally meant to be ceiling mounted. Behind the display shelves over the back counter, ribbed glass diffuses the dimmable fluorescent lighting.

WINDOW TREATMENTS

Crinkly curtains are clipped to metal rings on wire "rods." Spacing the clips widely allows the panel to droop casually.

WELL-CHOSEN WINDOW TREATMENTS ARE MORE THAN A NICE FINISHING TOUCH; THEY ARE A HARDWORKING COMPONENT OF ANY ROOM.

They can filter light and create atmosphere while softening harsh afternoon glare. They can provide privacy while offering an extra measure of security. They can conserve energy, helping you warm or cool a room with a flick of your wrist. Some window treatments even help control noise. And every window covering, like it or not, makes a style statement in your home.

As you read about different options on the following pages, think about what jobs you want your window treatments to perform. Privacy, for instance, is more important in bedrooms than in kitchens, and more important at night than by day. In terms of light control, blinds and shutters provide the option of modulating light throughout the day.

Window treatments can also solve less obvious problems. They can obscure unattractive moldings. They can "correct" architectural defects, such as windows that are mismatched or proportionally wrong for the room. You can "extend" or "shrink" a window depending on where you mount the treatment: placed up near the crown molding, a panel curtain or valance will heighten a window. Sheers can disguise an undesirable view, just as curtains that blend with the walls can frame a fabulous view without detracting from it. Shutters add architectural interest to a plain room. An arched, padded cornice softens the lines in a room and draws the eye upward.

Given all the possibilities for window coverings, all the magic tricks they can perform, it's hard to know where to hang them. Following are some helpful guidelines.

* Window treatments typically begin 5 inches above window opening.

* You may also hang a treatment just below the ceiling, at the bottom of crown molding, or halfway between the ceiling and window opening.

* Valances typically begin 8 inches above the window opening.

- Window treatments typically end in line with either the window apron or the floor.

- Apron-length treatments should end 5 inches below the window opening.

- Floor-length treatments should end 1/2 inch short of the floor.

- Shades usually extend 1 inch beyond the trim board on each side of window, or 2 inches beyond window opening if there's no trim board.

SHOPPING FOR WINDOW TREATMENTS

Retailers have come a long way in their ready-made window-treatment offerings. Lowe's now stocks a wide selection of off-the-shelf curtain panels, hardware, and shades. Curtain tiers come in a variety of lengths: 24, 36, and 38 inches. Widths are usually 60 inches. Drapery and sheer panels come in both 63- and 84-inch lengths. Their widths vary from 39, 40, 65, 80, and 90 inches. For custom fabric window treatments, consult the Yellow Pages under "Window Coverings". Home-decorating fabric stores, too, sometimes have workrooms; these services will send someone to your home to advise you on fabric, style, and hardware choices as well as to take measurements, fabricate the window treatments, and install them. If you are confident with a sewing machine, step-by-step books and patterns are available to help you whip up exactly what you want.

ABOVE: Checkered semisheer panels with a tucked border at the bottom hang from behind an antique mirrored cornice. A sheer "slip" on the nearby chair sounds the same romantic note.

LEFT: Pinch-pleated panels make the most of a striped silk fabric. With the pleats spaced to enfold only the ivory stripes, the taupe sections dominate the heading. As the panels open toward the bottom, the lighter stripes are revealed.

curtains and draperies

Curtains and draperies are the softest of the window-treatment options, with their yards of fabric to soak up noise and their undulating folds to "cozy up" hard expanses of glass and wall. Most curtains these days are gathered onto a rod or hung from one with rings, clips, or tabs. Because of this, hardware has become almost as much of a design statement as the fabric itself. (For more on hardware options, see page 349.) Draperies, hung from traverse rods and operated with cords or wands, are less common than they were in the past.

Simple fabrics whose colors blend with that of the walls will draw the eye through the window to a view beyond; the more contrast and pattern and detail you add to curtains, the more the eye will tend to stop at the window treatment itself. Also, small rooms will appear larger if the curtains blend with the walls, extending from floor to ceiling and beyond either side of the windows.

Unless you prefer an airy and casual look, you will probably have to line your curtains or draperies. A lining gives a curtain body and improves the way it hangs, protects the decorative fabric from sun and from any dirt or dust that drifts through the window, and presents a finished look from outside. Black-out linings can offer total light control as well, a nice option for bedrooms.

1 DRAPERIES are pleated panels hung from hooks that attach to small slides on a traverse rod; a cord or wand moves the slides along the track to open and close the draperies. Pleat options are diverse, from traditional pinch pleats to Paris pleats, goblet pleats, box pleats, inverted pleats, and many others. Here, silk pinch-pleated draperies are an elegant solution for a bow window. A custom-bent traverse rod was painted to blend with the plaid.

2 PLEATED CURTAINS, attached to rods with rings or clips, have the more finished and formal look of draperies but open and close by hand and hang from decorative rather than traverse rods. Preferences in pleat styles change as often as any other design trend. Here, a Paris-pleat curtain in fabric that coordinates with the wall covering hangs from a curved, wrought-iron rod with matching wrought-iron rings.

3 ROD-POCKET CURTAINS are by nature stationary, as it's difficult to pull them back and forth over the rod. They can be held to the side with tiebacks or allowed to hang straight down, as here.

4 TAB-TOP CURTAINS are simply panels with tabs, loops, or ties at the top edge, or heading. They adapt easily to a variety of windows, window-treatment hardware, and fabrics. Usually tabs are made of the same fabric as the curtains, but cording, ribbon, and braid can add eye-catching detail. Few tab-tops move across the rods as easily as do curtains on rings, so think of them primarily as stationary panels. Here, a stationary panel in a tropical print dresses up bamboo blinds that control light.

5 SHEERS, sometimes referred to as "glass curtains," diffuse light, provide partial privacy, and soften the shine and hard surface of glass. They are especially helpful in masking an unattractive view and giving daytime privacy without blocking light. Sheers with woven patterns, with decorative top stitching, or in an interesting metallic fabric can easily stand on their own—or they can be layered behind curtains or draperies.

6 STATIONARY CURTAINS, usually hung at the sides of a window and mounted so that they cannot be pulled closed, serve a purely decorative purpose. Because the panels don't close, less fabric is required. Here, silk fabric panels draped with a valance stay put at the sides to soften the look of the shutters. The rod is covered in the same fabric as the valance to visually unite the sides.

7 CAFÉ CURTAINS, which cover only the lower half of a double-hung window, are a minimalist choice in every way. They are mounted inside the window frame or directly on it, most often in a lightweight or sheer fabric that provides some privacy while admitting maximum light. Clip rings make it easier to open and close the curtains, though café curtains are usually left closed.

shades

Although they run the gamut from hardware-store vinyl roller shades to voluminous silk cloud shades, these coverings are generally chosen by those seeking an uncluttered, practical window treatment. Shades require less fabric than do curtains or draperies, which also makes them more economical. Because of their trim profile, they are especially suited to corner windows, where curtains might pose a problem.

Where shades are mounted should be planned carefully. Outside-mounted shades are secured above the window on the frame or wall and extend beyond the sides and bottom of the window. Inside-mounted shades sit inside the frame, close to the glass. Outside mounts offer more light control and insulation and can make the window appear larger, whereas inside mounts show off handsome frame moldings.

1 ROMAN SHADES, flat panels that draw up into neat, flat, horizontal folds, give a crisp, clean look with a minimum of fabric. Soft-fold Romans form loops of fabric when lowered. Here, striped Roman shades maintain their crisp pleats by means of narrow dowels slipped into stitched pockets. The fabric takes its color cue from the wall, unifying the room while highlighting the French doors and their sidelights.

2 WOVEN SHADES, made from split wood, bamboo, or natural reeds or fibers, offer a distinctly natural coloring and texture. If left unlined, they allow more light and view to filter through. They may roll up, like roller shades, or fold up, like Roman shades. When buying woven woods, look for straight-grained, smoothly cut strips; kiln-dried wood is going to be more resistant to warping.

3 LONDON SHADES have a more relaxed look than Roman shades but are simpler than cloud shades. Their inverted pleats are widely spaced, and the sides most often hang down. Here, an unlined linen shade filters light and softens a pair of casement windows; sisal buttons are the only details.

4 CLOUD SHADES are shirred at the top and drawn up by means of cords and rings sewn onto their back sides; when they're fully raised, fabric poufs form at the lower edge. They require more fabric than do Roman or London shades. Here, celadon silk shades dress bedroom windows in quiet, elegant color. A thick welt, knotted at the ends, finishes the upper edges, and tassel fringe links the window treatments to the walls and furnishings.

5 ROLLER SHADES, mounted on simple hardware at the top or bottom of a window, are perhaps the simplest of all window treatments. However, they needn't be merely utilitarian: they can be made of many different light- to midweight fabrics, beautifully hemmed at the bottom and accented with jewel-like pulls. Because they open flat, they are especially suited to panels of fabric with a large pattern or repeat. Roller shades can also be a useful, unobtrusive partner to other window treatments—such as sheers, stationary panels, or swags—that don't cover the whole window. Choose from the standard spring roller mechanism or a bead chain, which is easier to use and minimizes fingerprints.

6 CELLULAR SHADES, with their familiar honeycomb design, are simple and contemporary in style. Their main advantage is their energy efficiency, since their pockets trap air. Pleat sizes range from 3/8 inch to 2 inches, and the color and texture ranges are impressive. Cellular shades are opaque, so they offer total privacy. They can be top, bottom, or center mounted and collapse into a very small space when closed. They can also be custom fitted to arched and angle-top windows.

7 WINDOW SHADINGS are a high-tech cross between a sheer and a blind. With gossamer-sheer fabric on the front and back and opaque fabric slats in between that tilt like horizontal blinds, they offer maximum light and privacy control as well as flexibility. Like cellular shades, they can be top or bottom mounted and custom fitted to odd-shaped windows and skylights. Their simplicity makes them well suited to contemporary settings, but they adapt to more traditional homes when paired with decorative top or side treatments.

shutters, blinds, and screens

Window treatments made of wood, plastic, or metal offer a simpler and highly practical alternative to fabric treatments. Blinds, for instance, offer maximum light control: they can be closed completely; tilted to allow light to be directed up, down, or straight into the room; or raised to disappear behind a valance or cornice. Shutters have the same tilt function as blinds, but they also fold open to the sides to provide architectural interest.

These highly functional treatments do not, however, lack style. The natural beauty of wood brings a richness and glow to windows. Blinds blend well with both traditional and contemporary furnishings, and can be paired with fabric treatments to dramatic effect. Few window treatments can match plantation shutters for lending a room character and architectural interest. And Shoji screens say "Asian elegance" as no other window covering can.

1 HORIZONTAL BLINDS made of metal or vinyl come in a wide array of finishes and colors. Standard 1-inch miniblinds are appropriate for most windows and decorating styles. Micro-miniblinds, available in $\frac{1}{2}$- or $\frac{5}{8}$-inch sizes, work well for smaller windows or those with shallow sills. Venetian blinds, with 2-inch slats, can have either a contemporary or a retro feel. Blinds may be a different color on each side, making it easier to coordinate them with both exterior and interior paint. Some are available with a heat-reflective surface on one side. If space or light is an issue, keep in mind that wider slats mean fewer are needed and thus require less stacking space. Step-by-step instructions for installing blinds are given on pages 398–399.

2 WOOD BLINDS are timeless and add grace to any room. They offer a finished look on their own but are frequently paired with fabric treatments or topped with a cornice or valance. They come in a variety of woods and finishes, from rustic pine to rich walnut, or they can be painted to coordinate with your windows' trim paint. Wood-look blinds made of polymer won't warp or fade, even in high-moisture or variable-temperature rooms. Vertical cloth ladder tapes are options for wood blinds to reflect the room's decor.

3 VERTICAL BLINDS, especially useful for sliding doors and large picture windows, are sold in many textures and materials, but the look is always contemporary. They create visual height, are excellent for controlling light and providing privacy, and collect less dust than do horizontal treatments. Vertical blinds can hang loosely from the top, slide in a track at both top and bottom, or be connected by a chain at the bottom.

4 TRADITIONAL SHUTTERS, with $1\frac{1}{4}$-inch louvers in frames that are hinged to the window, are light in scale and work best in smaller windows or for café-style treatments. Narrow louvers restrict the light and block the view more than wider ones do, but they provide more privacy when fully open. How to install shutters is shown in photos and step-by-step directions on pages 400–401.

5 PLANTATION SHUTTERS, with $2\frac{1}{2}$-inch or larger louvers, work well in most interiors. The larger louvers open up the view and allow in more light than do narrower traditional shutters. Although the initial cost of plantation shutters is quite high, they last forever and add to a home's value.

6 SHOJI SCREENS are a staple of traditional Japanese homes, their translucent rice-paper panels bathing the rooms evenly in light. Generally used over sliding glass doors and windows, shojis either glide in a track or fold back on hinges, as shutters do. Shojis have inspired innovative shutterlike panels with solid inserts ranging from decorative privacy glass to woven reeds and rattan.

top treatments

Cornices, valances, swags, scarves, and other top treatments are a window's crowning glory. If privacy and light control aren't needed, top treatments can be used alone to add interest without the fullness of curtains. Or they can be used in combination with curtains, shades, or blinds to hide their hardware and add another decorative dimension. An arched or scalloped top treatment will soften the strong perpendicular lines of windows. Top treatments can unify windows—two or more windows so close that they are separated only by molding, for instance, can be brought together under one valance or swag. (Two windows that meet in a corner can also be united in this way.) Tall windows are ideally suited to top treatments over traversing or stationary panels. Although arched or scalloped valances may be too fussy for smaller windows, they add grace to taller windows and doors. If you're using these treatments over a picture window or short window, keep in mind that a deep valance overhanging the window will accentuate its width; a gently scalloped valance or shaped cornice mounted above the frame, just skimming the top of the glass, will create the illusion of a slightly taller window.

1, 2, 3 FABRIC VALANCES can be paired with matching stationary panels for a formal look, or with hard-working blinds or shades for a casual one. The standard valance length is 12 to 18 inches at the center, though some styles are longer at the sides. Many valances are simply a shortened version of curtains, drapes, or fabric shades. **Rod-pocket valances** are still a classic top treatment for curtain or drapery panels; **box-pleated valances** offer a more tailored look. A **Kingston,** or **bell, valance** is a hybrid treatment, part swag and part pleated valance.

4 SWAGS AND SCARVES are lengths of fabric that have been artfully pleated, gathered, and draped over the top of the window, usually over a rod or board or through swag holders, scarf holders, or sconces mounted at the windows' top outside corners. These holders are often quite decorative themselves (for more about these accessories, see the hardware chart on the next page). Light- and midweight fabrics that drape well are most easily folded and gathered into swags. Although swags may appear to have been casually draped, arranging the fabric successfully is quite an art form. Decorator-fabric stores offer tips to make the job somewhat easier, but you may find it worthwhile to hire a professional window-treatment fabricator to handle the installation. Scarf treatments are more casual, more loosely hung, and easier for the beginner to create. Here, floral swags are lined with a contrasting fabric; the longer tail matching the swag is called a cascade, and the shorter plaid piece with the rosette is called a jabot.

5, 6 CORNICES can be either upholstered or solid wood that has been painted or stained. They neatly hide the heading and hardware of any treatment underneath, and—because they are closed at the top—they block drafts. They are a natural partner for blinds and shades, which can look unfinished on their own. **Upholstered cornices** give windows a softer look and allow you to use a small amount of quality fabric effectively; the lower edge can be arched, scalloped, pointed, or straight. Possible embellishments include piping, braid, and fringe. Some **wood cornices** mimic the look of deep, decorative crown molding, but they can also be cut with artfully shaped lower edges for a more whimsical or countrified effect. Flat cornices can be decoratively painted, stenciled, or covered with a strip of wallpaper border. Cornices are usually mounted just outside of the window frame; it is especially important to accurately measure the depth needed to accommodate any window-treatment hardware that will be under the cornice.

hardware

Window-treatment hardware was once strictly functional, meant to do its job in a low-profile way. Interesting rods, rings, and finials were hard to come by. But thanks to a shift toward more casual window treatments as well as to a surge of interest in home decorating, the selection of hardware has burgeoned with interesting materials and innovative designs. Traditional or contemporary, high-tech or arty, window-treatment hardware is available to suit every style and budget. You'll find these items at Lowe's. Step-by-step instructions for installing decorative rods and hardware are on pages 402–403.

1 RODS vary from functional to highly decorative. Concealed rods come in numerous configurations to handle various window treatments. Traverse rods (see page 316, photo 1) allow draperies to be opened or closed with a wand or cord; they contain carriers or slides into which you slip drapery hooks. When the draperies are closed, the rod is hidden; when they are open, the rod is visible unless covered by a top treatment. **Decorative rods,** meant to be used with tab-top, rod-pocket, or ring-hung pleated curtains, come in many diameters and materials. Finished wood, wrought iron, brushed aluminum, and verdigris brass are all common and are sold in fixed or adjustable lengths. **Finials** are the rod's decorative end pieces; they may be part of the rod or separate elements that screw into the rod ends. You'll find traditional balls and spears; thematic leaves, stars, and seashells; and whimsical, jewel-like creations made of glass, beads, and other artistic components. Photo 1 shows a few of the decorative rods and finials available at Lowe's. As you shop for rods and finials, look for coordinating brackets to support the rods; if the rod is longer than 5 feet, you'll need a center brace as well.

2 SWING-ARM RODS are hinged so that you can swing the rod and its curtain away from an open window or door and back again when you want the glass covered. These are most often used with simple fabrics such as sheers and linens that have a uniform appearance on both sides.

3 WIRE RODS lend a high-tech look to window treatments. The rod consists of a length of wire, special brackets, and a center support. You attach the curtain (lightweight fabrics are recommended) to the wire with decorative clips, ribbon, or cording.

4 PEGS are a unique alternative to traditional rods; they are especially suited to country or eclectic decors. Curtains hung on pegs are stationary, though they can be tied back on the sides. Tied tabs best accommodate the pegs' perpendicular aspect. Here, the curtain's top edges and the tie tabs are sewn from a contrasting iridescent, copper-colored semisheer.

5 RINGS, CLIPS, AND HOOKS, once a utilitarian means to hang curtains from rods, are now seen in an array of clever metal and wood designs to coordinate with your rods. Photo 5 shows a few of the possibilities available at Lowe's. As you choose yours, think about how the clip or ring will fasten to your window treatment and which way it will turn the fabric once it's hung on the rod. **Swag and scarf holders** are ornate brackets or loops that fabric is pulled through or wrapped around; they are attached to the upper corners of the window frame or to the walls just beyond them. Decorative shade pulls put a finishing touch on simple roller shades.

6 HOLDBACKS are any of a number of different types of decorative hardware for holding curtains and draperies to the side of the window. Some styles can also be mounted at the top of the window and used as swag or scarf holders. Holdbacks usually jut out several inches in order to accommodate the folds of fabric; some are shaped into hooks, and others have a decorative front piece, such as a large shell or medallion, behind which the curtain is tucked.

7 PASSEMENTERIE is the term used for trims such as braid, cord, fringe, gimp, and tassels—the finishing touches that give your window treatment a custom look and accent its shape and form. These items range in price depending on the workmanship and fibers used, but as they tend to be expensive, they should be chosen thoughtfully. The most reasonably priced versions are found in home-decorating fabric stores; more lavishly constructed items are available through designer showrooms. As you choose, keep in mind the weight of your window treatment's fabric as well as the care and cleaning requirements of any trims.

FABRICS

This blue-and-yellow swiveling rocker gets gussied up with skirt fringe and a practical patchwork of fabrics. Multicolored braiding smoothes the transition between the fabrics, giving the lines of the chair and ottoman definition and much-deserved attention.

WHETHER GRACING YOUR FURNITURE OR FRAMING YOUR WINDOWS, FABRICS EXUDE PERSONALITY WITH THEIR COLORS, PATTERNS, AND TEXTURES.

Use them to set the room's mood—be it fresh and cheerful, elegant and refined, or clean and contemporary. Before you begin to pick and choose, it's useful to know something about how different fabrics perform, as well as where you can find the best selection.

FABRIC FUNDAMENTALS

Fabrics are made of natural or synthetic fibers, or a blend of the two. Natural fibers include cotton, linen, silk, wool, and mohair; man-made fibers include rayon, polyester, nylon, acetate, acrylic, and metal. Each of these fibers can be woven into a wide range of fabrics. Cotton, for example, can be woven into a sheer batiste, a lightweight chintz, or a heavy canvas.

Fiber content, in large part, determines whether or not a fabric will be practical for your needs. Some fibers are much more durable, stand up better to sunlight, or are easier to clean than others. In many cases, a blend combines the best qualities of two or more fibers: natural fibers gain durability, easier care, and a lower price tag when blended with man-made fibers; synthetic fibers take dyes better and are softer and more "breathable" when blended with natural fibers. In general, a blend of 60 percent synthetic and 40 percent natural fibers provides the greatest benefit. Less than 10 percent of one fiber in a blend makes little difference. The following lists will give you an idea of the advantages and disadvantages of different fibers.

NATURAL FIBERS. These are valued for their aesthetic appeal, and have been used for millennia.

COTTON is a durable, versatile fabric that takes color very well. It is available in countless weights, weaves, textures, and patterns, and is reasonably priced. However, it can fade and rot in sunlight and can shrink when washed. It's also highly flammable.

LINEN is woven from flax; it's cool to the touch and launders easily, but it creases and wrinkles easily, too. It is considered a strong fabric and is fade resistant. Although linen is most often seen in light, natural colors, it actually takes dyes very well. Like cotton, it's highly flammable.

SILK is a luxury fabric that drapes exceptionally well and takes color beautifully. However, it fades and rots in direct sun, stains easily (even from water), and is very difficult to care for; like linen, it wrinkles and shrinks with humidity. Silk also picks up static electricity. Although flammable, it's self-extinguishing.

WOOL is resilient and strong, drapes well, and contributes warmth. New processes have reduced the "itch" factor in most wools. Unless treated, 100-percent wool is susceptible to moth damage.

MOHAIR, from Angora goats, is a popular new choice for upholstery. It's soft but strong and very resilient. Cleaning it can be a

Mixing fabric patterns and soft shapes sets off this bay window seat and breakfast nook. While the shell fabric is key to the design, the black-and-white prints and large velour fruits link and "spread" its palette around the room. A solid plus a medium-scale diamond print and a large-scale shell motif equal a three-pattern success.

challenge, but a well-maintained, mothproofed mohair sofa will last for decades.

Other new naturals making their way into the decorating fabrics market include hemp and ramie. Hemp is almost like burlap, with its loose weave and rugged texture; it comes in "natural" colors such as browns and beiges. Ramie is like a soft, fragile blend of cotton and linen, breathing well but wrinkling easily.

SYNTHETIC FIBERS. Primarily 20th-century inventions, synthetics are known for low cost and practicality.

RAYON is the synthetic counterpart of cotton in its versatility and ability to blend well with other fibers. It, too, drapes well and takes color beautifully; it can have a deceptively natural appearance and feel. However, rayon will shrink, wrinkle, and mildew; depending on its finish, it can also be hard to care for.

POLYESTER is stable and durable as well as being colorfast, washable, and resistant to everything from rot, moths, and mildew to shrinking, stretching, and wrin-

Mixing patterns in a two-color scheme sends a fresh message via these period pieces. The Regency sofa is rejuvenated by its red-and-marigold plaid, with four variations of complementary patterns on the pillows; the armchair echoes the sofa's statement. Provincial side chairs are covered in a whimsical star fabric, relieving the stiffness of their traditional styling.

kling. It blends well and can take on the look of silk, with a nice drape and feel. It gives strength to natural fibers and will never go threadbare; most commercial-grade fabrics have a high percentage of polyester.

NYLON is stable, durable, strong, washable, and wrinkleproof; it's also very resilient, easy to care for, and inexpensive. However, it doesn't breathe: in the winter it's going to feel cold, and in summer it can become sticky.

ACETATE can mimic the look, feel, and drape of silk while resisting mildew, shrinking, stretching, and pilling. But it is a weak fiber that will weaken even further in the sun. Acetate is most often used in commercial fabrics.

ACRYLIC often simulates wool: it shares wool's warmth and strength but not its high price tag. It resists fading, mildew, and moths better than wool and is slower to soil. But acrylic pills easily and is less comfortable than natural fibers. Because it retains pleats and creases well, it's a good choice for tailored dust skirts and formal draperies.

METAL makes its way into decorating fabrics as metallic fibers, especially in window treatments; these fibers give luster and that sought-after "scrunched" look.

WEAVE. Along with fiber content, weave determines whether a fabric is right for a given job. Loosely woven fabrics are generally better for graceful window treatments; tighter weaves, because they're more durable, are best for upholstery. Lightweight fabrics such as cotton and linen suit pillows and other soft furnishings, but avoid using them to cover sofas or chairs that will get a lot of use. For free-flowing curtain panels, you'll want a fabric that drapes well. Sofas and

For a sleek, glamorous approach to bedding, start with a solid foundation: a padded and tufted headboard and base softened by pinkish beige plush velvet. A fluffy comforter covered in bold stripes is drawn back to reveal its flip-side pinstripe option. Stacked sleeping pillows are underscored by a decorative queen-size bolster.

Vintage-look floral linens in muted colors—fennel green and soft golds—complement the Asian-inspired furnishings of this guest room. The comforter cover reverses to a small check in silk taffeta, offering a lighter look for the summer months. Accents on the pillows—fine ruffles, braid, tone-on-tone toile, and brush fringe—give the ensemble depth and just a touch of decadence.

chairs should have a nice "hand"—that is, feel good. For superior durability, home decorators are increasingly choosing from the array of commercial-grade fabrics developed for retail spaces. These fabrics are generally available only through designers.

BUYING TIPS

While shopping, ask for samples of all the fabrics that you are considering. If the store doesn't have a check-out policy for its samples, buy a quarter-yard or however much you need to see the fabric's whole pattern. Once you have gathered more than enough samples, bring them home and look at them in context. Spread them out on the furniture you'll be re-covering, or tack them up over the window. How do they look with the walls, with the floor, and with other elements in the room?

When you've narrowed down your candidates, calculate exactly how much fabric you'll need. Interior designers, upholsterers, or fabric salespersons should be able to help you with this task. Try to buy all your fabric from a single bolt, checking it thoroughly for flaws such as color or pattern inconsistencies. If you must buy from more than one bolt, ask your salesperson to ensure that the dye lots match. Finally, determine whether the fabric should be laundered before it is cut; in general, if the fabric is for something you'll be washing, such as a slipcover, comforter cover, or curtain, you should prewash and then dry it. If it is a dry-clean-only fabric, do not prelaunder it. It is almost always a good idea to have upholstery fabric treated for stain resistance, either by the manufacturer or by a service that comes to your home once the furniture is delivered.

Upholstery fabrics are available from a multitude of sources. Lowe's can special-order some fabrics, and most large clothing fabric stores will have at least a small selection of "decorator fabrics" that are heavy enough to be used for upholstery or draperies. You'll find a larger selection at stores entirely devoted to home-decorating fabrics; there you'll also benefit from staff who are knowledgeable about decorating and upholstering. The fabrics at these stores are often organized to make selection easy for the do-it-yourself decorator, and the prices tend to be moderate. Be sure to ask the salesperson if your bolt is a "second"—that is, if it contains minor flaws that may or may not be noticeable.

Where do you find the fabrics featured in the advertisements and articles in upscale design magazines? Although some high-end upholstery shops and design studios have designer fabrics on display and available to order, the broadest selection can be seen at to-the-trade fabric showrooms. "To the trade" or "trade only" means you must be accompanied by a designer to order or even just to look. Chances are that you will be glad to have a professional's assistance, as the vast array of fabrics in these showrooms can be overwhelming. Most design centers can put you in touch with a designer, but it's better to find one by talking to friends and other trusted references. Once you've chosen your fabric, you can either buy it through that professional or see if it's available to consumers on the Internet (search by the fabric manufacturer's name).

Many retail furniture stores and department stores have their own collection of fabrics in a range of "grades" (in other words, the price of the sofa or chair depends on which grade of fabric you choose). They may also sell you their upholstery fabric by the yard. (It's a good idea to buy extra fabric in case you need to make future repairs.) In general, choose the best fabric you can afford, as price does correlate closely with quality in this case; keep in mind that imported fabrics are almost always more expensive than their domestic equivalents.

Creative slipcovers are a great way to throw tradition a curve and reinvent the personality of a seating piece. Overlapping tiers are welted to emphasize their scalloped edges.

SOFT FURNISHINGS

Aside from the two major uses of fabric in the home—upholstery and window treatments—there are several other places where textiles come into play: pillows, slipcovers, and bed coverings are chief among them.

PILLOWS. Though no longer used in the generous quantities of earlier decades, accent pillows can still lend a room spark and instant personality. Given the sheer variety of shapes, styles, and sizes of pillows, there is a perfect one for your every need. And because only a small amount of material is needed, this is one place you might want to splurge on expensive fabric, down filling, and gorgeous trimmings.

The size, shape, and fabric of a pillow should be suggested by its "parent" sofa or chair, as well as by the comfort preferences of whoever will be using it. For instance, if the pillow is meant to make the corner seats on a sofa more inviting, a square pillow nearly as high as the sofa back placed at each end will do the job nicely. A round pillow will visually soften a boxy sofa. A rectangular pillow at the center of a sofa's back is less expected; it can also provide lower-back support and enable a short person to sit comfortably, with her feet touching the floor. Whatever pillows you choose, don't overdo it with too many. Simplicity is the design direction of the future, and unless the sofa or chair is oversize or very deep, most pillows will end up on the floor, anyway.

As for fabric, consider the pillow to be an opportunity for contrast—in color, texture, or both. If the sofa is a sumptuous, textured chenille, add a tightly wrapped, smooth silk throw pillow. Or warm up a leather sofa with a soft mohair pillow in a complementary color (see "combining colors" on page 232). And pillows are a great medium to show off smaller pieces of vintage fabrics or inherited needlework;

Turquoise, orange, and red fabrics heighten the fun factor in this gender-neutral playroom. Plaids, stripes, and swirls happily commingle and make the inevitable stains less noticeable. The fabrics are mixed and matched again in the piping, an appropriately simple and easy-care trim for kids'-room cushions.

simply "frame" the prized panel with some simple velvet or silk.

Finally, consider welcoming each new season with a different set of throw pillows (or at least different pillow covers); the change will help you shift the mood of your home accordingly. You might use bright cottons in the summer, richly hued mohairs in the fall, jewel-toned velvets for the holidays, and pastel silks in the spring.

SLIPCOVERS. Popularized in the 1980s with the advent of "shabby chic," slipcovers are especially at home in a casual setting. Like a fresh change of clothes, they can completely alter the look of a piece of furniture—even of an entire room. A mohair sofa might cool off for the summer months with white cotton duck covers (scattered with fresh pillow covers in seasonal colors). Velvet slipcovers might dress up folding

chairs called into service for a large winter dinner party. For dining chairs and ottomans, in particular, slipcover options are as rich and varied as those for throw pillows when it comes to fabrics, styling, and trimmings. These smaller pieces offer a great opportunity to introduce bold patterns without worrying that you're overdoing it, or committing to it indefinitely.

Slipcovers are also enormously practical, protecting the furniture's original upholstery and extending its life. Once older upholstery has been worn threadbare or badly stained, adding a slipcover may be preferable to reupholstering, because it is easier to clean; this option is especially practical for households with pets or young children. (Keep in mind that all but prewashed cotton slipcovers need to be dry-cleaned, and even cotton loveseat and sofa slipcovers are too voluminous to fit in a home washing machine.)

But don't think of slipcovers primarily as cover-ups; when well made, they definitely enhance furniture. Unless you are a confident and experienced seamstress, seek out a company that specializes in

All-white slipcovers throughout instantly gave this Seattle lakeside cottage a fresh look. "It's light and airy year-round, no matter how gray it is outside," says the designer-homeowner. The soft matelassé cotton was washed and dried three times before it was cut and sewn, so it can be tossed into the washing machine whenever necessary.

slipcovers to do the job—and be sure you've seen examples of their work. If they say they don't need to have the sofa or chair in the shop as they work, chances are it won't be a properly fitting slipcover, and you should look elsewhere. And though there are many advantages to slipcovers (having two different looks is chief among them), economy is not necessarily one of them: a properly made slipcover is likely to cost just as much as reupholstering.

BED COVERINGS. Comforter covers, bedspreads, bed curtains, and pillows all perform many tasks, but providing comfort and style tops the list. As on sofas and chairs, pillows in the bedroom are fewer than they were in the past, perhaps as a matter of practicality: where do you put all of those pillows when you want to get into bed at night? The formula is now as easy as two plus two: For a queen-size bed, two 26-inch European squares covered in an upholstery fabric go against the headboard, with two decoratively shammed standard pillows in front of them. An accent bolster can add a third fabric by day and provide under-the-knee support for a back sleeper at night. Another approach is to stack two layers of standard pillows, one on top of the other, which couldn't be easier. Some prefer to keep the "sleeping pillows" under the bedspread—a good option if they are covered in a sheeting that doesn't contribute to the aesthetic mix.

Dust skirts provide another opportunity to introduce pattern and style. Full gathers have a feminine look, box pleats a simpler, tailored look. Consider repeating the dust skirt fabric on your decorative shams and using a complementary solid color or pattern on the comforter cover. Some fitted bedspreads drop all the way to the floor, eliminating the need for a dust skirt.

The traditional canopy frame is covered at the top, with a 12- to 14-inch valance dropping over its railings; formal canopies will also have floor-length curtains pulled back to each of the four posts of the bed, suggesting the possibility of total privacy. A lighter, more contemporary version would be a wrought-iron canopy frame with scaled-down tab-top curtains pulled back to the corners.

TRIMMINGS. Known as "passementerie" by design and fabric professionals, trimmings are the tassels, cords, buttons, and braids that can change an ordinary pillow or window treatment into something truly special. Gorgeous and tempting as they are, it is important to make sure these extras are in keeping with the weight, scale, and fabric they are paired with, as well as with the overall feel of the room. Cost may also figure into how heavily trim is used: the most sumptuous examples can be very expensive. Be sure to bring all of the fabrics you're considering along when shopping for trim, as well as accurate measurements.

FACING PAGE: Gleaming silk and nubby cotton fabrics, some hand-painted in gold, share a similar visual "temperature." Neutral sheers add pattern and texture.

BELOW: Decorative pillows bring all the colors in this room into balance. The braid picks up the periwinkle of a nearby sofa (see page 151). Note how a strip of fabric is used in two ways as trim: on the bias to create a diagonal pattern and straight for a gingham look. "Tassels are best used on purely decorative cushions—otherwise they can get in the way," says Los Angeles designer Gigi Rogers.

lighter fabrics

When we hear the word fabric, we tend to think first of lightweight cloths, including sheers and semi-sheers. Most sheer and lightweight fabrics are made of cotton, silk, linen, or synthetics. Sheer, or translucent, fabrics are best suited to light window treatments, to table skirts and toppers, and to bed canopies and dust skirts. Opaque yet still lightweight fabrics can be used for these same applications as well as for draperies, windowtop treatments, bedspreads, pillows, screens, wall coverings, and some slipcovers. Think twice about using lighter fabrics for upholstered seating, though, as they won't wear well over time.

1 SHEERS AND SEMISHEERS This see-through class of fabrics includes lace, netting, organdy, organza, dotted swiss (a muslin), batiste, and gauze. These are usually sold in shades of white and cream, simply because deeper colors are less transparent. As sheers and semisheers cannot provide privacy, particularly at night, they are often paired with curtains of a heavier fabric. If privacy is not an issue, generous quantities of sheer fabric can be draped or tied back for an ethereal, informal look.

2 LINEN PRINTS A natural for slipcovers (as shown here), linen prints provide a shabby-chic, country casual, beach house look. Their tendency to wrinkle, stretch, and even shrink in humid climates can be minimized by including synthetic fibers in the fabric. Although linens will eventually become threadbare when used for seating, they drape nicely and show off their weave beautifully as tab-top window panels.

3 TAFFETA A close, plain weave with a slight cross ribbing, taffeta is smooth and crisp, usually shiny, and available in a range of solids, plaids, and stripes. It is almost always seen in more formal settings; on this loveseat and ottoman, it is striped with silk sateen and gold metallic accents. Traditionally made of silk, taffeta is now available in synthetics as well.

4 TOILE DE JOUY The name refers to the printed design rather than to the fabric itself, which is usually a light- to midweight cotton. It depicts scenes of French country life—originally in a single color against a white or off-white background, but now frequently in a two-color scheme. This traditional print is found not only on fabrics but on wallpapers as well; here, the two are matched. Toile de Jouy is ideal for window treatments, slipcovers, bedding, and light-use upholstery.

5 SHANTUNG This is a plain weave, usually of silk, with elongated horizontal nubs caused by irregular-size yarns; these imperfections are what give the fabric its interest and natural beauty. Used in formal and elegantly casual settings alike, shantung comes in a spectrum of intense colors and has a lovely sheen. It is especially well suited to pillows, window treatments, and bedding, but it can be used for upholstery as well.

6 MOIRÉ A ribbed, plain weave of cotton, silk, or rayon, with a distinctive "watermarked" appearance, moiré is a traditional fabric that's at home in elegant interiors. Here, apricot and charcoal combine in a strikingly modern adaptation.

7 CHAMBRAY Made of light- to midweight cotton, chambray has a smooth, tight, plain weave. Whatever color it takes has a "frosted" appearance, due to the material's interwoven white threads. Chambray conveys a casual, fresh feeling and is easy to care for, making it especially appropriate for children's rooms, breakfast nook seating, and family rooms. Lightweight chambray is suitable for curtains and sheets, midweight better for slipcovers and upholstery.

8 CHINTZ Almost always made of cotton, chintz has a close, plain weave. It is usually printed with traditional florals, checks, and stripes and glazed for a smooth, lustrous finish. It is common to mix a "family" of chintzes in one room, on everything from upholstery to table skirts to window coverings.

heavier fabrics

Medium-weight fabrics such as damask, chenille, canvas duck, and mohair are good choices for heavier draperies and for most upholstery tasks, as well as for pillows. The lighter canvases and damasks are also fine for use as slipcovers, bedspreads, screens, and table coverings. Fabrics of heavier weight, including matelassé, velvet, tapestry, and leather, guarantee the longest life for upholstery.

1 DAMASK Available in a variety of fibers and weights, damask is woven into designs that alternate matte and sheen, creating a reversible pattern in a tone-on-tone or two-tone color scheme. This very traditional and formal fabric is typically used for fine table linens, draperies, and upholstery, but if washed and left unpressed it can make a sumptuous casual slipcover.

2 CHENILLE Usually made of cotton or wool, chenille has the plushness and light-catching nap of velvet, but with a texture woven into its cut pile. Though durable, chenille is very soft to the touch and gives informal furniture a quiet elegance. On a large sofa, as here, its texture and nap make an expanse of one solid color more interesting.

3 MOHAIR Once-fuzzy mohair is now often mixed with cotton and wool and sold in more subdued forms, such as twill and pile (as shown here). It has made a strong comeback recently among upholstery fabrics, being second in popularity only to leather. New treatments have largely eliminated the itchy quality once associated with it. Mohair takes dyes beautifully, so look for it in vivid hues. Be sure to follow the care instructions to the letter.

4 DUCK This broad term covers cottons and some linens made in strong, plain, firm weaves; it is also known as canvas and sailcloth, and is traditionally treated and used for sails and outdoor cushions. Here, a vibrant red-checked armchair is complemented by the bright, primary-color pillows and window seat; the casual look and practicality of the fabric suit this family room well.

5 MATELASSÉ A quilted pattern woven into thick cotton, matelassé is typically seen in shades of white and cream. The patterns range from old-fashioned floral motifs to more contemporary geometric designs. Matelassé is traditionally used in bedspreads but has been seen more recently on tablecloths and shabby-chic-style slipcovers (see page 333). It works in formal settings as well as in more casual schemes.

6 VELVET A luxurious, cut-pile weave in silk, cotton, wool, or synthetic fibers, velvet can be embossed, striped, solid, patterned, or—for a less formal look—crushed or "antiqued," as shown here. It may have a lustrous finish that shimmers in the light, or a dull finish. Lightweight versions are stunning in elegant draperies, slipcovers, pillows, and even bed dressings; heavier weaves are suitable for upholstery.

7 TAPESTRY Woven on a Jacquard loom, this fabric is meant to look like tapestry wall hangings. It is rougher and more substantial than its brocade and damask cousins but features the same floral and pictorial motifs. Often used on accent pillows and small chair seats, tapestry can be overwhelming if distributed with too heavy a hand. Here it is reinterpreted in a small geometric design for a more updated look.

8 LEATHER The most popular choice for upholstery, leather is simply treated animal hide. It is so durable that it is now being used for flooring (see page 301). Leather comes in many natural colors as well as in a rainbow of dyed hues, and will adapt beautifully to formal as well as casual furniture, traditional as well as contemporary homes.

FURNITURE

FURNITURE, PERHAPS MORE THAN ANY OTHER DECORATIVE ELEMENT, EMBODIES THE MARRIAGE OF FORM AND FUNCTION.

A rattan chair with plush cushions brings both texture and comfort to this warm neutral scheme. A leopard-print stool adds a touch of whimsy.

So many daily activities rely on it: eating, sleeping, working, reading, and socializing, among others. Sofas, chairs, and tables can also help organize and define spaces and traffic patterns within a home. And given the infinite possible combinations of wood, fabric, metal, and glass, furniture choices can express your taste and personality as well as serve your daily patterns.

ASSESSING YOUR NEEDS. Before you set foot in a furniture store, consider the big picture: are you starting with an empty room, looking to replace a piece or two, or filling in some holes? Inventory and measure the pieces you will keep. Then list the characteristics and functions of new pieces you will need. If you are starting with a blank slate, you'll have wonderful flexibility—but you may also feel the psychological and financial burden associated with "filling up" a room.

Many designers recommend buying only essential pieces at first, of the finest quality you can afford, rather than compromising quality and durability in order to furnish an entire room in one go. This leaves you the time and space to acquire pieces as you fall in love with them, giving your room an evolved, layered look. (If you want matching upholstered pieces, do order them all at the same time to make sure sufficient fabric is available and that all the pieces age together.)

If you simply want to replace a chair or sofa that is showing signs of wear, consider reupholstering what you have. If the piece is comfortable, has classic lines, and is well constructed, new upholstery can extend its life. Although this will not always save you money, it will spare you the hassle and waste of getting rid of the old furniture.

When adding to pieces you already own, don't be overly burdened by trying to match what you have. Aside from providing more visual interest, mixing and matching styles and materials can also give you more flexibility if you later want to move furniture from room to room or house to house.

Even if you choose to add pieces over time, it's best to start with an overall plan of which pieces you want, where they will be used, and what your home's overall color palette is. This foresight will ensure that all your future choices will work together, and it will help you avoid regrettable impulse buys.

UPHOLSTERED FURNITURE

Once you've settled on the general style and scale of a piece you're looking for (see pages 346–349 for design guidance), it's time to determine what's underneath it all.

VALUE FOR MONEY. Made-to-order sofas and chairs are available in mid- to high-end price ranges from furniture stores, department stores, and designer showrooms. Upholstered furniture is one purchase that justifies the saying "you get what you pay for," so think hard about how long you want your piece to last, and compare that with what you are willing to spend. Wherever you buy your sofa, be sure to consider these points:

❖ The highest-quality, longest-lasting seating will have a kiln-dried oak, maple, or poplar frame at least ³/₄ inch thick; softwood frames will cost less and be less durable.

❖ Joinery should be dowelled or double dowelled; look for corner blocks, which give the frame extra stability.

Upholstered furniture offers comfort, style, and color in one package. Here, a mix of matching pieces, the blue-and-white sofa and chair, and a contrasting piece, a chair covered in a warm-hued awning stripe that matches the draperies, demonstrates how upholstered furnishings can make a room cozy.

WORKING WITH ANTIQUES

*M*any people inherit antique furniture from family members or friends; others buy vintage furniture at estate sales, flea markets, and antique malls because it can be an economical way to make a unique statement with furniture. Antiques can bring a wonderful sense of craftsmanship and history to a home, and inherited pieces offer emotional comfort as well.

How do you work these one-of-a-kind pieces into your home? Don't be a slave to them, believing that if you have a country pine dining table, every one of your wood pieces should be country pine. Rather, consider the overall style of a piece: Is it formal or casual? Simple in detail, or elaborately carved? Delicate and graced with curves, or more angular and massive? Rather than trying to match styles or even periods, focus on repeating design lines and (as always) maintaining appropriate scale.

If you feel that a beloved antique just doesn't work with the furnishings and architecture in your main living areas, try incorporating it into a less used space such as a guest room. Or move it to the foyer or landing, where it is more likely to shine on its own.

If you plan to acquire antiques, how do you know whether you will be getting good value? Take the time to familiarize yourself with a period that appeals to you—ask antique dealers about the history of any piece you are interested in, read books and magazines, visit antique shows.

Otherwise, judge it as you would any other piece. Do you love it? Is it in your price range? Are its moving parts in good working order? Check for warpage, water damage, and missing hardware. Is it stable, and are its dimensions truly useful? ∼

ABOVE: Three inherited antiques—the tall secretary, the desk in the window bay, and the scalloped table in the foreground—came out of storage to mingle with a tansu chest and other newer pieces in this Victorian-era living room. The underlying warm brown and gold tones of the floor and area rug help tie together the eclectic collection, and the warm chamois-colored walls provide a quiet backdrop. Note how the large, heavier case goods are positioned on the perimeter of the smallish room, while lighter pieces inhabit the room's airy core.

- Legs that are an integral extension of the frame are preferable to screwed-in legs, which may wobble over time.

- Eight-way, hand-tied springs are by far the most supportive; the lesser alternative is zigzag, or sinuous, springs. You should not hear the springs when you sit down.

- Seat cushions with their own internal springs will be the most supportive, followed by those of high-density foam. Either may be wrapped with a down blend or with Dacron. Down blends can be used alone for very soft back cushions, but they are seldom recommended for seat cushions.

- Because made-to-order upholstered pieces are built by hand from the frame out, it can take anywhere from 10 to 16 weeks from the day you put down your deposit to their arrival at your door. If delay is a concern of yours, ask about delivery time.

Made-to-order furniture isn't within everyone's means, of course. Medium-priced retailers are now selling certain lines of furniture online and through catalogs; just be sure to check their return policy and shipping charges. Another alternative is to frequent estate sales or furniture-consignment stores. Second-hand furniture with "good bones" can be updated with a slipcover or new upholstery.

COMFORT. Whatever your price range, comfort is paramount. Sit on lots of sofas and chairs while asking about their filling; compare foam with down and with polyester fiberfill-wrap cushions. What's more important to you: softness or support?

Pay attention to the piece's dimensions. Overall dimensions such as length and depth simply help you determine how it will fit in the room. Seat height, seat depth, seat back height, and armrest height are often overlooked "comfort" measurements. If your household's occupants vary in height, choose seating that will accommodate the tallest person, and get an extra cushion to prop against the seat back for shorter family members.

Here are a few other things to note as you shop: Is the frame sturdy and free of creaks and wobbles? Is it well padded, especially at the corners and edges? Do the cushions fit snugly? Do moving parts work smoothly? Are the cushions reversible? Are details well sewn? Does the piece support your arms, neck, and head? Is the angle of repose comfortable? Finally, be extra careful when buying a piece that you can't try out first, especially if it's nonreturnable.

Upholstered pieces play the starring role in this living room. The ottoman doubles as a coffee table and becomes the key to the color mix. The chenille sofa in solid persimmon is accented with striped and plaid pillows, while the armchairs introduce another, larger-scale pattern. Tight color sequencing and a range of small to medium print sizes make up a formula for success.

A handcrafted cupboard in contrasting woods provides behind-closed-doors storage at top and bottom. In the middle, a desk pulls down, giving the unit depth and revealing three display niches. This piece fills an awkward space in a useful as well as artful way.

CASE GOODS

The term *case goods* is used for furniture that is task oriented and primarily of wood, metal, or other hard, man-made material (rather than upholstered). Dining sets, desks, chests, benches, armoires, occasional tables—these pieces, with their rich wood grains, interesting paint or lacquer finishes, carved details, or eye-catching shapes, give a room character. Case goods can also evoke past eras of refinement or embody the simplicity of modern design.

Three main factors should be considered as you choose case goods: function, style, and budget. Once you've determined the pieces you need and the purpose each must serve, look at other furniture in your home or in magazines and catalogs to help you focus on style.

Most furniture styles are available in a wide range of prices; their cost depends on the materials used and the quality of construction. The general categories to choose from (roughly in order of decreasing cost) are designer or handcrafted pieces, antiques and collectibles, reproductions, modular or mass-produced furniture, and unfinished or ready-to-assemble (RTA) furniture.

As for materials, hardwood means the wood of deciduous trees: cherry, maple, mahogany, and walnut, to name a few. Softwoods, such as pine and fir, are often less expensive than hardwoods and usually more casual in style. Still less expensive are medium-density fiberboard (MDF) and particleboard; these can be heavier or more prone to water damage and chipping, but they are also more stable and warp resistant than solid wood. Plywood is the strongest alternative to solid wood, and is in many cases much stronger.

Most reproduction and mass-produced furniture is no longer made of solid wood but of veneer—thin sheets of a decorative wood glued onto a cheaper solid material. Today's veneers are less prone to chipping and peeling than they were in the past, and they are increasingly the only economically and environmentally sound option. If case goods are labeled as "solid wood," it applies only to the visible areas of the furniture; unseen portions are probably of MDF, particleboard, or plywood. If owning solid wood furniture is important to you, look for antique pieces, Asian imports, or custom-made pieces.

A wood's finish not only protects it but can change its appearance dramatically. A clear finish, such as an oil or a wax, will allow the grain and other characteristics of the wood to show through. Stain and paint add color. "Distressed" finishes are sometimes chosen in more casual homes, especially for high-traffic areas or for furniture that will see heavy use. Whatever finish you choose, be sure to ask how to care for it.

Wood is the material most often used in case goods, but you'll also find wrought iron combined with glass or wood, which brings a bit of the garden indoors. Other metals, such as aluminum, steel, copper, and chrome, lend a more modern look.

As you shop for your case goods, keep an eye out for the following hallmarks of quality:

❖ Do the drawers have smooth glides and stops, as well as dust panels between drawers? Are the interiors nicely finished?

❖ Are all the joints, including those in the drawers, secure? Screwed joints are stronger than stapled or glued joints. Dovetail and tongue-in-groove construction is also very strong, but the craftsmanship they require adds significantly to their cost. Weight-bearing joints should be reinforced with corner blocks.

❖ Do the doors fit well, opening and shutting freely?

❖ Is the piece stable and free of squeaks and wobbles?

❖ Do long shelves have center supports beneath them?

❖ Is the hardware sturdy and securely mounted?

❖ Does the finish feel smooth and appear to be evenly applied?

❖ If the piece will hold equipment such as a TV, stereo, or computer, are there holes for the electrical cords to pass through?

❖ Will the shelving in a television cabinet or armoire support the weight of your TV or computer? What about the swivel or pull-out tray for it?

The curves of this American Queen Anne–style dining suite in quarter-sawn oak echo those of the coved ceilings and soft archway opening to the living room beyond. Curves continue in the sofa, iron-and-glass coffee table, and barrel chairs.

sofas and loveseats

Settee, davenport, or couch—call it what you will, the sofa is likely to get more use than any other piece of furniture in your gathering room. For this reason, many designers consider it the one to treat as an investment. Buy a sofa with simple, classic lines and solid construction, and it will last a lifetime—with a few reupholstery jobs to refresh it along the way. And because it is usually the largest, most used, and most expensive piece of furniture, it's wise to make it your first purchase, building the room around it.

To narrow your choices, consider some of the following questions. How long a sofa do you want? Sofas come in 7- and 8-foot lengths; you should allow approximately 3 feet of space on either end for traffic flow. (Also, measure to ensure that the sofa will fit through your door when it is delivered.) Some people opt to go shorter altogether with a loveseat (or pair of loveseats) in the 5- to 6-foot range—too short for most adults to recline on.

If naps are important to you, by all means stretch out on sofa models in the store, looking for lower, rounded arms. How many seat cushions would you like? Keep in mind that rarely do more than two people sit on a sofa at the same time, so one or two cushions may be adequate. Some other styling considerations: Do you want finished wood legs, bun feet (low, rounded legs), or a skirt (either tailored or gathered) to hide the legs?

Also, do you need the option of extra sleeping space? Many sofas can be bought as sleepers; mattresses with springs are likely to be the most comfortable for your guests. Futon couches—collapsible frames with a fabric-covered pad forming the seat and back—have come a long way in both comfort and design. They do, however, tend to take up more space than sleeper sofas, and typically come with a full-size, not queen-size, mattress.

There are innumerable variations on sofa styles; knowing a few names and characteristics will help you communicate with salespersons and designers.

1 A LAWSON SOFA is the most traditional style, with rounded arms and fitted but unattached or semi-attached seat cushions. It comes with two or three cushions and either exposed legs or a skirt.

2 A CAMELBACK SOFA has a tailored look, with its tight, bell-curved back, rolled arms, and (usually) exposed legs.

3 A SETTEE is benchlike, with an exposed structure and padded seating. If you prefer an airy look, have a small space, or like to see the beauty of the frame, a settee may appeal to you.

4 A TUXEDO SOFA is distinguished by straight or slightly flared arms that are as high as the tight seat back. Other tight-backed sofas have tufted or channeled styling.

5, 6 A CONTEMPORARY SOFA has clean, squared-off lines, with straight arms and often a lower-than-traditional back.

7 SECTIONAL SOFAS AND MODULAR SEATING can be configured into just about any shape to suit your space. The array of different pieces—armless, corner, ottoman, chaise, and others—can be taken apart and reconfigured (or used separately) at will. This is a nice option if you like to rearrange your furniture with the change of seasons or for different entertaining needs.

8 VINTAGE PIECES, such as this forties loveseat, give a room instant panache and usually blend nicely with both contemporary styles and furniture of other eras. Also, if an older piece still feels solid after decades of use, it's a good bet that it will hold up for you as well.

chairs

Many of the principles that apply to selecting a sofa also apply to buying upholstered chairs. But if you think the array of sofas is impressive, the choices among chair styles are dizzying. Consider how you will use the chair: Do you love curling up to read a good book? Perhaps *you want a pair of chairs for intimate conversation? Do you need "oppositional seating" facing the sofa? Chairs with swivel mechanisms make it easy to redirect seating to accommodate all of these needs. Dining chairs should fit (but not necessarily match) the dining table.*

1 A CLUB CHAIR is the most classic and enduring armchair choice, perhaps because of its comfortable styling: rounded arms at a comfortable height, a generous seat cushion, and a supportive back cushion. Club chairs come in a range of sizes and interpretations but tend to take up more space than other styles.

2 WINGBACK CHAIRS are highly traditional; people who are tall and like to sit in an upright position find them comfortable, as they offer good head and neck support. However, the tight, straight back doesn't provide the lower back support that most women need.

3 DINING CHAIRS must above all be comfortable; be sure that your feet rest naturally on the floor when you're seated and that nothing protrudes into your back. Slipcovers will protect the upholstery of padded seats. Mixing and matching different chairs not only creates an interesting, eclectic look, but also helps accommodate people of various dimensions.

4 A CHAISE, with its elongated seat and built-in footrest, is one of the most comfortable types of seating. Often a chaise has just one arm, making sitting in and rising from it more graceful. Though traditionally associated with bedrooms, chaises are now making appearances in family rooms and any other room where people might like to unwind.

5 A CHAIR-AND-A-HALF is just what it says: bigger than a single chair but smaller than a loveseat. It is large enough for two average adults to snuggle in or for a parent and two kids to cozy up in to read a book. It is almost always paired with a generous ottoman to provide a chaise effect. Some even harbor a twin-size sleeper.

6 RECLINERS have enjoyed a renaissance as their styling has been revolutionized. Whether you prefer a wood-framed Arts and Crafts look, a classic leather club chair, or a trim floral-chintz wingback, you can find it

as a recliner. New mechanisms mean that recliners can be placed as close to the wall as 3 inches.

7 OTTOMANS aren't just for feet anymore. This useful and multipurpose piece can be deployed as extra seating in a pinch—or, with a large tray on top, a coffee table. Some even open up to provide storage space for blankets or toys. Ottomans come in many shapes, from long and narrow to square to round. Ideally, an ottoman should be an inch or more lower than the chair it will be paired with. However, if it is to be used primarily as a coffee table, it should be an inch or two higher than the seating. Finally, if it is heavy or large, consider putting it on casters so you can more easily employ its versatility.

8 ARMLESS CHAIRS come in a variety of styles and sizes, but in general they take up less space in a room, both physically and visually. Lacking supportive armrests, they are seldom as comfortable as armchairs but are useful where you need to fill a small space or sit for a short time: in a foyer or near a card or writing table, for instance.

8

case goods

If it's not upholstered, it probably fits into the category of case goods. Tables, dressers, desks—beds—these are some of the hardest-working pieces of furniture in your house, so they deserve to be well-planned purchases.

Before going shopping, it pays to measure the spaces you have to fill; carry those figures—and a pocket tape measure—with you at all times. You may find the perfect piece when you least expect it.

1 DINING TABLE decisions should be based on a number of factors, some of them obvious: Is it to be used for everyday meals or for occasional formal dining? Do you want to be able to adjust the size of the table depending on the number of diners? (Be sure any leaves not only fit properly but also match the table's graining and finish.) Typically, a 6-foot-long rectangle will seat eight people comfortably. A narrower trestle- or refectory-style table offers more intimacy but allows little space for serving dishes or centerpieces. A circular dining table is considered "democratic" and conducive to conversation for groups of four to eight; some have leaves that extend them into ovals. Be sure the table isn't too large for the room: allow at least 32 inches from it to the walls on all sides. Ideally, there should be 7 inches of clearance from the tabletop to the chair seat beneath it; the underside of the table should also be snag free.

2 A COFFEE TABLE is typically long and low, placed in front of a sofa. Depending on the layout of the room, it may also be a large square or two or three tables of similar height grouped together. Many coffee tables now have thick glass tops with display space for books or collectibles underneath, leaving the top clear for entertaining. Don't forget to consider the softer option of an ottoman as a coffee table (see page 343).

3 OCCASIONAL TABLES are small conveniences placed near each seating area to accommodate beverages, reading material, or lamps. End tables of medium height set at either end of a sofa; round skirted tables draped with one or several layers of decorative fabric, perhaps topped with glass; and long, narrow consoles that may back a sofa or grace an entry to support lamps or display photos are examples. Stacking tables—three or more tables of descending sizes that nest together—are particularly useful, as they can be moved around the room when needed. A general rule of thumb for selecting any occasional table is that it be proportional in scale and height to the seating it serves.

4 A HUTCH, china cabinet, or sideboard not only provides storage and display space for dishes but adds character to a dining room or kitchen; some styles even include a buffet surface. A sideboard can also be used in an entry or behind a sofa (depending on its height). Here again, consider your storage needs first, and whether you want to display the contents. Glass doors and mirrors will add light to a room. Your piece doesn't need to match the room's other case goods, but it should complement them in shape, style, scale, and materials.

5 WRITING DESKS serve a largely decorative function, but placed near an entry they make a good dropping-off place for keys or gloves; others may be used for writing a quick note. These desks tend to be smaller than their hardworking office counterparts and are often tucked into a corner of the living room or into a guest room, for both ornamental and utilitarian purposes. An antique secretary fills the bill in period-style homes, while Art Deco–inspired versions such as this one fit nicely in more contemporary settings.

6 COMPUTER DESKS should be deep enough for a good-size computer monitor; they must stow a keyboard, mousepad, printer, and the computer itself, and have adequate holes for all those components' cords. Most people also require at least one file drawer and one shallow supplies drawer. Do you want built-in cubbies or stacking trays for sorting papers? Enough surface area on which to do paperwork and use a phone? Will you need a lamp, or built-in lighting? What about a fax machine? Sit at the desk to make sure that you have adequate leg room and that the desktop and keyboard tray are at ergonomically suitable heights for you. More furniture makers are designing home-office armoires like this one that blend with traditional furniture in a bedroom or living space and neatly hide the desk when it's not in use.

Continued on next page >

... case goods

7 A BED FRAME can be as simple as a metal "Harvard" frame covered with a dust ruffle or as elaborate as a grand **four-poster bed** draped with fabric—and every variant in between. A headboard is a versatile middle-ground option. It can be padded and lavishly upholstered or slipcovered (making it easier to clean and change), or it can be affixed to the wall behind the bed—bordered wallpaper, a quilt hung on the wall, even picket fencing cut to the width of the bed.

8 A CAPTAIN'S BED, with storage drawers beneath it, and a **trundle bed,** which pulls out from under the bed for sleepovers, are two useful options for children's rooms. This efficient model combines the two styles.

9 A DAYBED is topped by a regular mattress within a three-sided frame; a pop-up trundle bed below it can turn a twin into a king-size bed. Although the mattress surface offers great sleeping comfort, the back is nothing more than throw cushions, and the seat may be too high for most people.

10 NIGHTSTANDS don't have to match the bed, nor must you have a pair of them. Instead, consider the needs of the individual who will use it: Should there be space for a lamp? Reading material? Clock radio? Concealed storage? Depending on your needs, any occasional table can be used—or a small dresser, a wall-mounted shelf, a trunk, even a rustic chair. Some contemporary beds actually incorporate adjoining nightstands. Whatever your choice, the nightstand's top should be at least as high as the mattress. Its width should be in proportion to the bed's size; a nightstand one-third the width of the bed is about right.

11 DRESSERS are a must for bedrooms without sufficient built-in storage. A small dresser or **lowboy** (shown) can double as a nightstand—or even as a diaper-changing table in a baby's room. A tall **highboy** fits a lot of storage into a small footprint. A **Dutch bureau** is ideal for a guest room, providing a few drawers on the bottom, bookshelves on top, and a writing desk as well. Think carefully about the size and number of drawers you would like. Shallow drawers at hip height are convenient for socks and other small items, whereas deeper drawers down low work for sweaters and blankets.

12 ARMOIRES are another option for bedrooms as well as family rooms and living rooms. Useful for storing everything from clothing and linens to books, TVs, and even entire home offices, they take up less floor space than some alternatives because they use vertical, rather than horizontal, space. The armoire below conceals a TV.

12

built-in storage

Efficient storage is a must for an efficient house—not just in the kitchen and closets, but in the living areas as well. Books, collections, throw blankets, games, and photo albums are only a small part of the problem; our increasingly complex entertainment systems, including all their tapes, CDs, and remotes, require substantial, well-planned storage. Often the best way to achieve this is with a built-in unit.

Though expensive, built-ins allow you to customize your storage to the number and type of items that need a home while maximizing available space. For instance, when you design a custom wall unit, you're able to build all the way up to the ceiling. Painted the color of your walls and finished with matching trim, wall units blend in and take up less visual space as well. One caveat: Built-ins typically can't be moved, so consider them a long-term investment in your home. If you anticipate moving, the modular wall units available in many furniture stores can be assembled to accommodate a variety of storage needs and spaces, offering some of the look and functionality of built-ins.

Once you know the function of the piece you need and the space it will occupy, start collecting pictures of looks and details that you like: hardware, door styles, moldings, types of wood, and finishes. Think about how your choices will fit in with the rest of the room. Do you want something more casual and functional, or a piece that almost stands on its own from an artistic standpoint?

When you have gathered your thoughts and examples, seek out a cabinetmaker by asking friends for references or calling those whose work you've seen. If necessary, get a second quote. Before a single plank of wood is cut, make sure the cabinetmaker himself measures the space.

1, 2 WALL UNITS Here are a few things to consider as you plan your storage. Do you need mostly concealed storage, or would you like display space as well? One smart design for a wall unit is to have deeper, closed storage up to counter height, then shallower, open shelves up to the ceiling for books or photos and other display objects. A combination of drawers and cupboards gives you the greatest flexibility. Glass doors will keep delicate or prized possessions safe from small hands and dust. Put infrequently used items up high. A sliding ladder gives you access to top shelves and lends that authentic library look. Lighting can also be installed in the unit to display collectible objects; glass shelves allow the light to travel up and down. Both traditional and contemporary wall units are shown here, to suggest the range of styles available in custom cabinetry.

3 HUTCHES Kitchen cabinets are built-ins of a sort, but some are more furniturelike than others. Here, a hutch was custom built to the dimensions needed for the owners' dishes and other kitchen items and then artistically painted to give it country charm.

4 HIDDEN STORAGE Built-ins needn't be a pricey focal point in a room. In this bedroom, simple shelves behind the bed store books and favorite objects and can be concealed with curtains—a softer, space-saving alternative to doors that swing open.

5 MEDIA CABINETS Measure the television as well as key accessories such as other media equipment and CD, DVD, or videotape collections. Think carefully about what height you would like the screen to be relative to where you will be sitting. Do you want it on a pull-out tray, a swivel tray, or both? Do you want to be able to conceal it when it's not in use? Consult your owner's manual to determine the weight; many of today's larger TVs require a stronger base. Will you want to place speakers in the unit? Note that, if media components are to be operated with a remote control, they will probably have to be on open shelves or behind glass.

6 DESKS If you are creating a unit to serve as a desk, think about how you plan to use your office, how much and what kind of storage and table space you need, and what kind of computer and peripheral equipment you have. How many people will be using the space? Lighting is crucial in an office; you might consider having it built into the unit.

HOME DECORATING TECHNIQUES AND PROJECTS

"I DID IT MYSELF!" EVERY TIME YOU PAUSE TO ADMIRE A CHARMING BORDER YOU'VE STENCILED AROUND YOUR BEDROOM WALLS, or to place a cherished item on a decorative shelf you've installed on your family room wall, you can take special pride in knowing you created it yourself. When you have a clear vision of how you want your rooms to look, it's a wonderful feeling to give that vision shape with your own two hands. If working with hammer and paintbrush is your cup of tea, this chapter will serve up just what you want. From practical projects, such as installing door trim and baseboards, to room-enhancing paint techniques like colorwashing and sponging, you'll find more than two dozen fully illustrated, step-by-step projects to keep you happily occupied. So get your brushes and tools ready, and go creative!

decorative painting basics

Most decorative painting projects—from sponging and colorwashing to combing and stamping—start with the same preliminary steps. You need to mask adjacent surfaces that aren't to be painted and you'll need to apply a base coat. This base coat is the paint layer on which you will add your decorative coat, a blend of paint and thinner called glaze. This project shows how to perform these preliminaries.

With all the paint brands and finishes available, buying paint you'll be pleased with can be a dizzying prospect. All the decorative painting projects in this book feature Lowe's latex-base, satin finish American Tradition Valspar paint. One advantage of latex paints is that they dry quickly and can be cleaned up with soap and water. Alkyd or oil-based paints have a stronger odor, give off solvents as they dry, and can only be cleaned up with thinner.

Before applying a base coat, wash dirt and grease off walls with warm water and a household cleanser. Fill cracks and holes with spackling compound, sand patches smooth, and apply a primer to them. For applying a latex base coat, you'll need a roller with a nylon cover. For "cutting in" edges, it's a good idea to invest in a good-quality 2- or 3-inch synthetic-bristle brush. Wear disposable latex gloves when painting; they will protect your skin and allow greater flexibility than rubber gloves.

MATERIALS
❖ Paint (Latex-base, satin finish American Tradition paint, "Martinique Morn," paint chip 316C, shade -2)

TOOLS
❖ 3-inch synthetic-bristle brush
❖ Nylon roller
❖ Plastic paint tray
❖ EasyMask™ painting tape
❖ Latex gloves

1 MASKING ADJACENT SURFACES
Starting at the top of the wall, lay 2-inch painting tape along the wall that won't be painted. Align the sticky half of the tape flush with the corner. Painting tape is coated with a quick-release adhesive that won't pull off existing paint. Working your way down the wall, firmly press the tape in place so paint won't leak beneath it (left). Cut the top end of the tape straight and flush with the ceiling. At the baseboard, lay the tape along the upper edge to form a ledge to catch paint drips. Tape off edges of the floor with 2-inch masking tape, then cover the floor with a drop cloth.

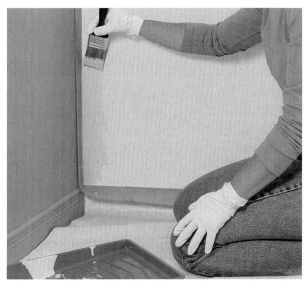

2 CUTTING IN THE EDGES With latex paint, cutting in can be done before rolling paint on the wall. Pour some paint into a roller tray and dip a synthetic-bristle paintbrush into the paint, coating about a third of the bristles. Brush off excess paint on the edge of the tray. Cut in first along the ceiling, followed by door and window trim, then along adjacent walls and finally the baseboard. At an adjacent wall, start about two brush lengths from the ceiling and brush up to the corner. Move down and brush upward to join the wet edge, continuing until you cut in from the baseboard (above) to the wet edge above it.

3 ROLLING ON THE PAINT To reach the upper sections of the wall, attach an extension to your roller. Load up the roller in the tray and roll off the excess. Starting a few feet from one top corner of the wall, apply the paint in an "M" shape to a 3- to 4-foot square section (above). Work toward the adjacent wall, overlapping the cut-in edge along the corner.

4 FILLING IN WITH THE ROLLER Without recharging the roller with paint, roll back over the same section of wall to fill in unpainted spaces (above). Still without adding any fresh paint, make a third pass to even out any marks left by the edge of the roller. Apply more pressure for this third pass. Continue rolling paint on the wall in sections and filling in, until you've covered the wall.

TIPS

The edge of the roller closest to the handle tends to leave more of a visible mark on the wall than the other edge. To compensate for this, turn the roller around when making the third pass.

colorwashing

Colorwashing can transform an otherwise dull room into a lively, airy space. Surfaces are "washed" with a diluted paint and glaze mixture applied in broad crisscrossed strokes, then passed over a second time with a dry brush. The sweeping texture that results is reminiscent of rustic plaster—helpful in disguising small imperfections—and makes an interesting contrast to painted woodwork. Color psychology is especially effective in this technique. Pale blues can create the effect of a cool underwater world, while yellows can give a room with little natural light a sunny disposition. The rich brown tones chosen for this project create a mood of warm intimacy—ideal for a dining room. Colorwash colors are usually kept to the same family, with the glaze a darker shade of the base color; light tones over dark ones tend to look chalky and make the brush strokes obvious.

MATERIALS

❖ Lowe's American Tradition paints, satin finish 264A-4 Autumn Acorn (base coat), 294-6 Copper Penny
❖ Valspar translucent pearl glaze

TOOLS

❖ 4-inch paintbrush
❖ Plastic paint tray
❖ Stirring sticks
❖ Mixing containers
❖ Painter's tape
❖ Drop cloth
❖ Latex gloves

Drips and dribbles indicate the paint and glaze mixture is too thin. Thicken the mixture with more paint.

❖

Your brush strokes can be crude as you apply the glaze, but keep an eye out for drips and immediately brush them out.

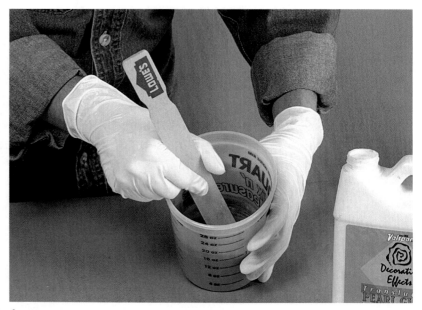

1 PREPARING THE PAINT AND GLAZE MIXTURE Complete the base coat and allow it to dry for the recommended time: two days for latex paint; two to three days for alkyd paint. Tape off adjacent ceiling, woodwork, and wall surfaces you don't wish to paint. Prepare a mixture of equal parts paint and glaze and two-thirds part water (above)—32 ounces (2 pints) for an average-size room (10 feet by 12 feet)—and pour some into a paint tray.

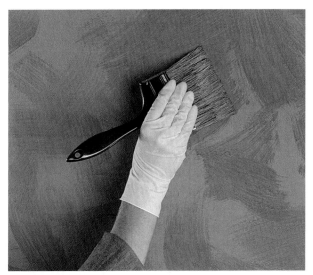

2 BRUSHING ON THE GLAZE MIXTURE Working top to bottom from one end of the surface to the other, apply the mixture to a 3-foot-square section with a 4-inch paintbrush. Holding the brush by the base, make sweeping crisscross strokes, moving your wrist to vary the angle. Cover no more than half of the section and leave large spaces between series of strokes while the brush is fully loaded (above). Work along edges and into corners only once the brush has been partially discharged.

3 BLENDING BRUSH STROKES Fill in spaces and even out effect intensities as the brush becomes less saturated (above). Continue blending in with the discharged brush, feathering the edges of strokes.

4 STARTING SUBSEQUENT SECTIONS Reload the paintbrush and begin the next 3-foot-square section at the center, working back to the completed section without overlapping the edges (above). Blend in the section, then continue the same way along the surface. Vary the starting point of sections both vertically and horizontally to avoid noticeable demarcations.

5 BLENDING SECTIONS Blend in sections by brushing the spaces between strokes with a partially loaded brush (above). Brushing directly over previous strokes risks intensifying the effect and leaving noticeable demarcations. Continue blending in with the discharged brush, feathering the edges of strokes.

combing

Combing can be applied to create a variety of lined textures. Effect variables include the thickness of the teeth and spaces of the graining comb as well as the pattern employed. Three common patterns are straight—shown in this project—basketweave and moiré (horizontal and diagonal strokes added to vertical ones). Beginners beware: The technique isn't as easy as it looks. Maintaining straight, uninterrupted lines and completing ceiling-to-floor sections before the diluted paint and glaze mixture dries can be challenging. The good news is that errors are easily wiped away and practice improves your performance. As with most faux finishes, two tones of the same color produces a subtle, refined effect—and small imperfections aren't obvious.

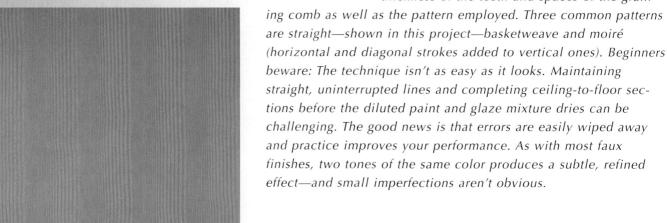

MATERIALS

❖ Lowe's American Tradition paints, satin finish: 248-2 Clear Horizon (base coat), 248-4 Dover Straights
❖ Valspar translucent pearl glaze

TOOLS

❖ Plastic paint tray
❖ Stirring sticks
❖ 3-inch paintbrush
❖ 4-inch paint roller
❖ Triangular rubber graining comb
❖ Carpenter's level
❖ Painter's tape
❖ Plastic lid
❖ Hobby knife
❖ Straightedge
❖ Drop cloth
❖ Latex gloves

1 TAPING GUIDELINES Complete the base coat and allow it to dry for the recommended time: two days for latex paint; two to three days for alkyd paint. Tape off adjacent ceiling, woodwork, and wall surfaces you don't wish to paint. Prepare a mixture of equal parts paint, glaze, and water—32 ounces (2 pints) for an average-size room (10 feet by 12 feet)—and pour some into a paint tray. Mark points for a vertical line every 2 feet along the surface with a carpenter's level, then lay painter's tape along each series of points (above). Don't skip this step—even experienced pros require guidelines.

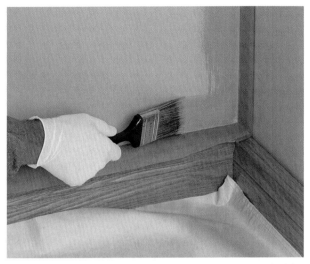

2 CUTTING IN ALONG EDGES Working from one end of the surface to the other, apply the diluted paint and glaze mixture top to bottom on a section equal in width to the graining comb—here, 8 inches. Cut in along edges with a 3-inch paintbrush (above).

3 ROLLING ON THE GLAZE Fill in the section with a 4-inch paint roller, making overlapping vertical passes (above). Noticeable edges will tend to blend in once the surface has been combed.

4 COMBING THE SECTION Hold the graining comb flush against the ceiling and the adjacent wall. Maintaining uniform pressure, drag the comb smoothly and steadily down the surface to the bottom in one uninterrupted pass. Wipe glaze mixture off the teeth of the comb immediately with a damp cloth. Apply glaze mixture to the next section, cutting in with the brush and filling in with the roller. Comb the surface using the previous section and first taped guideline as reference. Continue along the surface the same way (above), removing the taped guidelines as you go.

5 HANDLING END CORNERS Chances are the width of the last section of the surface will be less than the width of the comb. To complete this section, make a comb from the lid of a plastic container. Trace the outline of the comb's teeth onto the lid (above), then cut the lid to size with a straight-edge and a hobby knife. Apply glaze to the last section, then comb the surface with your homemade tool.

stamping

Once an ancient printing method, stamping is a popular decorative painting technique in which a pattern is repeated over a surface. You can stamp a design across an entire wall or confine it to a border, as shown in this child's room. Although stamped borders often follow the ceiling line, some motifs, such as the sun stamp used here, work best if located a few inches below the ceiling.

Decorative painting stamps are traditionally hand-carved, but you can buy rubber and foam stamps. Foam stamps, like the one from Lowe's shown here, hold more paint than rubber ones and can give your design a spongelike texture. If you plan to stamp the same design in more than one color, as in this example, buy one stamp for each color so as not to contaminate your colors.

In choosing colors for stamping, make sure the stamp colors complement the base coat color, but differ enough to stand out without clashing. This project was executed with Lowe's latex, satin-finish American Tradition paints. Ivory Castle (paint chip 232, shade 2) was laid down as the base coat, and Bright Chartreuse (paint chip 228, shade 6) and Crispy Lettuce (paint chip 227, shade 3) were stamped over it.

MATERIALS
- American Tradition paints, satin finish: 227-3, 232-2, 228-6
- Valspar translucent pearl glaze
- Plaid Stamp Decor stamp 5362

TOOLS
- Yardstick
- 1-inch artist's brushes
- Mixing containers
- Stirring sticks
- Rags
- Latex gloves

1 MARKING BORDER GUIDELINES Apply the base coat on the wall to be stamped and let it dry. Then mark light pencil lines 3 inches down from the ceiling at several points along the wall. Join the marks with a yardstick. Draw a second line below the first so the distance between them will accommodate your design. In this example, featuring three rows of 4 by 4-inch motifs, the lines are 9 inches apart. Beginning at the end of the wall that is most visible when you enter the room, mark off both lines at 4-inch intervals with short vertical lines (above).

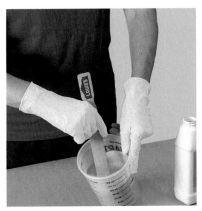

2 PREPARING THE GLAZE MIXTURES
Set aside a plastic container for each stamp color. In this example, there are three. Pour a little of each paint—about 4 ounces—into a separate container; here, we also mixed together 2 ounces of each stamp color in another container, creating a third color. Add 4 ounces of glaze to each container and stir each mixture thoroughly with a clean paint stick (above). The glaze serves to thin the paint to the proper consistency for stamping.

3 APPLYING PAINT TO THE STAMPS
Load up a 1-inch artist's brush with one of the glaze mixtures, and lightly apply the paint to one side of the stamp (above). Avoid putting too much paint on the stamp, as excess paint can collect in gaps and bleed into your design. Using a different brush for each stamp will prevent the colors from being contaminated.

4 TESTING THE STAMP Draw border guidelines on your test piece of cardboard and practice stamping the colors on it to help you work out a pleasing arrangement for your design (above). This example features the green Crispy Lettuce for one stamp at the top of the border and the yellow Bright Chartreuse for another at the bottom. A third stamp between the first two uses the green for the sun's corona and the green-yellow blend for the core.

5 STAMPING THE PATTERN Load up the stamp with your first color and discharge the excess on the piece of cardboard. Beginning at one end of the wall, center the stamp between the first two vertical lines, directly under the upper guideline. Press the stamp onto the surface. Repeat between the third and fourth vertical lines, allowing a 4-inch space between the two impressions (above). Continue stamping until you reach the opposite end of the wall.

6 COMPLETING THE PATTERN Align the stamps of the bottom row directly below those of the upper row, positioning them the same distance from the lower guideline. Center the stamps of the middle row horizontally and vertically from the stamps of the top and bottom rows. Remember to load up the stamp (above) and blot the excess each time you use the stamp.

TIPS

Stamping a border for a whole room requires surprisingly little paint. Eight ounces or a half pint of each color will be sufficient for an average-size room (10 by 12 feet).

❖

Stamping with water-base paint and glaze is very forgiving. Keep a clean, damp rag on hand, and you'll be able to "erase" mistakes.

❖

Coat a piece of cardboard with your base color. You'll use it for testing your stamps in step 4.

stenciling

Stencils can bring a touch of Victorian elegance to a dining room, a sense of fun and whimsy to a child's bedroom, or a taste of homespun Americana to an otherwise ordinary kitchen. A border is the most popular form of stencil application, and many stencils are specifically designed for this purpose—including the one shown here. In this project, three stencils make up the complete image; each one is numbered according to the order of its application. Many stencil packages suggest a color palette, but you may opt for changes depending on the color of the base coat. Here, the pebbled effect of the stencil brush work complements a sponged-on application. Because the stencil requires very little paint, artist's colors sold in tubes can be used. Acrylic rather than oil is preferable since quick drying time speeds the application of overlapping motifs. Interior latex paint, used in this project, is also suitable.

MATERIALS

- ❖ Lowe's American Tradition paints, satin finish: 293-1 Vanilla Wafer (base coat; 293-2 Pekin (sponged on); 293-3 Golden Den, 293-5 Covered Wagon, 295A-3 Autumn Wheat, 295A-5 Oak Root, 341-2 London Smoke, 341-4 Bewitch, 285-5 Mistletoe Kiss (stenciled on)
- ❖ Stencil Decor 26727 Townhouse Row

TOOLS

- ❖ Low-tack masking tape
- ❖ Release tape
- ❖ Carpenter's level
- ❖ Hobby knife
- ❖ Stencil brushes
- ❖ Artist's brush
- ❖ Mixing containers
- ❖ Plastic tray
- ❖ Drop cloth
- ❖ Latex gloves

1 POSITIONING THE FIRST STENCIL Mark reference points along the surface at the desired height of the stenciled border with a carpenter's level. Lay low-tack masking tape along the points as a guideline. Check each stencil closely; use a hobby knife to clear any portion of the pattern that is stamped but not cut out completely. Start the stenciled border at a conspicuous spot—such as the edge of a central window. Line up the lower edge of the first stencil with the guideline and secure the stencil along the upper edge with release tape (above).

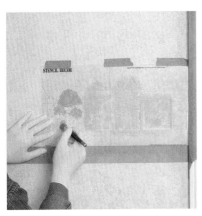

2 APPLYING THE PAINTS In this project, the first stencil calls for four colors. Lay out the colors in separate containers together with a stencil brush for each color and a plastic tray. Paint the cutouts as much as possible in sequence to avoid missing one. Using a circular motion, swirl the brush in the color, then blot excess off onto the tray—the brush should be almost dry. Lightly pounce the brush into the cutout (above), being careful not to touch areas assigned to another color. Vary the angle of the brush to achieve a textured, pebbly effect, allowing some of the base color to show through.

3 REPOSITIONING THE STENCIL Continue the full length of the border with the first stencil; mistakes are easier to make if you switch to the second and third stencil in order to complete one section at a time. Remove the stencil and reposition it along the guideline, matching up the register marks on the stencil with the pattern painted on the surface (above). Apply paint to the cutouts, then reposition the stencil and continue.

5 APPLYING SUBSEQUENT STENCILS Two stencils complete the border image. Match up the registration marks on the second stencil with the pattern painted at your starting point; secure the stencil with tape. The colors for the second and third stencils are successively darker tones of those for the first stencil, so brushes can be wiped—not washed—and assigned to the next closest color. Because the second and third stencils add details, apply slightly more brush pressure than with the first to create a more opaque surface (above). Complete applications of the second stencil, then apply the third stencil.

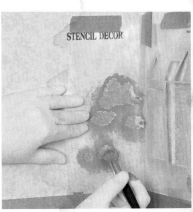

4 HANDLING CORNERS Chances are the full pattern of the stencil won't fit onto one surface at a corner. Fortunately, an acetate stencil is flexible enough for the pattern to be applied on both sides of the corner without a visible break. Register the stencil with the pattern painted and tape this side of the stencil in place. Gently press the stencil into the corner, bending but not creasing it, and tape the other side in place. Apply paint to the cutouts, working as far into the corner as possible (above); slight gaps can be touched up later.

6 MAKING FREEHAND TOUCHUPS Correct errors and fill in gaps after completing applications of the stencils. Many stencils have uncut sections, called bridges, to hold a pattern together; the gaps left will need to be filled in. With an artist's brush, also fill in where cutouts were missed (above) or details need sharpening. Work with an almost dry brush and pounce the surface lightly.

sponging on

Sponging on is a quick and easy painting technique that is surprisingly versatile. Sponges were once living creatures and therefore unique, so examine each one closely before making your selection. Those with a varied, porous surface will create the most dramatic effects. Working with two or three different sponges will avoid a repetitive pattern. The technique, though, depends on more than just the sponge. It is the paint and glaze mixture that helps create the transparent effect, allowing the base color to come through. In a successful sponging-on project, impressions of the sponge itself should disappear in a textured uniformity. Choosing colors of contrasting hues can create dramatic effects, but results are often difficult to achieve since inevitable imperfections are more eye-catching. A safer approach is to choose paints from the same color family. The two American Tradition paints used in this project are from one panel of six paint chips, each separated by two yellows of successively darker tones.

MATERIALS

❖ Lowe's American Tradition paints, satin finish: 230A-4 Summer Haze (base coat); 230A-1 Blazing Star
❖ Valspar translucent pearl glaze

TOOLS

❖ Faux Creations Atlantic sea sponge
❖ Plastic paint tray
❖ Stirring sticks
❖ Mixing containers
❖ Release tape
❖ Drop cloth
❖ Plastic bucket
❖ Latex gloves

1 PREPARING THE SPONGE Complete the base coat and allow it to dry for the recommended time: two days for latex paint; two to three days for alkyd paint. Tape off adjacent ceiling, woodwork, and wall surfaces you don't wish to paint. Prepare a mixture of equal parts paint and glaze—32 ounces 2 pints) for an average-size room (10 feet by 12 feet). Pour some of the mixture into a paint tray, then dip the sponge into the mixture and blot it (above). The ideal sponge for pouncing is loaded without its pores being clogged. An overloaded sponge will leave thick, wet prints.

2 POUNCING THE SURFACE Work end to end across the surface in sections from top to bottom so drips are covered and don't run into completed areas. Pounce the surface with the sponge at varying angles, making light hand gestures and moving your wrist from side to side (above). Leave large spaces between pounces at the outset when the sponge is fully loaded. Fill in spaces and even out effect intensities as the sponge becomes less saturated. Don't overdo the pouncing: Allow about 50 percent of the base color to show through.

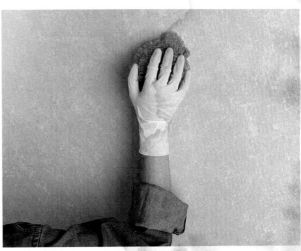

3 FILLING IN AND BLENDING Once the surface is completed, stand back and look for gaps and uneven areas. Fill in the gaps and blend in the uneven areas with an almost dry sponge—adding too much paint risks creating an unwanted contrast. Pounce lightly with the sponge without overlapping covered areas (above) to avoid increasing their intensity.

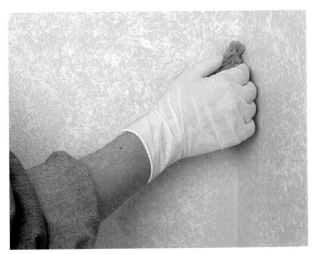

4 HANDLING CORNERS AND EDGES Corners and edges along the ceiling or woodwork can be handled as you go or at the end of the project. Sponges, fortunately, are very flexible and can be torn down to the size needed for these special-attention areas. Tear off a piece of sponge about 3 inches in diameter and pounce as much as possible into the corner (above) or along the edge. Tear off a smaller piece to pounce spots not reached with the larger piece. Blot the pieces well so some of the base color shows through.

TIPS

If the sponge becomes tacky or clogged, rinse it in warm water, then squeeze and pat it dry before resuming.

❖

Fix sponging "errors" with sponged on dabs of the base coat color.

❖

Be careful not to rotate the sponge on the surface, or the glaze will smear.

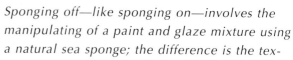

sponging off

Sponging off—like sponging on—involves the manipulating of a paint and glaze mixture using a natural sea sponge; the difference is the texturing with the sponge is done by removing mixture rather than by applying it. Because the mixture is diluted with water, the finished effect of sponging off tends to be more subtle than sponging on. Sponging off registers soft imprints of the sponge. A completed surface appears pebbly and dappled—similar to textured plaster or a sandy beach. Experimenting with contrasting colors is risky, but can result in surprising and dramatic effects. Keeping with colors from the same family ensures easier-to-live-with effects.

MATERIALS

- ❖ Lowe's American Tradition paints, satin finish: 316-2 Martinique Morn (base coat), 316-4 Green Pastures
- ❖ Valspar translucent pearl glaze

TOOLS

- ❖ Faux Creations Atlantic sea sponge
- ❖ Mixing containers
- ❖ Plastic paint tray
- ❖ Stirring sticks
- ❖ Painter's tape
- ❖ 4-inch paint roller
- ❖ 2-inch paintbrush
- ❖ Drop cloth
- ❖ Plastic bucket
- ❖ Latex gloves

2 POUNCING THE SURFACE Dip the sponge into a bucket of cold water and squeeze it drip-dry, then pounce the surface lightly at varying angles (center). Leave large spaces between pounces at the outset when the sponge is fresh. Feather edges and even out effect intensities as the sponge becomes mixture-saturated. The more pouncing you do, the lighter will be the effect. Rinse the sponge and squeeze it drip-dry when it no longer lifts off mixture—two or three times per section. Roll a new section 6 to 12 inches larger or smaller than the first (so the edges of sections won't be noticeable), then pounce with the sponge. Continue in this manner.

1 ROLLING ON THE GLAZE Complete the base coat and allow it to dry for the recommended time: two days for latex paint; two to three days for alkyd paint. Tape off adjacent ceiling, woodwork, and wall surfaces you don't wish to paint. Prepare a mixture of equal parts paint, glaze, and water—32 ounces (2 pints) for an average-size room (10 feet by 12 feet)—and pour some into a paint tray. Working top to bottom from one end of the surface to the other, apply the mixture to a 3-foot-square section. Cut in along edges of the surface with a 2-inch paintbrush, then fill in with a 4-inch paint roller, making crisscross passes to avoid creating noticeable edges that will be difficult blend in (top).

3 HANDLING EDGES AND CORNERS Edges and corners along woodwork or the ceiling can be handled as you go or at the end of the project. Sponges, fortunately, are very flexible and can be torn down to the size needed for these special-attention areas. Tear off a piece of sponge about 3 inches in diameter and pounce as much as possible along the edge (bottom) or into the corner. Tear off a smaller piece to pounce spots not reached with the larger piece. Keep the pieces at a uniform dampness to maintain the consistency of the effect.

refinishing furniture

Stripping painted furniture can reveal concealed treasures. A small table painted years ago for a child's room, for example, can fit your decor elsewhere once the beauty of its natural surface is uncovered and refinished.

Refinishing furniture used to be a messy job. Paint strippers were generally made from chemicals that gave off powerful—and potentially harmful—fumes. You can now buy less toxic but equally effective strippers. Safety remains paramount, however, so keep the following precautions in mind: Only use paint stripper in a well-ventilated area. Wear safety goggles and neoprene rubber gloves.

Once the wood is bare, you have a couple of options. You can stain the piece and follow with a clear protective finish, as shown here, or proceed directly to the clear finish. Bear in mind that a stain doesn't only color the wood. A good-quality stain will also bring out the wood's natural highlights. Either way, all the tools and materials you need for stripping and refinishing your treasure are available at Lowe's.

MATERIALS

- ❖ Citristrip Stripping Gel
- ❖ Citristrip Paint Remover Wash
- ❖ Minwax Wood Stain: Cherry 235
- ❖ Olympic water-based polyurethane, satin finish

TOOLS

- ❖ 180- and 220-grit sandpaper
- ❖ 220-grit waterproof sandpaper
- ❖ 0000-grade steel wool
- ❖ Tack cloth
- ❖ Wooden paint scraper
- ❖ Corner stripping tool
- ❖ Sanding block
- ❖ 2-inch paintbrush
- ❖ Foam applicator
- ❖ Putty knife
- ❖ Neoprene rubber gloves
- ❖ Safety goggles

TIPS

If the piece has multiple layers of paint, you may have to apply several coats of stripper.

1 APPLYING THE STRIPPER Lay a sheet of newspaper or cardboard on your work surface. Wearing neoprene gloves and goggles, use a 2-inch natural-bristle paintbrush to apply a generous coating of stripper to the flat sections of the piece (left). Let the stripper sit on the surface for the time suggested by the manufacturer. While you're waiting for the stripper to "activate," coat another section.

Continued on next page >

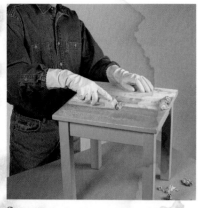

2 SCRAPING OFF THE FINISH Run a wooden paint scraper across the surface to check if the stripper is activated. The paint should bubble and be easy to scrape off. If not, wait a little longer. If the paint comes off easily, work parallel with the wood grain to remove it (above). Continue applying stripper and scraping off the paint.

3 STRIPPING DETAILS AND CORNERS Removing paint from corners and crevices will take a little extra care and requires special tools. With a metal stripping tool, scrape old finish from these areas (above). Avoid gouging the surface. Use a stripping tool with concave edges for rounded surfaces such as chair legs. A nut pick or cuticle stick can be used on carved details.

4 CLEANING THE SURFACE Once most of the paint has been stripped off, remove loosened residue with paint remover wash. Soak the stripping pad supplied with the wash and scrub all surfaces of the piece (above).

5 SANDING THE WOOD Scratches and other signs of wear can usually be corrected with sanding. Hold a lamp or flashlight close to the surface at different angles to better see flaws. Then, fit a sanding block with 180-grit sandpaper and sand the surface at a slight angle to the grain (above). Once the blemishes are gone, go over the surface again with 220-grit paper. Work with the wood grain to achieve a smooth surface. Remove dust with a tack cloth or a soft brush.

6 MAKING SURFACE REPAIRS A gouged or dented surface can be repaired with wood filler. If you plan to stain the piece, chose a stainable filler. Other wood fillers are available in a variety of colors corresponding to the type of wood you are repairing. With a putty knife, apply the filler and spread it evenly (above). Allow the filler to dry for the recommended time, then lightly sand with 220-grit sandpaper. Clean away dust with a tack cloth.

TIPS

In addition to removing stubborn particles of paint, paint remover wash will clean the surface and prepare it for a new finish without raising the grain of the wood.

7 APPLYING THE STAIN Staining a softwood such as pine may require the application of a conditioner before staining, as variances in wood density can cause a stain to penetrate the surface unevenly. If you are unsure whether or not your furniture is softwood, try this little test. In an inconspicuous section, press your fingernail against the surface. If an impression is left in the wood, the piece is definitely softwood and should be treated. Choose a conditioner recommended by the stain manufacturer. Next, apply the stain with a 2-inch natural-bristle brush in even strokes following the wood grain (above). Work from the top of the piece down so you can easily remove drips.

8 WIPING OFF EXCESS STAIN Removing excess stain from a wood surface will help ensure that it colors evenly. Allow the stain to penetrate the wood for the recommended time, then wipe the surface with a clean, soft cloth (above), paying special attention to joints and other areas where stain collects.

9 APPLYING A FINISH Once the stain has dried, apply the finish; use a foam applicator for a water-based polyurethane finish. Hold the applicator almost perpendicular to the surface, starting with grooves and joints, and cover one section at a time. Spread the finish in light, even strokes (above). If any bubbles form, pass an almost dry brush back over the surface. Let the first coat dry for the recommended time.

10 SANDING BETWEEN COATS For best results, apply three coats of finish. Between each coat, lightly scuff the surface to improve adhesion. Regular sandpaper on a finish tends to clog, so use 220-grit waterproof paper. Sand in the direction of the grain (above), then remove the dust with a tack cloth.

adding a wallpaper border

Hanging a wallpaper border is an easy adornment. Borders are available in a wide array of styles and colors. Follow the same techniques for hanging a border as you would for hanging any other wallpaper. Surfaces should be in good condition and clean. A prepasted wallpaper border, such as the one used in this project, is applied simply by soaking it with water. If you are applying a border over an existing wallpaper, coat the surface under the border with an opaque primer-sealer and use vinyl-to-vinyl adhesive to hang it. Wallpaper borders are typically sold in 5-yard spools. To find out how much you need, measure the length of the surface you intend to border and add 10 percent for waste.

MATERIALS

❖ Warner Sculpted Borders Wallpaper SCU-1054F 17830, run B2

TOOLS

❖ Plastic bucket
❖ Sponge
❖ Dishwashing liquid
❖ Carpenter's level
❖ Tape measure
❖ Trimming guide
❖ Utility knife
❖ Wallpaper trough
❖ Smoothing tool
❖ Seam roller

TIPS

Before installing a border over a new wall covering, let the paper dry thoroughly so the weight of the border won't pull it away from the wall.

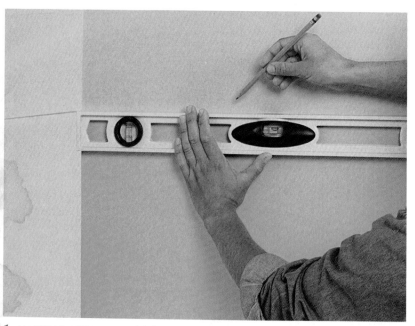

1 MARKING GUIDELINES Make any necessary spot repairs. Wash the surface with a solution of dishwashing liquid and warm water, then rinse it thoroughly and allow it to dry. Draw a reference line along the surface at the desired height of the wallpaper border with a carpenter's level (above).

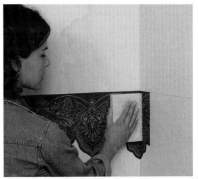

2 PREPARING THE BORDER Cut the border as needed into a manageable 4- to 6-foot strip with a utility knife and a trimming guide. Fill a wallpaper trough about two-thirds full with warm water. Loosely roll the strip paste-side out and immerse it in the water, then allow it to soak for the time specified by the manufacturer. Lift out the strip by the top edge and gently fold it into 6-inch pleats, paste-side to paste-side (above), without making creases. This is called "booking." Then let it sit for the time recommended by the manufacturer.

3 HANGING THE FIRST STRIP Hang the first strip against the frame of a door or window or at an inconspicuous corner. Align the strip with the marked guideline and press it into place. Smooth bumps and wrinkles out of the strip with a smoothing tool (above). If necessary, trim the end of the strip to fit flush using a trimming guide and a utility knife.

4 HANGING AT AN INSIDE CORNER At an inside corner, cut a strip long enough to run an inch or two past the corner. Soak and book the strip, then hang it. Press the strip into the corner with a damp sponge to crease it (above). Hang a strip on the opposite side of the corner so it overlaps and aligns with the pattern of the first. Carefully cut through both strips along the corner with a trimming guide and a utility knife. Lift the second strip to remove the waste pieces, then press it back into the corner.

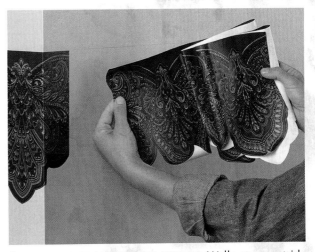

5 DOUBLE-CUTTING SEAMS Ends of strips may be simply butted together, but double-cutting seams ensures a perfect pattern match without a gap. Hang a second strip so it overlaps the first and the patterns are aligned. With a trimming guide and a utility knife, carefully cut through both strips (above). Lift off the end of the second strip and remove the waste pieces, then press it back into place. Wait for the time recommended by the manufacturer, then roll the seam with a seam roller.

6 HANGING AT AN OUTSIDE CORNER Walls at an outside corner are seldom perfectly plumb—if you simply continue around the corner, the border isn't likely to be level on the other side. Double-cutting a seam at the corner ensures the best possible pattern match. Cut the first strip long enough to run an inch or two past the corner and hang it. Hang the second strip on the opposite side of the corner (above) so it overlaps and aligns with the pattern of the first as closely as possible within the marked guideline, then double-cut a seam.

wallpapering below a chair rail

Chair rails give you an opportunity to use two different decorating treatments on the same wall. In this example, the portion above the molding is painted; the section below will be covered with wallpaper. The chair rail can already be in place, as shown here, or be installed afterward. Bear in mind that you can follow these same steps if you want to apply wallpaper to an entire wall that has no chair rail.

Preparation is the key to success with this project. Patch any cracks with spackling compound and sand the patches smooth. Wash the surface with a household cleaner to remove dirt, grease, and mildew. Set up a clean worktable large enough to hold a wallpaper trough, and cut wallpaper strips before you hang them.

Lowe's carries a wide variety of styles and types of wallpaper, including the sample shown here. Two main types of paper are available. Prepasted paper can be soaked in warm water, as in this project, or you can apply an activator. For unpasted papers, you need to brush or roll wallpaper paste onto the back of the paper.

MATERIALS
❖ Village Prepasted Wallpaper 5801866, run No. 3

TOOLS
❖ Hammer
❖ Finishing nail
❖ Plumb bob
❖ 24-inch straightedge
❖ Smoothing tool
❖ Trimming guide
❖ Utility knife
❖ Seam roller

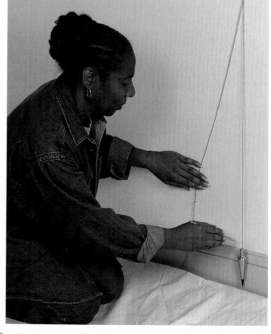

1 LAYING OUT A VERTI-CAL CENTER GUIDELINE Tack a finishing nail to the center of the wall just below the chair rail, then hang a plumb bob from the nail to just below the baseboard. (It's better to work outward from the midpoint of the wall and end with equal strips at each end than to have a full strip at one end and a partial one at the other.) Mark two points on the wall in line with the plumb line (above). Remove the plumb bob and nail, then draw a line between the points with a straightedge. Alternatively, use a carpenter's level to mark a vertical center guideline.

2 CUTTING THE FIRST STRIPS Measure the distance between the chair rail and the baseboard and add about 3 inches. Unroll the wallpaper, pattern side down, and transfer your measurement to the back. Trim the paper with a straightedge and a utility knife (above). This will be the top edge of your first strip. Turn the strip over so the pattern faces up, then unroll the paper for the second strip beside it. Fold back the top edge of the roll so the pattern at the fold aligns with the first strip, then cut the paper at the fold. Cut the second strip to the same length as the first. Cut a third strip as you did the second.

3 ACTIVATING THE ADHESIVE Fill a wallpaper trough about two-thirds full with warm water. Roll up the first strip and set it in the trough, gently pressing down to remove air bubbles. Let the paper soak for the time recommended by the manufacturer. Lift the strip out by its top edge, allowing the water to drip back into the trough (above).

4 BOOKING THE PAPER Before hanging the paper, allow the wet paste to activate for a few minutes . Folding the wet wallpaper over on itself—like a book—will prevent it from drying out during this time. With the strip pattern side down on an absorbent cloth or towel, gently fold each end of the strip to the center, taking care not to crease the paper (above). Cut and book two or three strips before applying them to the wall, arranging them on your work surface in order.

5 HANGING THE FIRST STRIP Once the first strip is ready to be hung, gently lift it by the top edge, keeping the bottom half folded. At the wall, align one edge of the strip with the plumb line and overlap the chair rail by 2 inches. Pass a smoothing brush over the surface (above), creasing the paper at the chair rail. As you reach the middle of the sheet, open the bottom section. Continue smoothing the paper on the wall. When you reach the bottom of the wall, crease the paper at the baseboard, allowing the excess to overlap the molding.

6 TRIMMING THE EXCESS Once the sheet is flat on the wall and the top and bottom are creased, trim the excess. Press a trimming guide into the crease at the baseboard, then cut through the excess with a utility knife (above). Repeat for the crease bordering the chair rail.

7 HANGING SUBSEQUENT SHEETS Hang the second strip, gently butting its edge against the first. Shift the strip up or down as necessary to align the pattern, making sure to overlap the chair rail by about 2 inches. Smooth and trim the paper as you did the first strip. Hang several strips, then smooth the seams with a seam roller (above). Avoid applying too much pressure, or you will force paste out from under the paper. Once all the paper is hung, sponge the surface to remove any excess glue and pat dry with a towel.

covering switch plates and outlets

When you're wallpapering, the cover plates for switches and outlets threaten to stand out and interrupt the continuity of the pattern. The best approach is to proceed with your project, then return and wallpaper the cover plates. Shut off electricity to the switches and outlets before removing the cover plates. With the cover plates out of the way, you can paper over the boxes, then trim the paper neatly along the edges of the boxes. As a final touch, paper the cover plates so the pattern aligns with the surrounding surface.

Lowe's carries several brands and styles of wallpaper, including the pattern shown on these pages. You'll also find all the tools you need for covering walls at Lowe's.

MATERIALS
❖ Sunworthy Wallcoverings DES 1261010, lot E1

TOOLS
❖ Wallpaper scissors
❖ Utility knife
❖ Straightedge
❖ Masking tape

TIPS

When buying wallpaper, remember to get extra for cover plates. Note that the cover plate for a switch is the focus of this project; apply the same procedure for the cover plate of an outlet.

1 REMOVING THE PLATE Turn off the switch, then shut off the electricity to the circuit at the service panel. Next, undo the screws that hold the cover plate in place and take it off (above).

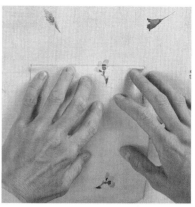

2 CUTTING AROUND THE BOX Apply the paper to the wall, covering the box for the switch. With a utility knife, make diagonal cuts between corners of the box, forming four flaps of wallpaper. Trim the flaps, running the knife blade from corner to corner along the inside edge of the box (above).

3 ROUGH-FITTING THE PATTERN Cut a sheet of wallpaper large enough to cover the switch plate and match the pattern surrounding the switch box. Hold the sheet over the box, align the patterns and lightly mark the sheet with a pencil 1½ inches outside the edges of the box. Cut the sheet at the marks. Position the cover plate on the box and place the sheet over it (above), matching it to the surrounding pattern. Lightly fold the sheet around the back of the top edge of the cover plate.

4 MATCHING THE PATTERN Because the cover plate projects from the wall, you need to adjust the placement of the wallpaper sheet on it slightly to align the patterns perfectly. Position the cover plate and the sheet on the wall and slide the sheet down on the cover plate by about ⅛ inch (above). Once the patterns on the cover plate and wall align, firmly crease the paper across the top, sides and bottom of the cover plate.

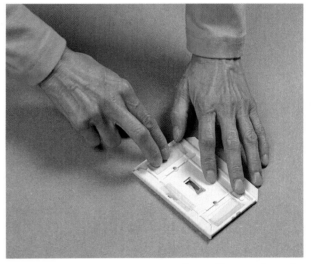

5 TRIMMING THE PAPER FOR THE PLATE Trim the sheet of wallpaper to ½ inch outside the edges of the cover plate. Holding the cover plate and sheet together, outline the opening for the switch toggle on the sheet. Set the cover plate aside and cut diagonally between marked corners of the opening, forming flaps. With wallpaper scissors, trim the corners of the sheet to the creases (above).

6 COVERING THE PLATE Prepare the wallpaper sheet for gluing following the manufacturer's directions, then set it facedown on a work surface. Position the cover plate facedown on the sheet, aligning its edges with the creases. Fold the edges of the sheet onto the back of the plate and secure them with masking tape (above). Tape the flaps around the switch toggle opening the same way. Allow the paper to dry, then pierce holes through the sheet at the cover plate's screw hole locations.

installing running baseboard

Baseboard molding plays a key role in the decorating scheme of many rooms. If the baseboards you have now don't fit into your plans, replacing them with new molding is a relatively straightforward project. Many styles of baseboard, like the type shown here, come with matching corner blocks that greatly simplify running molding around corners. The blocks are installed first, then straight lengths are cut at 90 degrees to fit in between.

For corner blocks made of hardwood, drill pilot holes through the pieces before driving nails, or the wood may split. If you plan to paint your new moldings, apply a coat of primer before installation.

Some baseboard is paired with quarter-round shoe molding, usually nailed to the baseboard or to the floor in front of it. Remove shoe molding first, using the same method shown in step 1.

MATERIALS

❖ Baseboard molding and corner blocks (Profiles, No. L163E, 9⁄16 x 5¼ inch)
❖ Wood shims
❖ 2-inch finishing nails
❖ Latex caulk (Alex Painter's Acrylic Latex Caulk)
❖ Nonshrinking latex hole filler

TOOLS

❖ Utility knife
❖ Putty knife
❖ Pry bar
❖ Hammer
❖ Nail puller
❖ Miter box
❖ Stud finder
❖ Measuring tape
❖ Nail set
❖ Electric drill
❖ Bevel gauge

1 REMOVING OLD BASEBOARD If the baseboard is fused to the wall with layers of paint, cut through the paint between the molding and wall with a utility knife to open a gap large enough for the blade of a putty knife. Slip the knife into the gap near one end of the baseboard and push a wood shim behind the blade to protect the wall. Use a small pry bar to pry the baseboard ½ inch away from the wall. Continue along the wall with the pry bar and shim (above) until you can pull off the entire length of molding. Use a nail puller to remove the nails.

2 PREDRILLING THE OUTSIDE CORNER BLOCKS The outside corner block shown is nailed in place through the front corner. The pilot holes for the nails are best drilled with the corner block clamped facedown to a work surface atop a scrap board. Fit an electric drill with a bit of the same diameter as the nails, then drill two pilot holes straight through the block (above). Guide the drill so the bit exits at the front corner of the block. Locate the holes about an inch from the top and bottom of the block.

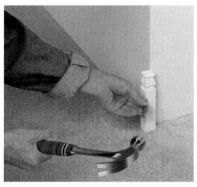

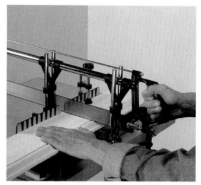

3 FASTENING THE OUTSIDE CORNER BLOCKS Hold the outside corner block in position, making sure it is flat on the floor and flush against both wall surfaces. Drive a finishing nail into each hole to anchor the block to the wall. To avoid marring the wood, leave ¼ inch of the nails protruding, then sink the heads below the surface with a nail set (above).

4 ANCHORING THE INSIDE CORNER BLOCKS Hold an inside corner block in position, then drill two pilot holes through each face of the block, locating them about an inch from the top and bottom and offsetting them as shown. Drive a finishing nail into each hole to anchor the block to the wall, then sink the heads. In case your walls aren't perfectly square, check the angle of the corner blocks before cutting a straight length of baseboard to fit between them. Holding the handle of a bevel gauge against the floor, adjust the blade so it rests flush against the inside corner block (above). Adjust the angle of your miter box to the angle set on the bevel gauge.

5 CUTTING STRAIGHT LENGTHS OF BASEBOARD Measure the distance between the inside and outside corner blocks and transfer your measurement to a straight length of baseboard by marking two cutting lines. With the baseboard face up on the base of the miter box, align one of your cutting marks with the blade and make the cut (above). Measure the angle of the outside corner block, as shown in step 4, adjust the saw accordingly and cut the other end of the baseboard.

6 NAILING STRAIGHT LENGTHS OF BASEBOARD With a stud finder, locate and mark the wall studs along the walls between corner blocks just above where the baseboard will sit. Fasten straight lengths of molding to the wall with a pair of 2-inch finishing nails at each stud mark, locating the nails 1½ inches from the top and bottom edges of the baseboard (above). Sink the nail heads with a nail set.

7 FINISHING THE JOB With a caulking gun and latex caulk, fill any gaps between the baseboard and the wall (above). Conceal the nail heads with a non-shrinking latex hole filler. Let the caulk and filler dry according to manufacturer's directions, use fine sandpaper to smooth them and apply a finish to the baseboard.

TIPS

You can apply a finish to molding either before or after it is installed. If you are planning to wait until after, finish the back face of each piece before starting to keep it from warping.

❖

If you are installing shoe molding, cut it to fit along the bottom edge of the baseboard, making 45 degree cuts at corners. Install shoe molding flush against the baseboard, nailing it to the floor with 2-inch finishing nails 16 inches apart.

installing door trim

Few decorating projects can transform the look of your home's doorways as effectively as replacing the door trim, also known as door casing. If the trim framing your doors is banged up or simply visually uninteresting, removing the old and installing new trim that suits your decorating scheme is easy to carry out.

Lowe's stocks various types and styles of door trim, from simple to ornate. It's a good idea to choose a style and size that complements adjoining baseboards. The trim featured here, for example, comes with plinth blocks for the bottom of the doorway and rosettes for the top that match the trim. Not only do these accents have a traditional Victorian look, the rosettes eliminate the need to make tricky miter cuts at the top corners. Lengths of trim that butt against rosettes can simply be cut at 90 degrees.

The trickiest part of this installation is keeping the trim level and plumb in relation to the door frame. Marking a "reveal" line around the frame (step 2) will give you the same professional advantage that finish carpenters enjoy.

If you are installing hardwood door casing, it's best to predrill pilot holes before driving the nails to prevent splitting the stock. If you plan to paint the trim, apply a coat of primer to the pieces before installation.

MATERIALS

❖ Door trim with rosettes and plinth blocks (Profiles, No. 623, ⁹/₁₆ x 3¼ inch)
❖ 2-inch finishing nails
❖ Spackling compound

TOOLS

❖ Hammer
❖ Safety goggles
❖ Nail puller
❖ Combination square
❖ Utility knife
❖ Putty knife
❖ Small pry bar
❖ Nail set
❖ Adjustable miter saw
❖ Measuring tape

TIPS

To break any paint bond between the old trim and the wall, cut along the seam with a utility knife to open a gap large enough for the putty knife.

1 REMOVING THE OLD TRIM Wearing goggles, pry up the bottom end of a length of side casing with a putty knife and slip in a wood shim. Remove the knife and slip in a small pry bar, using the shim to protect the wall. Pry away the trim, gradually moving upward (above). Pry off the other length of side casing and the head casing the same way. Use a nail puller to remove the nails from the door casing and wall.

2 MARKING THE REVEAL A reveal line serves as a guideline for fastening door casing just inside the door frame, revealing a narrow portion of the frame (typically ¼ inch). Adjust the end of the ruler on a combination square ¼ inch from the handle. Then, holding the handle flush against one side doorjamb and a pencil against the end of the ruler, slide the handle and pencil along the edge of the jamb, marking the reveal line. Mark the head jamb and the other side jamb the same way.

3 INSTALLING THE PLINTH BLOCKS Place one of the pinth blocks on floor, lining up its inside edge with the edge of one side jamb. (Plinth blocks are aligned with the door frame rather than the reveal line.) Drive a 2-inch finishing nail through the block, about 1 inch above the floor, into the jamb. Fasten the three other corners of the block to the wall and doorjamb the same way (above). To avoid marking the block, leave about ⅛ inch of the nails protruding. Then, with a nail set, sink the nail heads just below the surface. Install the other plinth block on the opposite side of the doorway.

4 INSTALLING THE ROSETTES Like the plinth blocks, the rosettes are aligned with the door frame. Position one of the rosettes so it aligns with a top corner of the frame. Drive a 2-inch finishing nail through the bottom corner of the rosette into the jamb. (The three remaining corners will be fastened to the wall in step 5.) Attach the other rosette on the opposite side of the door the same way.

6 INSTALLING THE SIDE CASING Measure and cut lengths of side casing to fit between the rosettes and the plinth blocks. Fix them in place one at a time, aligning their inside edges with the reveal line (above). Nail the side casing to the jambs and wall as you did the head casing. Fill the nail holes with spackling compound, let it dry, and lightly sand. Wipe the trim with a clean, dry rag, then apply a finish to the wood.

5 FASTENING THE HEAD CASING Measure the distance between the rosettes, then transfer the measurement to the casing and cut it in a miter box. Aligning the bottom edge of the head casing with the reveal line along the head jamb, fasten its midpoint to the jamb with a 2-inch finishing nail. Drive two more nails into the trim and jamb, each one about 1½ inches in from the end of the casing. Drive three more nails along the top edge of the casing opposite those along the bottom. Hold each rosette flush against the head casing and fasten its three remaining corners, then sink all the nail heads with a nail set (above).

adding a chair rail

Chair rails were originally installed, mainly in dining rooms, to protect plaster or paneled walls from being dented by chair backs; hence the name. Although chair rails serve a decorative purpose rather than a functional one these days, they generally maintain their traditional profile. A length of flat, thin molding features a rounded projecting element that serves as a bumper for chair backs. Other profiles are available—or you can create your own design by doubling up two styles of chair rail, installing one below the other.

Chair rails can be added to virtually any room of the house. Installed about 36 inches above the floor, chair rails divide walls visually, creating an ideal opportunity to employ two different but complementary wall treatments. Options include painting above the rail and wallpapering below or applying a different paint color on either side of the divide.

Lowe's carries the chair rail featured in this project as well as several other styles. Installation is fairly straightforward. You can pick up all the tools and materials needed for the job at Lowe's.

MATERIALS

❖ Chair rail: Profiles No. 310, ¹¹⁄₁₆ x 2⅝ inch
❖ Interior primer
❖ 2-inch finishing nails
❖ Wood filler

TOOLS

❖ Chalk line
❖ Carpenter's level
❖ Backsaw and miter box
❖ Hammer
❖ Nail set
❖ Stud finder

TIPS

If you plan to paint or finish the chair rail after installation, coat the back face beforehand. This will prevent the molding from warping.

❖

For an outside corner, the front face of the molding will be longer than the back; for an inside corner, the front face is shorter. Set the direction of the saw blade accordingly.

❖

For hardwood molding, drill pilot holes through the chair rail before driving the nails.

1 PRIMING THE TRIM You can paint or finish chair rail before or after installing it. If you plan to cover the molding before installation, apply an even coat of finish with a brush about the same width as the chair rail (above). Allow the pieces to dry.

2 LAYING OUT LEVEL GUIDELINES Measure up 36 inches from the floor at both ends of each wall and mark your measurements on the walls. For each wall, drive a finishing nail into the wall at one of the marks, then hook the end of a chalk line to the nail. Extend the line to the other mark and snap a chalk line on the wall. With a carpenter's level, check that the chalk lines are level (above). If not, draw a level line above or below the chalk lines using the top edge of the level as a straightedge.

3 MARKING THE WALL STUDS Chair rail should be fastened to wall studs, which are typically spaced at 16-inch intervals. Locate the studs with a stud finder. For the electronic type shown, pass the device back and forth on the wall. The light at the top will indicate when the stud finder crosses the edges of a stud. Mark the center of each stud—about ¾ inch from the edges—on the guidelines.

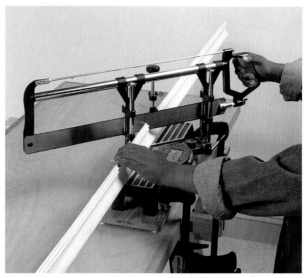

4 MITERING THE TRIM For chair rail trim with a simple profile—like the style shown here—the pieces can be joined at corners with miters. For each wall, measure the distance between the corners, then transfer your measurement onto the back face of the molding. Set the chair rail upright in a miter box with the back face of the molding flush against the fence. Adjust the blade angle for a 45 degree cut and saw the chair rail (above).

5 FASTENING THE TRIM Position the trim on the wall, aligning the top edge with the guideline and mitered ends with corners. Test-fit the corner joints—you may have to sand the mitered ends to close gaps. Fasten the chair rail to the wall with a pair of 2-inch finishing nails at each stud mark, locating the nails ½ inch from the top and bottom edges of the trim (above). To avoid marring the wood, leave ¼ inch of the nails protruding, then sink the heads below the surface with a nail set.

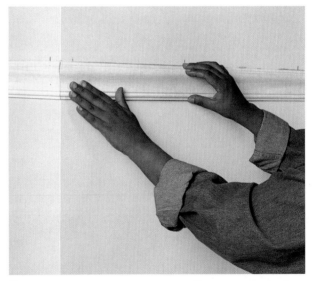

6 LOCKING OUTSIDE MITER JOINTS To ensure a snug fit at outside corners (above), drill a pilot hole for a 1¼-inch finishing nail through the joint from each side of the corner, then drive in the nails. Sink the nails and fill all the holes with wood filler.

making a plate rack

A plate rack enables you to display dishware, rather than stack plates unseen in a cabinet.

A plate rack is essentially a wall-mounted shelf. A decorative accent railing is anchored around the perimeter of the shelf, allowing the plates to be displayed upright.

Plate racks aren't readily available "off the shelf," but crafting your own is quite easy. The rack featured in this project was made with 1 by 4 oak and decorative accent railing available in oak or maple in lengths of 2, 4, 6, and 8 feet. Lowe's carries both as well as all the other tools and materials required for this project.

The plate rack shelf in this example is cut 24 inches long, but whatever the length of yours, the plates will be heavy so it's best to secure the shelf brackets to wall studs, which are located at 16-inch intervals. Also make sure the shelf is level. For best results, work with a level—don't try to level the shelf by eye.

MATERIALS

- ❖ 1x4 oak
- ❖ Decorative shelf brackets
- ❖ Kok's Woodgoods Decorative Accent Railing GR-48 oak
- ❖ Wood filler
- ❖ Wood plugs
- ❖ ¾-inch finishing nails
- ❖ 1½-inch No. 6 wood screws

TOOLS

- ❖ Backsaw and miter box
- ❖ Tape measure
- ❖ Corner clamps
- ❖ Electric drill
- ❖ Hammer
- ❖ Nail set
- ❖ Stud finder
- ❖ Carpenter's level

1 CUTTING THE RAILING Cut the shelf to the desired length, then make two marks on the railing, each mark centered between two spindles, that will leave it ½ inch shorter than the shelf. Set the railing upright in a miter box with one side flush against the fence, adjust the blade angle for a 45 degree cut, and saw the railing at one of the marks (above). Miter the railing at the other mark the same way. Cut two more lengths of railing, each one ¼ inch shorter than the width of the shelf, mitering one end of each piece at 45 degrees.

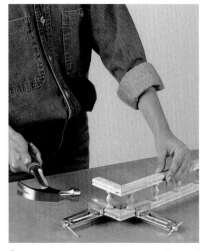

2 ASSEMBLING THE RAILING Spread wood glue on all the mitered ends of the lengths of railing, and assemble each corner in a corner clamp. Then drill a pilot hole for a ¾-inch finishing nail through each corner and drive a nail into each hole (above). Countersink the nails with a nail set, then conceal the nail heads with a wood filler that matches the color of the rail. Once the glue is dry, remove the clamps.

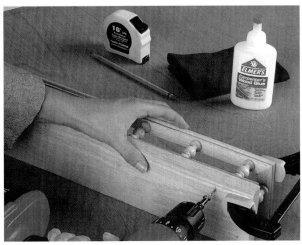

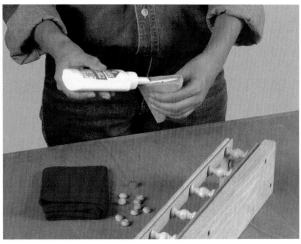

3 ATTACHING THE RAIL TO THE SHELF Mark light pencil lines at the front corners of the shelf ¼ inch from the edge and ends. Then glue and clamp the assembled railing to the shelf so its edges align with your marks. Turn the shelf on its back edge and, using a tape measure, mark its underside at the midpoint of the front railing piece. Mark two more points 3 inches in from each end of the shelf and two more at the midpoint of each side railing piece. With a combination bit, drill a pilot hole for a 1½-inch No. 6 wood screw into the shelf and railing at each point (above). Drive a wood screw into each hole. Once the glue is dry, remove the clamps.

4 ATTACHING SHELF BRACKETS Position two decorative shelf brackets on the underside of the shelf 16 inches apart and the same distance from the ends of the shelf. Mark the locations of the brackets on the underside and top of the shelf, spread wood glue on one bracket's short edge and reposition it so the long edge is flush with back of the shelf. Glue the other bracket to the shelf the same way (above). Clamp the brackets in place, then drill a pilot hole for a 1½-inch No. 6 wood screw into the top of the shelf at each mark. Drive a screw into each hole, then cover all the screw holes with decorative wood plugs matching the shelf. Once the glue is dry, remove the clamps.

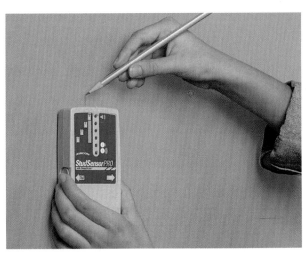

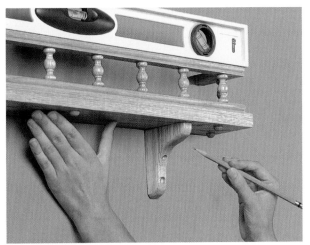

5 MARKING THE WALL STUDS At the location and height of the plate rack, find the nearest wall studs with a stud finder. For the electronic type shown, pass the finder slowly back and forth over the wall. The light at the top will glow when the stud finder crosses the edges of a stud. Mark the center of the stud, about ¾ inch from the edges (above).

6 LEVELING THE PLATE RACK Position the plate rack on the wall so that one of the shelf brackets aligns with a stud mark. With an electric drill, drive one of the wood screws supplied through a predrilled hole in the bracket and into the wall. Then set a carpenter's level on the plate rack railing, level the rack, and mark a line on the wall along the underside of the shelf (above). Remove the level and, with the shelf aligned with the pencil line, drive the three remaining screws through the brackets and into the wall.

installing crown molding

Crown molding is employed to add a formal look to a room, but it once played a practical role by concealing the joint between walls and ceilings. Widths and styles vary from simple flat molding to the more commonly used sprung moldings featured in this project. Wider, more elaborate moldings tend to need larger spaces and higher ceilings to appear well proportioned. For a room with 8-foot-high ceilings, choose a molding that is about 3¼ inches wide.

Crown molding is available in several materials, all suitable for painting, including medium-density fiberboard (MDF) and polyurethane. Unlike wood, these materials will not warp, twist or contain knots. Of course, nothing replaces the natural beauty of wood. The wood molding featured on these pages is made by Profiles (No. L49) and measures ⁹⁄₁₆ x 3¼ inches. This and several other types of crown molding, as well as all the tools and materials required for installation, are available at Lowe's.

MATERIALS
- Crown molding (Profiles, No. L49, ⁹⁄₁₆ x 3¼ inches)
- 1¼-, 2-, and 2½-inch finishing nails
- Wood glue
- Construction adhesive
- Wood filler

TOOLS
- Tape measure
- Carpenter's square
- Chalk line
- Stud finder
- Bevel gauge
- Protractor
- Hammer
- Nail set
- Small putty knife
- Sliding compound miter saw
- Electric drill
- Utility knife

1 MEASURING THE MOLDING PROJECTIONS Before you can install crown molding, you need to determine where the trim will rest on the walls and ceiling. Place a short length of trim against a carpenter's square so one arm of the square represents the wall and the other the ceiling (above). Record the "vertical projection" (how far down the wall the trim will extend) as well as the "horizontal projection" (how far along the ceiling it will extend). For this project, the 3¼-inch-wide molding has vertical and horizontal projections of 2⅜ inches.

2 MARKING THE MOLDING LOCATION Beginning at one corner, measure and mark the vertical projection down from the ceiling on both adjacent walls. Next, measure and mark the horizontal projection on the ceiling. Mark the same measurements at the opposite corners of the room. Attach a chalk line to a small finishing nail driven into the wall at one of the marks. Unwind the chalk line to the mark at the other end of the wall and snap the line. Snap similar guidelines along the other walls and along the ceiling (above). With a stud finder, locate and mark the studs along the top of the walls, marking their locations just above the guidelines. Also locate and mark ceiling joists that lie perpendicular to the walls.

3 CHECKING OUTSIDE CORNERS FOR SQUARE Outside corners are not always 90 degrees—especially in older homes—so a standard 45 degree miter cut won't result in a tight joint if the corners in your home aren't square. This step will help you cut a better-fitting corner joint. Cut a length of molding and hold it along the guidelines, extending it a few inches beyond the corner. Mark a line on the ceiling along the top edge of the trim, extending your line the full length of the piece. Repeat the procedure on the adjacent wall (above), intersecting your first mark.

4 DETERMINING THE MITER ANGLE Use a bevel gauge to measure the angle of the corner and to set up the cutting angle of your saw. Hold the handle of the gauge against one of the walls and open the blade so it aligns with the corner and the point where the lines drawn on the ceiling intersect (above). Lock the angle of the gauge and lay it against the adjustable base of a sliding compound miter saw. Set the base and tilt the blade of the saw to the angle on the bevel gauge.

5 CUTTING THE MOLDING Place the molding upside down on the saw base with the bottom edge—the edge to be installed on the wall—flush against the fence. If the molding will be installed to the left of the corner, place it to the right of the blade. If the trim will be to the right of the corner, set it on the left side of the blade. Holding the molding against the fence with your hands clear of the blade and aligning your cutting mark with the blade, saw the molding (above).

6 FASTENING THE MOLDING IN PLACE Align the molding with the chalk lines and its mitered end with the corner, then fasten it with a 2½-inch finishing nail at each wall stud and ceiling joist. For hardwood, first drill pilot holes through the trim. If the joists run parallel to the wall, fasten the trim to the ceiling with a nail at each end and construction adhesive in between. Spread wood glue on the mitered ends of both lengths of molding, then fasten the second piece (above). Drill a pilot hole for a 1¼-inch finishing nail through the joint from each side of the corner, then drive in the nails. Sink the nails with a nail set as you go.

7 FASTENING TRIM AT AN INSIDE CORNER Adjust the bevel gauge to the angle of the corner, then measure the angle with a protractor. Set the angle of your saw to one-half the angle. Place the molding right side up on the saw base and miter the pieces as in step 5. Fasten the molding in place (above), driving 2½-inch finishing nails into the wall studs and ceiling joists. Use nails and construction adhesive if the joists run parallel to the wall. Sink the nails with a nail set as you go. Fill the nail holes with wood filler if you will be applying a clear finish; use a latex hole filler if you will be painting the molding.

TIPS

If the wall does measure 90 degrees, you may be able to buy a precut corner piece for your style of molding.

❖

Join two lengths of molding along a wall with a scarf joint. Cut the contacting ends of the two pieces at 45 degrees in a miter box, making the cuts in opposing directions so that the joint will be invisible when the molding is installed.

installing decorative wall shelves

Decorative wall shelves are a traditional favorite for displaying anything from books to bric-a-brac, giving your walls an attractive focal point. Installing shelving isn't a complicated job, but there are a few pitfalls to avoid. Number one: Be sure to provide adequate support. It's best to secure shelf brackets to wall studs, which are located at 16-inch intervals. If, as in this project, the brackets are installed less than 16 inches apart, fasten one to a stud and the other to the wall with a plastic wallboard anchor. Number two: Make sure the shelf is level. For best results, work with a level—don't try to eyeball the height of the shelf brackets.

This project features a rectangular "trophy shelf," but Lowe's carries many other styles of decorative shelving, including semicircular corner shelves.

MATERIALS
❖ Lewis Hyman trophy shelf supplied with brackets and fasteners (1½-inch wood screws)
❖ Plastic wallboard anchor

TOOLS
❖ Stud finder
❖ 2-foot level
❖ 24-inch metal ruler
❖ Cordless drill

TIPS

The brackets should rest squarely against the wall. If they don't, remove the brackets and readjust the screws, easing them out slightly or driving them deeper into the wall.

❖

A 2-foot level is ideal for leveling short shelving units.

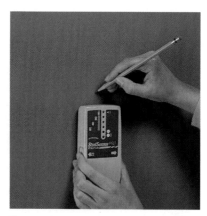

1 MARKING THE WALL STUDS Select the location and height of your shelf, then find the nearest wall studs with a stud finder. For the electronic type shown, pass the finder slowly back and forth over the wall. The light at the top will glow when the stud finder crosses the edges of a stud. Mark the center of the stud, about ¾ inch from the edges.

2 MARKING A LEVEL LINE FOR THE SHELF Place a level against the wall 1 inch below the shelf location, crossing the stud marks. Lightly mark a level line on the wall along the top edge of the level (above).

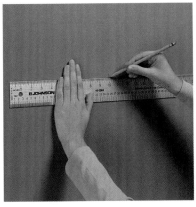

3 MARKING THE FASTENER LOCATIONS For the shelving unit shown here, the brackets are located 10 inches apart, 3 inches in from each end of the shelf. Mark a point on the level line, aligned with a marked stud location. Mark another point 10 inches from the first, again on the level line (above).

4 DRILLING A HOLE FOR THE ANCHOR Choose a plastic wallboard anchor to fit the screws provided with the shelving unit. Fit an electric drill with a bit of the same diameter as the anchor, then drill a hole into the wall at the second point you marked in step 3 (above).

5 INSERTING THE WALLBOARD ANCHOR Insert the plastic anchor into the hole and lightly tap it with a hammer (above) until the sleeve of the anchor is flush with the wall.

6 INSTALLING THE FASTENERS With a screwdriver, fasten one of the screws supplied with the shelving unit into the anchor (above), leaving ¼ inch of the screw projecting from the wall. With the drill, drive a second screw directly into the wall at the marked stud point, again leaving ¼ inch protruding.

7 INSTALLING THE BRACKETS AND SHELF Engage the metal fitting in each shelf bracket with a projecting screw head (above), then tug the brackets downward to secure them.

8 CENTERING THE SHELF Set the shelf on the brackets, centering it in place, so the ends extend past the brackets by about 3 inches (above).

making a fabric picture frame

Fabric frames are a great crafts project that will add personality and zing to your home decor. They also make attractive gifts with a personal touch, allowing you to show off some artistic flair. The double-mat method shown here is a popular framing technique. Three cardboard mats mounted back to back are enveloped in fabric. The outer front mat has a "window" cut out of its middle. Quilt batting gives it about an inch of thickness and quarter-round shoe molding glued around its perimeter lends rigidity. Fabric covers the mat, batting, and molding. The middle mat, wrapped in contrasting fabric, has a window sized to frame the photo or artwork you want to show-case. The middle-mat window should be about an inch smaller all around, than the outer one. The backing mat is left intact and sheathed in the same fabric as the outer mat.

The wood molding and all the tools required for this project are available at Lowe's. You can get the materials at most hobby and fabric stores. Any fabric is fine; this project uses two by Waverly, which has a variety of attractive patterns.

MATERIALS
❖ 2 square yards of fabric
❖ Enough mat board for three 11-x-13-inch mats
❖ 2 square feet of quilt batting
❖ ½-inch quarter-round shoe molding
❖ White arts-and-crafts glue
❖ Clothespins
❖ ¾-inch masking tape

TOOLS
❖ 18-inch metal ruler
❖ Wet square
❖ Backsaw
❖ Miter box
❖ Utility knife
❖ Cutting board
❖ Fabric scissors

1 CUTTING WINDOWS IN THE MATS Begin by cutting all three mats to the same dimensions. Next, place the middle mat on a smooth cutting surface and, with a T square and ruler, measure in from each side to draw guidelines for the window. Size the window to overlap the photo or artwork by about ⅛ inch. Cut out the window along the guidelines with a utility knife and a straightedge (above). Begin the cut in a corner, stopping just short of the next corner. Turn the mat around to cut the next line, starting from the incomplete corner. Cut all four sides in this way. Next, set the middle mat over the outer mat, lining up the sides, and trace the window onto the outer mat. Measure and mark a new guideline 1 inch outside the traced line. Cut out a window in the outer mat the same way as the first.

2 CUTTING THE MAT OUTLINES IN THE FABRIC Lay out the piece of fabric for the middle mat face down on your work surface. Center the mat on the fabric and, with a pencil, trace both the window and perimeter of the mat on the fabric. Set the mat aside. Next, fix ¾-inch masking tape along the inside of the window outline on the fabric and on the outside of the perimeter line (above). Mark a smaller window outline 1 inch in from the inside edge of the tape and cut through the fabric along this outline with fabric scissors. Discard the square of fabric. Next, mark a larger perimeter outline 2 inches outside the tape and, if necessary, cut it out. Discard the fringe of fabric. Repeat to cut the fabric for the outer mat.

3 GLUING THE FABRIC TO THE MIDDLE MAT At each inside corner of the window in the middle-mat fabric, cut at a 45 degree angle from the corner to the masking tape, forming four flaps. Remove the masking tape. With the fabric face down, reposition the mat on it, lining up the mat inside the perimeter tape on the fabric. Apply a zigzag bead of white glue on the mat opposite the fabric flaps (above). Fold the flaps back and press them down on the glue. Hold the flaps in place with masking tape.

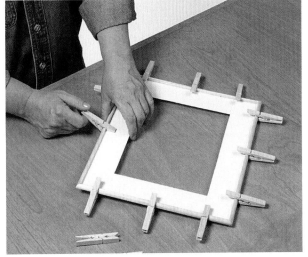

4 GLUING THE OUTSIDE EDGES OF THE FABRIC Apply a bead of glue around the perimeter of the mat, then fold the four outer fabric flaps onto the back of the mat, smoothing them in place. Secure the fabric with masking tape. At each corner, fold the excess fabric over the mat to form a flat triangle. Tape the folded fabric securely in place (above). Set the middle mat aside for now.

5 FASTENING MOLDING TO THE OUTER MAT Measure and mark four lengths of shoe molding to frame the outer mat. Miter the ends of the molding at 45 degree angles with a backsaw and a miter box. Spread glue on the bottom of the molding pieces and position them around the perimeter of the mat. Hold the molding in place with clothespins until the glue dries (above).

Continued on next page >

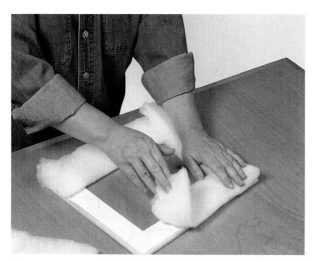

6 GLUING THE BATTING TO THE OUTER MAT Once the glue is dry, remove the clothespins and prepare four strips of batting, cutting them to the same length and twice the width of each side. Apply a zigzag bead of glue along the window border inside the molding. Next, press each section of batting onto the glue covering the border (above). Extend the outside edges of the batting over the molding.

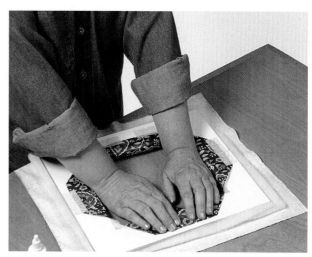

7 ATTACHING THE FABRIC TO THE OUTER MAT Lay the fabric for the outer mat face down and set the outer mat face down on top, aligning its outside edges with the tape outline you put down in step 2. Glue and fold back the inside window flaps (above), taping them in place as you did with the middle mat. Do not attach the exterior sides of the fabric yet.

8 BONDING THE MIDDLE AND OUTER MATS Lay the middle mat face down on the back of the outer one, lining up the mats' outside edges. Apply glue around the perimeter of the middle mat and fold back the fabric of the outer mat onto it, smoothing the flaps over the glue (above). Secure the fabric with tape. When the glue is dry, remove the tape. Fold back the corners as you did with the middle mat fabric and tape them securely in place.

9 ADDING THE PICTURE AND BACKING Trim the fabric for the backing mat to the same size as the fabric for the outer mat. Glue the fabric to the mat as you did for the other mats, omitting window flaps. Next, center the photo or artwork you want to showcase on the back side of the middle mat. Apply a bead of glue along the perimeter of the back of the middle mat, then lay the backing mat over it with the fabric-covered side up, lining up the edges of all three mats (above). Tape the backing mat in place until the glue is dry, then remove the tape. Stitch two hanger rings to the fabric on the back of the mat, placing them about 2 inches in from the top and each side. Attach picture wire between the hangers.

making a frame with a removable back

A home never seems to have enough picture frames. The build-it-yourself wood frame featured here has a removable back, which makes it easy to change "exhibits." If your household has artistic youngsters with prolific output, this is the project for you. Rabbets cut along the inside edges of the frame pieces enable the plastic front, cardboard back, and artwork to be slipped in and out. Plastic strips that hold everything in place pivot out of the way.

You'll need a router to cut the rabbets as well as to round over the edges of the frame pieces. A miter box is a must for cutting the angled corners of the frame. With a little woodworking skill and the step-by-step instructions that follow, you can execute this project confidently.

The frame can be any size that suits your decor. The top and bottom frame pieces are cut 11¾ inches long, and the sides measure 15½ inches, yielding a frame with inside dimensions of 8 by 12 inches. All the lumber, tools, and other materials for this project are available at Lowe's.

MATERIALS
- ❖ 1-x-2-inch pine
- ❖ ⅛-inch acrylic plastic
- ❖ ⅛-inch cardboard
- ❖ ½-inch quarter-round shoe molding
- ❖ 1½-inch No. 8 wood screws
- ❖ ¼-inch wood plugs
- ❖ Wood glue
- ❖ Olympic Interior water-based polyurethane satin finish
- ❖ Pivoting clips
- ❖ Eye hooks
- ❖ Picture wire

TOOLS
- ❖ Router
- ❖ Miter saw
- ❖ Electric drill
- ❖ Screwdriver
- ❖ Measuring tape
- ❖ Miter clamps and quick-action clamps
- ❖ Sander

TIPS

If you make your cutting marks on the rabbeted edge of the frame pieces, the distance between the marks on each piece will equal the inside dimensions of the frame. In this example, the marks would be 8 inches apart on the top and bottom pieces and 12 inches apart on the sides.

Continued on next page >

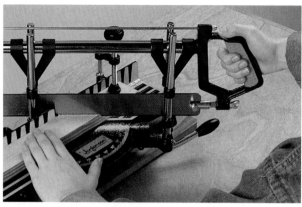

1 RABBETING THE FRAME PIECES Cut the four frame pieces a little longer than their finished lengths, then secure one of them atop a scrap board to a work table. Fit a router with a piloted rabbeting bit sized to cut a ⅜-inch-wide swath. Adjust the bit's cutting depth to the combined thickness of the plastic, cardboard back, and artwork—in this case, ¼ inch. Gripping the router firmly in both hands, set its base plate on the board at one end and guide the bit into the edge of the piece. Keeping the bit's pilot bearing pressed against the wood, feed the router at a slow, steady pace along the edge of the board (above) until you reach the other end. Rabbet the other three pieces the same way.

2 MITERING THE FRAME PIECES Mark the frame pieces to their finished lengths, then set one of them rabbeted side down in a miter box, aligning a cutting mark with the saw blade. Adjust the cutting angle to 45 degrees, then make the cut (above). Miter the other end of the piece, angling the saw 45 degrees in the opposite direction. Cut the remaining boards the same way.

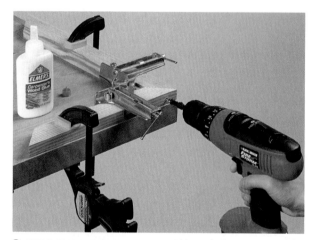

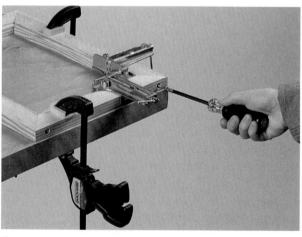

3 REINFORCING THE CORNERS Although the corners of the frame are glued together, screws will strengthen the connections. Apply wood glue to the contacting ends of the bottom and one side piece, and assemble the corner in a miter clamp, making sure the rabbets in the two pieces are in contact. Clamp the assembly to the table and drill a hole into the edge of the bottom piece 1 inch from the corner, using an electric drill fitted with a ⁵⁄₁₆-inch combination bit (above). This special bit produces a pilot hole for a screw with a wider section at the top for a wood plug. Adjust the bit's stop collar to drill as deep as the length of the screw plus ¼ inch.

4 ASSEMBLING THE FRAME Drive a 1½-inch No. 8 wood screw into the hole you drilled in step 3 so the head sits ¼ inch below the surface of the wood. Remove the pieces from the miter clamp and fasten the top and other side piece together the same way. With opposite corners assembled, join the remaining two corners one at a time (above).

5 CONCEALING THE SCREW HEADS
Dab the ends of four ¼-inch wooden plugs with wood glue, then insert one into each hole in the frame (above). With a hammer, gently tap the plugs in place, taking care not to mar the frame. With a sanding block fitted with 80- or 100-grit paper, sand the plugs flush with the surface.

6 ROUNDING THE OUTSIDE OF THE FRAME Clamp the frame face up to the table and fit the router with a piloted rounding-over bit. Set the depth for a shallow cut. With the bit clear of the wood, hold the router base plate on the frame and guide the bit into outside edge of the stock. With a slow, steady movement, guide the router counterclockwise along the edge of the frame, keeping the pilot bearing against the wood (above). Reposition the frame on the table as necessary.

7 ROUNDING THE INSIDE EDGES
With the same bit in the router, round over the inside edges of the frame. Follow the same procedure as for the outside edges, except that you should feed the router in a clockwise direction (above).

8 FINISHING THE FRAME To protect the frame, it's a good idea to add a finish to the wood. A clear furniture finish will fit the bill without altering the wood's natural color. For this project, Olympic Interior water-based polyurethane satin finish was used. Lightly sand the front and sides of the frame, then wipe the surface with a clean, dry cloth. Apply the finish with a foam applicator or a small synthetic-bristle paintbrush (above). Allow the finish to dry for the time recommended by the manufacturer before applying a second coat.

9 ADDING PIVOTING STRIPS AND EYE HOOKS When the final finish coat is dry, set the frame face down. At the midpoint of each frame piece, drive the screw of a plastic pivoting strip into the frame ¼ inch from the rabbeted edge (above). The strips will hold the backing, artwork, and plastic in place, and can be swiveled aside to remove the backing and artwork. Next, fasten an eye hook to each side piece about 3 inches below the top and 1 inch from the outside edge. Braid picture wire between the eye hooks. Place the sheet of acrylic plastic against the frame, cut to fit snugly in the rabbets. Add the artwork and the cardboard backing.

installing blinds

The horizontal vinyl blinds shown in this project are an ideal complement to a modern or contemporary decor. They also enhance the comfort of your home. Their adjustable slats enable you to control the amount of light entering a room.

Blinds are available in a range of materials including wood, polyvinyl chloride (PVC), vinyl, and aluminum. The slats come in a variety of widths, from less than an inch to 2 inches wide. Lowe's carries a wide choice of blinds, including those featured here.

Whichever type you choose, the installation steps will likely follow those pictured here. Once you've purchased blinds that fit your measurements, mounting brackets are anchored to the window frame and a head rail that holds the blinds is attached to the brackets. Hold-downs anchor the bottom of the blinds.

There are two ways to measure for blinds: inside or outside mount. Inside-mounted blinds, as shown here, are secured to the inside of the window frame. On an outside mount, the brackets holding the head rail are attached to the window trim or, if the window has no trim, a few inches out from the window. Take careful measurements before installing your blinds, then take your measurements to Lowe's. They will cut your blinds to the size you need.

MATERIALS

❖ Levolor Custom Size 1"
  Premium Vinyl Mini-Blinds,
  Dover 15184, 27" x 64"

TOOLS

❖ Tape measure
❖ Screwdriver
❖ Electric drill

1 MEASURING FOR AN INSIDE MOUNT Measure the distance between the side jambs of the window frame at three locations: the top, bottom, and middle (left). Record the smallest measurement. Also measure the height of the window at three spots: the middle and each side. Record the largest measurement. Take your measurements to Lowe's; they'll cut blinds to fit.

2 MEASURING FOR AN OUTSIDE MOUNT Measure the width of the window in three places as you would for an inside mount, but include the window's side casing on both sides in your measurement (above). If your window has no trim, measure the width of the window and add a few inches on each side. Measure the window's height in three spots, adding a few inches at the top for the mounting hardware and at the bottom for blocking light.

3 INSTALLING THE MOUNTING BRACKETS Hold one of the brackets supplied in position and mark its screw holes. For the inside mount shown here, position the bracket flush with the upper front corner of the window frame. Drill a pilot hole for the screws supplied at each mark and secure the bracket in place (above). Install the other bracket the same way at the opposite corner of the frame.

4 INSTALLING THE HEAD RAIL Insert the blinds into their brackets on the head rail, then hang the rail on the mounting brackets. Lock the rail in place following the manufacturer's instructions; in this case, you need to slide the face plate at each end of the rail into its bracket (above).

5 INSTALLING THE VALANCE Snap the valance into place on one side of the rail, lining up the ends of the valance and rail, and use a pencil to mark the excess valance at the opposite end of the rail. Cut the valance to length with scissors or a utility knife and install it on the head rail (above).

6 INSTALLING HOLD-DOWN CLIPS Position one of the hold-down clips in line with the blinds at the desired height on a side jamb of the window frame. In this example, the clip is positioned about 2 inches above the bottom of the window. Mark the clip's screw holes, drill a pilot hole for the screws provided at each mark, and fasten the clip to the jamb (above). Attach the other clip at the same height to the opposite side jamb.

TIPS

Wider blinds may come with a center bracket. Attach it to the head frame of the window midway between the end brackets.

installing
shutters

Interior shutters with movable louvers lend windows a traditional charm and are a practical and visually appealing way to control the light coming into a room. The type of shutters featured in this project are made of vinyl, yet appear to be painted wood. The main benefits of vinyl shutters over wood are that they will not warp or need painting.

Lowe's carries a number of types of louvered window shutters, including these café-style units, which cover the entire width of the window and about half its height. Also known as single-hung shutters, they feature four hinged panels that can be fastened together at the middle. These shutters can be installed inside or outside the window frame. Take your choice into account when measuring the window opening. Shutters are available in a range of sizes to fit snugly in standard-size window frames. If your window frame doesn't fit the standard exactly, don't despair. You can buy shutters that are up to 2 inches narrower than your window opening and use filler strips, sold separately at Lowe's, to extend the width of the shutters. The strips are attached to the shutters on one side and to the window frame on the other. Steps for preparing and using these strips are included here.

MATERIALS
❖ Basic Blindz Colonial
  Interior Shutter Set, 27" x 28"
❖ Filler strips

TOOLS
❖ Tape measure
❖ Backsaw and miter box
❖ Electric drill
❖ Screwdriver

TIPS

When drilling a pilot hole, use a bit slightly smaller than the screw you'll be driving.

1 MEASURING THE WINDOW OPENING Before shopping for shutters, measure the width of your window (above), taking measurements from the inside or the outside face of the frame—depending on where you prefer to hang the shutters. Take measurements at several heights; your frames may be slightly out of square. Record the narrowest result. Also measure the height of the window. If you will be using filler strips to install the shutters, trim the strips (step 2). Otherwise, proceed to step 3.

2 TRIMMING THE FILLER STRIPS Sold in 8-foot lengths, the filler strips must be cut to the same length as the height of the shutters. Measure the height of the shutters, transfer the measurement to a strip, and make the cut in a miter box set for 90 degrees (above). Cut a second strip the same way.

3 MARKING THE HANGING STRIP LOCATIONS The shutters come with two hanging strips that are fastened to the window frame; the shutters are then hinged to the strips. Position one of the hanging strips on edge against the window frame with its hinges facing out. Hold the strip about ¼ inch off the bottom of the frame so that the shutters can open and close without binding. With a pencil, mark the strip's two screw holes on the window frame (above). Repeat for the second hanging strip on the other side of the window. If you are using filler strips, prepare them (step 4). Otherwise, proceed to step 5.

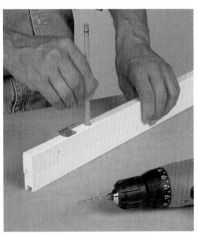

4 PREPARING THE FILLER STRIPS Engage one of the cut filler strips with the edge of one of the hanging strips. With the ends of the two strips aligned, mark the hanging strip screw holes on the filler strip (above). Slide the strips apart, then drill a pilot hole for the screws through the filler strip at each mark. Repeat for the second filler strip.

7 HANGING THE SHUTTERS Install the shutter panels one at a time, starting with one that has hinges on both sides. Engage its hinge pins with the cylinders on the hanging strip, making sure the notch on the louver tilt stick at the center of the panel is at the top. Hang a middle panel—one with hinges on just one edge—on the first panel (above). Hang the two remaining panels on the hanging strip on the other frame, then cover all the screw holes with the plugs supplied. Finally, fasten the knobs and latch to the middle panels using the screws supplied.

5 DRILLING HOLES IN THE WINDOW FRAME At each mark you made in step 3, drill a pilot hole for the screws supplied into the window frame (above).

6 FASTENING THE STRIPS TO THE WINDOW If you are using filler strips, reengage them with the hanging strips. Then, holding one of the strips in position on the window frame so its screw holes are aligned with the pilot holes on the frame, drive the screws to fix the strip to the frame (above). Fasten the other strip to the frame.

installing rods and hardware

Hanging window treatments is one of the simplest decorating projects you can undertake. But the payoff from dressing up an ordinary window with a little color and texture can be startling.

Perhaps the most challenging part of the job is choosing hardware of the appropriate size and style. That's why it is crucial to measure the window before buying materials. Curtains typically look best when they span just beyond the window casing. As for length, they can hang to the window sill or almost to the floor—or a point somewhere in between. Take your measurements to Lowe's—they'll help you select from among a range of ready-made window treatments and make sure you go home with the suitable hardware.

Whichever type or style of curtains and hardware you choose, installation generally follows the steps shown here. Brackets are mounted to the wall on each side of the window casing. The brackets (along with a center support) hold up a curtain rod, which in turn supports the curtains. For curtains that come with a valance, a valance rod completes the installation. Be sure to follow all the manufacturer's instructions.

MATERIALS

- Graber Structures™ 2½-inch Dauphine® Wide Pocket Rod & Curtain Rod Combination
- Designables™ Heather swag set and valance

TOOLS

- Tape measure
- Stud finder
- Screwdriver
- Electric drill
- Carpenter's level

1 MEASURING THE WINDOW WIDTH Although you can mount hardware right onto window casing, it's best to attach the brackets to the wall slightly outside and above the head casing. Measure the length of the head casing—including any rosettes (above)—and add 2 to 5 inches to the measurement. This extra width will ensure that the edges of the curtains won't be visible from outside. When shopping for window-treatment hardware, make sure the type you buy is adjustable to your final measurement.

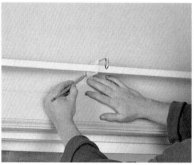

2 MEASURING THE WINDOW HEIGHT
To determine the length of curtains required, measure from the point where you want them to fall to the point where you plan to fasten the wall brackets—in this case, a few inches above the head casing (above).

3 INSTALLING THE WALL BRACKETS Hold one wall bracket in position—in this example, 2 inches outside and 4 inches above the head casing—and mark its screw holes. If there is a wall stud in line with the marks—use a stud finder to check—drill a hole for the screws supplied and attach the bracket (above). If there is no stud, drill a hole for the toggle bolts supplied and use them to fasten the bracket to the wall. With a carpenter's level, mark a level line across the wall from the top edge of the bracket to the other bracket location. Align the second bracket with the line and fasten it to the wall.

4 INSTALLING THE CENTER SUPPORT Hook the curtain rod onto the center support and snap the rod into place on the wall brackets. These wall brackets feature three fittings that enable you to hang the curtain rod at three different heights. Chose the height that best suits your decor. Use the tape measure to position the center support midway between the wall brackets. Then, mark the center support's fastener holes (above). Remove the curtain rod and secure the center support with the fasteners supplied.

5 HANGING THE CURTAINS Feed the curtains onto the curtain rod (above). Snap the rod into place on the wall brackets and center support.

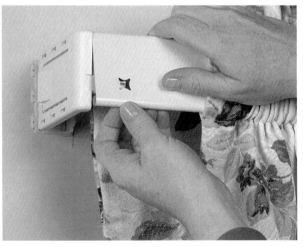

6 INSTALLING THE VALANCE ROD With the curtains in place, snap the end brackets supplied into the wall brackets so that they project the same distance from the wall as the center support. Feed the fabric onto the valance rod following the manufacturer's instructions, then hook the valance rod on the center support and snap the rod into place on the end brackets (above).

staining a wood floor

Refinishing a hardwood floor can transform the look of your entire home. Before you embark on this project, however, keep in mind that the condition of the floor will determine how much work you need to do. If the damage is limited to surface scratches, the floor can be sanded with a pad or vibrating sander before you refinish. But if the surface is painted or badly damaged, it will need three sanding passes with a drum sander and an edger.

Before renting a drum sander, check the thickness of the flooring. Hardwood flooring is usually ¾ inch thick and can be sanded several times. Thinner floors (½ or ⅜ inch thick) must be sanded carefully, as sanding can eventually damage boards or wear down to the nails. Once you've decided to go ahead, buy your floor stain and finish before sanding—you should apply them as soon as the sanding is done to keep the exposed wood from absorbing moisture.

Although both oil- and water-base stains and finishes are available, water-base products are generally preferred because of their quicker drying time and because, unlike oil products, they don't give off solvent fumes.

MATERIALS
❖ Sanding sheets and discs in 36-, 50-, and 80-grit
❖ Plastic sheeting
❖ Release tape
❖ Olympic Fruitwood stain
❖ Olympic polyurethane satin floor finish

TOOLS
❖ Dust mask
❖ Safety goggles
❖ Ear protectors
❖ Rubber gloves
❖ Pry bar
❖ Hammer
❖ Nail set
❖ Rental drum sander and edger
❖ Orbital sander
❖ Rental floor polisher
❖ Measuring tape
❖ 3-inch synthetic paintbrush
❖ Foam finish applicator
❖ Rags
❖ Vacuum cleaner

TIPS

Protruding nail heads are a problem, as they can tear sandpaper and cause damage to a drum sander. Inspect the floor closely and sink the heads of any protruding nails at least ⅛ inch below the floor surface with a hammer and nail set.

❖

Keep the sander moving at all times or the drum will gouge the floor.

1 PREPARING THE ROOM
Removing the shoe molding in the room will enable you to sand up to the baseboards or walls. With a pry bar, gently pull away the molding, using a thin wood shim to protect the baseboard and wall (right). Once all the shoe molding has been removed, prepare the room so as to contain the sanding dust. Close the door and cut a piece of plastic sheeting a little larger than the opening. Seal the sheeting on all four sides with release tape. If possible, place a box fan in an open window to provide ventilation.

2 SANDING THE FLOOR Have the clerk at the rental store show you how to load and handle the drum sander and edger. For the model shown, wear a dust mask, goggles, and ear protection, and loop the power cord under your belt. Load the sander with coarse paper—typically 36-grit. Position the sander at one corner of the room parallel to the length of the floorboards. With the drum off the floor, turn on the sander. Once the motor reaches full speed, begin moving forward and slowly lower the drum to the floor. Let the sander pull you forward at a slow, steady pace (left). As you approach the far wall, slowly lift the drum, then lower it and move the sander backward, pulling it over the same strip of flooring you just sanded. Once you're back at your starting point, raise the drum off the floor and jog the sander over by 3 or 4 inches. Continue sanding the floor in strips until you reach the opposite wall.

3 SANDING THE EDGES Sand edges missed by the drum sander with an edger. Load the edger with a sanding disc of the same grit used for the drum sander. Holding both handles, tilt the edger back on its casters and switch it on. Starting at a corner, slowly lower the front of the edger to the floor facing the wall. As soon as the disc makes contact, sweep it along the grain of the floorboards, working left to right in 1- to 2-foot sections (above). Continue until you reach the opposite wall. To sand along a wall at a 90 degree angle to the floorboards, move the sander in arcs from the wall to the edge of the drum-sanded area. Once you are done with the edger, vacuum the floor. Then sand the floor again with the drum sander and edger, each loaded with medium (50-grit) paper, and a third time with fine (80-grit) paper. Vacuum the floor after each pass.

4 APPLYING WOOD STAIN Sand corners and spots under radiators or toe-kicks with an orbital sander or by hand with a paint scraper. Vacuum the floor again. Wearing rubber gloves and goggles, apply the stain with a 3-inch-wide synthetic brush, working slowly and evenly in 4-foot-square sections (above). Work in the direction of the wood grain. After the stain has set—usually in 10 to 15 minutes—remove the excess with clean, dry rags. As rags become soaked, use new ones. Avoid touching stained areas of the floor with your hands or feet—they will leave a print. If this does occur, scrape and hand sand the area. Reapply stain and wipe. Allow the stain to dry for the time specified by the manufacturer.

5 APPLYING A FLOOR FINISH Prepare the finish according to the manufacturer's instructions—most water-based products require thorough mixing. Pour some finish into a paint tray and, with a foam applicator, apply it in 4-foot-square sections, beginning along the walls and following the wood grain (above). Let the finish dry according to the time specified. Apply a second coat. Once it has dried, lightly roughen the surface with a floor polisher loaded with a 150- or 180-grit screen. Apply a third or more coats of finish. Let the last coat dry for two or three days before moving furniture back into the room.

painting a floor

Painted flooring, common in the 19th century, is enjoying a revival. Stenciling, trompe l'oeil, faux finishes, and stain applications to mimic wood inlay can all be used. Some of these techniques require advanced skills, but simple geometric designs are easily achieved—and to great effect. By alternating painted boards and boards with a clear finish, as in this project, the wood grain is emphasized, creating an interesting contrast to the applied color. Choose a tone to match or complement the room's furnishings. A latex interior paint is suitable if the entire flooring is also covered with polyurethane.

MATERIALS
- Lowe's American Tradition paint, satin finish, 310A-4 Eucalyptus Tree
- Olympic polyurethane, satin finish

TOOLS
- Pry bar
- Hammer
- Nail set
- 80-grit waterproof sandpaper
- Pole sander
- Vacuum cleaner
- Tack cloth
- Tape measure
- Low-tack masking tape
- 4-inch paint roller
- Plastic paint tray
- 2-inch paintbrush
- Pole finish applicator
- Floor polisher with 180-grit screen
- Latex gloves

1 SANDING THE FLOOR
Remove the shoe molding to expose the flooring along the baseboards. Gently pull off the molding with a pry bar, protecting surfaces with a wood shim. Examine the flooring for protruding nails and sink the heads with a nail set and a hammer. Fit a pole sander with 80-grit waterproof sandpaper—regular sandpaper tends to clog on finished surfaces. Sand the flooring in the direction of the wood grain (above), changing the sandpaper as necessary. Once the sanding is completed, vacuum thoroughly and wipe the flooring with a tack cloth.

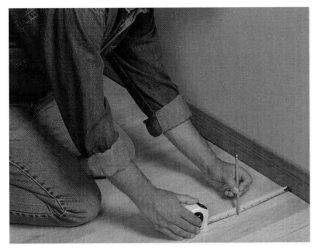

2 MARKING OUT THE DESIGN In this design, sets of two painted floorboards alternate with sets of three unpainted floorboards within an unpainted border at the perimeter equal to the width of three floorboards. To lay out the border, measure the width of three floorboards and mark this distance from the baseboard at several points on each end of the floorboards (above). Simply count three floorboards out from the baseboard where the floorboards run parallel to the baseboard.

3 TAPING OFF THE STRIPES With low-tack masking tape, mark off the outer edges of the border and the sets of floorboards to be painted (above). Press the tape down firmly along its entire length to ensure a good seal and overlap the ends.

4 ROLLING ON THE PAINT To avoid mistakes, make an X with masking tape in each area to be left unpainted. Pour a quantity of paint into a paint tray, then load a paint roller and roll off the excess. Working in the direction of the wood grain, apply paint to the floorboards (above). Start away from the taped edges while the roller is fully loaded, then work along them—there is less risk of bleeding under the tape with a partially loaded roller. Roll directly along the edges of the tape to ensure crisp painted edges. Let the paint dry to the touch, then peel off the tape—if you wait too long, the tape may lift paint along the edges. Lightly sand any bleed marks and wipe away dust with a tack cloth.

5 APPLYING A CLEAR FINISH Pour a quantity of clear finish into a paint tray and apply it to the floorboards, working in the direction of the wood grain. Cut in the edges of the flooring along the baseboards with a 2-inch paintbrush, then complete the rest of the flooring with pole finish applicator (above). Allow the finish to dry for the time recommended by the manufacturer, then apply a second coat and let it dry. Lightly sand the flooring using a floor polisher loaded with a 180-grit screen, then vacuum and wipe with a tack cloth. Make a final application of clear finish and let it dry for two or three days before moving furniture back into the room.

installing faux plaster rosettes

Rosettes are an ornamental feature of many older homes, adding elegance to any room by transforming a light fixture into a focal point. Rosettes were traditionally made from plaster, and they are still available in that form. But plaster rosettes are very difficult to install, particularly on drywall ceilings. An easier and equally attractive option is a rosette made from polyurethane. Available from Lowe's in a wide variety of designs and sizes for different fixtures and ceilings, these rosettes have the added advantage of not being subject to warping like wood. Once a polyurethane rosette is installed, you can paint it any color to match your decor.

This is a fairly straightforward project, but you will need to temporarily remove the light fixture where the rosette will go. Be sure to shut off electrical power to the fixture before starting work. You'll find all the tools and materials needed for this project at Lowe's.

MATERIALS
* ❖ Polyurethane rosette (Balmer VI Ceiling Center, 251 Deacon, 72815-25117)
* ❖ Latex caulk (Alex Painter's Acrylic Latex Caulk) or construction adhesive
* ❖ Nonshrinking latex hole filler
* ❖ 2½-inch trim-head screws

TOOLS
* ❖ Screwdriver
* ❖ Voltage tester
* ❖ Stud finder
* ❖ Electric drill

Drive the screws at or between decorative details on the rosette so that the heads will be as inconspicuous as possible.

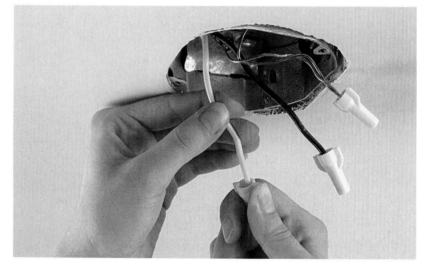

1 TAKING DOWN THE LIGHT FIXTURE Switch the light off, then shut off the power to the fixture at your service panel. Unscrew the fixture from the electrical box, then, without touching any bare wires, undo the wire caps from the wire ends. Use a voltage tester to confirm that the power is off, touching one of the tester probes to the box and the other to the black wire end. Repeat with the white wire and the bare copper ground wires. The tester should not glow during any test. If it does, return to the service panel and turn the power off to the correct circuit and retest. Once you're sure the power is off, disconnect the fixture wires from the cable wires, set the fixture aside, and twist wire caps on the cable wires (above).

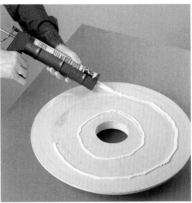

2 OUTLINING THE ROSETTE ON THE CEILING Hold the rosette in position on the ceiling, centered around the electrical box, and trace its outline on the ceiling with a pencil (above). Take the rosette down and set it aside.

3 MARKING THE CEILING JOISTS Although polyurethane rosettes are not heavy, it's a good idea to fasten them to the joists running across the ceiling. With a stud finder, mark the locations and direction of the ceiling joist that cross the outline you traced in step 2. Make the pencil marks just outside the outline (above) so that you will see them after the rosette is repositioned on the ceiling.

4 APPLYING ADHESIVE TO THE ROSETTE Set the rosette face down on a work surface and spread two rings of latex caulk or construction adhesive on the rosette's back face (above). Locate the rings about 1½ inches from from the inner and outer circles of the rosette, to prevent too much adhesive from squeezing out after you install the rosette.

5 INSTALLING THE ROSETTE Reposition the rosette on the ceiling within the marked outline, pressing it firmly into place. Fasten the rosette to the ceiling with three 2½-inch trim-head screws spaced evenly around the circumference of the rosette and located at ceiling joists (above). Using an electric drill, drive the screws without sinking them too deeply—this could damage the rosette.

6 PATCHING THE SCREW HOLES With a wet cloth, wipe away any adhesive that squeezed out around the rosette. Conceal the screw heads with a non-shrinking latex hole filler (above). Let the filler dry according to the manufacturer's directions, then use fine sandpaper to smooth the patches. To reinstall the light fixture, connect the wires and fasten the fixture to the electrical box. Restore power to the fixture at the service panel.

installing faux plaster crown molding

Unless your decorating scheme calls for crown molding with the look and feel of wood, faux plaster is a viable choice. In addition to being less expensive, faux plaster crown molding offers several other advantages over wood. Made from molded polyurethane, faux-plaster trim is free of surface flaws and it will not warp. Its lighter weight makes it easier to work with at ceiling level. And faux plaster molding is easier to install than wood, especially around corners. Faux-plaster crown molding comes with molded blocks for both inside and outside corners, so all you need to do is fasten them in place.

This project features egg-and-dart style crown molding. Lowe's stocks this and several other styles, ranging from simple to ornate. Whichever style you choose, installation is straightforward.

MATERIALS

❖ Polyurethane crown molding (CMF0800, CMFI800, CMFO800)
❖ PL Premium™ construction adhesive
❖ Latex caulk (Alex Painter's Acrylic Latex Caulk)
❖ Finishing nails

TOOLS

❖ Carpenter's square
❖ Measuring tape
❖ Stud finder
❖ Cordless drill
❖ Chalk line
❖ Miter box
❖ Hammer
❖ Caulking gun

If you position an outside corner block flush against an out-of-square corner, the installation will be thrown out of alignment.

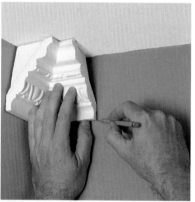

1 POSITIONING INSIDE CORNER BLOCKS Hold an inside corner block in position so that it contacts the ceiling and both walls. Mark pencil lines on the ceiling and walls along the top and bottom edges of the block (above). These marks will serve as guidelines for the straight lengths of molding.

2 CHECKING THE OUTSIDE CORNER FOR SQUARE Outside corners are not always square. To check, hold an outside corner block against the corner and mark a pencil line on the ceiling along the top edge of the block. Then place a carpenter's square on the ceiling with an arm of the square flush against one wall. If the other arm of the square is parallel to your pencil mark, the corner is square. Move on to step 3. If not, mark a new set of lines along the arms of the square (above). Reposition the block, aligning its top edges with the second set of lines, and mark lines on both walls along the block's bottom edges.

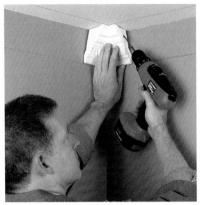

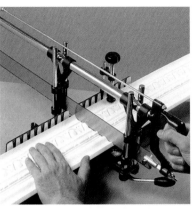

3 MARKING GUIDELINES FOR THE STRAIGHT LENGTHS Once all the corner block positions have been marked, you need to add level guidelines along the walls and ceiling between the corners. First drive a finishing nail into the wall at one of the corner marks. Hook the end of a chalk line on the nail and extend the line to the corresponding mark at the other end of the wall. Snap the line (above). Repeat for the guidelines along the ceiling. Next, use a stud finder to mark the wall studs and ceiling joists running perpendicular to the wall. Make your marks just outside the guidelines.

4 FASTENING THE CORNER BLOCKS Spread a thin layer of construction adhesive on the surfaces of the corner blocks that will contact the walls and ceiling. Position the blocks, aligning their top and bottom edges with your guidelines. With a drill, drive a 2½-inch drywall screw through each side of the blocks—the sides that will be hidden by the straight lengths of molding—angling the screws upward into the ceiling (above).

5 CUTTING THE STRAIGHT LENGTHS Measure the distance between the corner blocks, then transfer your measurement to a straight length of molding. Set the molding in a miter box; the model shown allows you to adjust the angle of the saw blade for the cut you need. Adjust the saw for a 90 degree cut, lining up the blade with your mark. Cut through the molding at the mark (above).

6 INSTALLING THE STRAIGHT LENGTHS Apply beads of adhesive along the edges of the molding that will touch the ceiling and wall. Press the molding firmly in place to make good contact with the wall and ceiling. Next, fasten the molding to the wall at each stud and ceiling joist mark; drive one 1⅝-inch drywall screw about 1 inch above the bottom edge of the molding (above), and another about 1 inch below the top edge, angled upward into the ceiling. Sink the screws just below the molding surface.

7 APPLYING FINISHING TOUCHES Fill gaps along the wall and ceiling with a bead of latex caulk (above). Also fill any gaps between the straight lengths of molding and the corner blocks. With a clean, damp cloth, wipe away any excess caulk. Fill screw holes with spackling compound, let it dry, and lightly sand the surface.

installing a ceramic tile backsplash

A ceramic tile backsplash is both attractive and functional, serving as an eye-catching and water-resistant wall surface above a kitchen counter-top. Laying a tile backsplash is a fairly easy job, but take the time you need to plan the tile lay-out, as shown in steps 1 and 2. All you need are the tiles and plastic tile spacers, which enable you to maintain uni-form spacing between the tiles. It's much easier to adjust your layout after a dry run than it is after pressing your tiles into fresh adhesive. The rest of the process is simple: spread adhesive on the wall, press the tiles into place, and fill the joints between tiles with grout.

The backsplash for this project was created with two rows, or courses, of 4-by-4-inch tiles. The bottom course comprises stan-dard glazed wall tiles, whereas each tile of the top course has a rounded top edge (called a bullnose) that rests flush against the wall. This bullnose edge prevents water on the wall from seeping behind the tiles. A bullnose tile goes at the ends of the bottom row, and a special bullnose tile with two rounded edges goes at the ends of the top row. Lowe's stocks wall tiles in a wide variety of sizes and colors to suit your decor.

MATERIALS

❖ Standard and bullnose ceramic wall tiles (American Olean, Biscuit White), tile spacers
❖ Laticrete Premium Multi-Mastic Tile Adhesive (white)
❖ Grout
❖ Silicone sealer
❖ Sanding block

TOOLS

❖ Rubber gloves
❖ Level
❖ Tape measure
❖ Medium-grit sandpaper
❖ Tile cutter
❖ Notched trowel
❖ Grout float
❖ Sponge

TIPS

Ceramic tiles do not bond well to paint. If the wall surface for the backsplash is painted, sand the paint off the wall under the level lines, using a sanding block fitted with medium-grit sandpaper.

❖

Remember to cut bullnose tiles for the ends of the bottom row with the bullnose edge facing out.

1 PLANNING THE TILE LAYOUT Set a plastic tile spacer on the countertop against the wall to be tiled and place a standard wall tile on the spacer. Mark a pencil line on the wall along the tile's top edge. Place another spacer on the tile's top edge, then hold a bullnose tile on the spacer with its bull-nose edge facing up. Mark another pencil line on the wall along the tile's bull-nose edge (above). With a level, extend the upper line along the entire length of the wall surface to be tiled. Measure the wall length to be tiled (in this case, from one end of the countertop to the other) and mark its midpoint with a vertical line that crosses the level line.

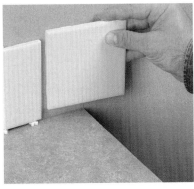

2 ADJUSTING THE LAYOUT Starting at the midpoint line marked in step 1, lay out a dry run of tiles along the wall. Be sure to place a tile spacer between every pair of tiles. The last tile at the end of the course should be at least one-half width (above). If the remaining space is smaller, adjust the midpoint line to one side or the other so both tiles at the end of the course will be at least one-half width.

3 CUTTING TILES Once you are satisfied with the tile layout, mark cutting lines across the bullnose tiles at the ends of the courses. Use a tile cutter to trim the tiles, leaving bullnose edge intact. For the model shown, set a tile on the base of the cutter so the cutting line is directly under the scoring wheel of the cutter. Pull the scoring wheel across the tile (above), then push down on the handle to cut the tile.

4 APPLYING THE ADHESIVE To protect the countertop from stray adhesive, tape a sheet of kraft paper to the surface. With a notched trowel, spread latex tile adhesive on the wall between the countertop and the level line, working from the midpoint line to one end of the countertop. Apply the adhesive carefully, so that the level line remains visible. Angle the trowel at 45 degrees and sweep it across the wall; the notches will produce ridges of adhesive of the correct height and thickness.

5 LAYING THE STANDARD TILES Starting at the midpoint line, set a pair of tile spacers on the countertop. Wearing rubber gloves, press the first standard tile into the adhesive; align one edge with the midpoint line and set the bottom on the spacers. Using spacers to maintain the correct gap between tiles, install the rest of the course the same way (above).

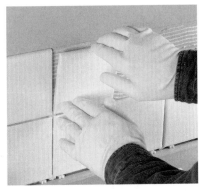

6 INSTALLING THE BULLNOSE TILES Install the bullnose tiles as you did the standard ones, inserting spacers between units and aligning the rounded edge of the tiles with the level line (above). To prevent the spacers from projecting beyond the top edge of the tiles, trim the top arm off these spacers before placing them. Lay a special bullnose tile with rounded edges at the top and one side for the end of the countertop. Then spread adhesive on the other side of the midpoint line and finish installing the backsplash tiles. Let the adhesive set overnight.

7 GROUTING THE JOINTS Prepare grout following the manufacturer's directions. With a grout float, spread grout across the tiles, holding the float diagonally to compact the grout into the joints. Scrape excess grout off the tiles with the edge of the float, then let the grout harden for about 15 minutes. Wipe the tiles clean with a damp sponge, let the grout set overnight, and clean off any remaining grout haze with a clean, damp cloth. After waiting for the time recommended by the grout manufacturer, brush a silicone sealer on the joints.

adding tile around a fireplace

A fireplace is the focal point of any room, generating physical warmth and a comforting ambience. Installing ceramic tiles on the hearth and surrounding wall will further enhance the beauty of a fireplace. Because the surfaces to be covered are relatively small, this is a fairly straightforward project. Pick your tiles carefully, choosing a color, size, and texture that will complement your decor and add a personal touch to the room. The tiles featured in this project measure 12 inches square, with ⅛-inch grout joints between units.

Very little preparation is required for this project. With the exception of wood paneling, virtually any surface—including plaster, drywall, or plywood—will accept tiling. Because the hearth will be subject to heat and a certain degree of traffic, start by laying cement backerboard as a base between the subfloor and the tiles. Cut a piece of backerboard to fit on the hearth, spread thinset mortar on the subfloor, and fix the backerboard in place with nails or screws.

MATERIALS
- ❖ Elegant Collection Porcelain Ceramic Tiles, Venetian Stone
- ❖ Cement backerboard
- ❖ Thinset mortar
- ❖ ⅛-inch tile spacers
- ❖ Grout
- ❖ 1-inch finishing nails
- ❖ ⁷⁄₁₆ x ¹¹⁄₁₆-inch quarter-round shoe molding

TOOLS
- ❖ Tape measure
- ❖ Notched trowel
- ❖ Rubber mallet
- ❖ Carpenter's level
- ❖ Torpedo level
- ❖ Tile cutter
- ❖ Masking tape
- ❖ Sponge
- ❖ Grout float
- ❖ Rubber gloves
- ❖ Sandpaper
- ❖ Backsaw and miter box
- ❖ Hammer
- ❖ Nail set
- ❖ Drop cloth

1 PLOTTING THE TILE LAYOUT ON THE HEARTH Protect the floor in front of the hearth with a drop cloth. You can plan your layout by dry-fitting tiles or using a story stick. Make a story stick by cutting a board a little longer than the hearth's longest dimension. Make a mark one grout-joint width from one end (here, ⅛ inch) and a second mark one tile width farther along (here, 12 inches). Continue marking the stick at ⅛- and 12-inch intervals until you reach the other end. To use the stick, lay it along one side of the hearth and transfer each grout-joint and tile mark to the backerboard base (above). Repeat along the front of the hearth, positioning the stick as needed so tiles at the edges will be the same size. Your marks will tell you how many tiles to lay and what size to cut those along the edges.

Start the layout at the top of the outline so that the tile that needs to be cut short to fit will be at the hearth, rather than at the top, where a short tile would be more visible.

2 CUTTING TILES TO FIT For the partial tiles around the perimeter of the hearth, measure the space between your last layout mark and the edge of the hearth. Transfer the measurement to the tiles to be cut, then cut the tiles one at a time. Set the tile in a tile cutter so that your cutting mark is directly under the scoring wheel. Pull the scoring wheel across the tile, then press down on the handle to snap the tile in two (above).

4 LAYING THE HEARTH TILES Starting at one edge of the hearth, set a tile spacer against the edge of the hearth and another against the wall. Press the first tile into the mortar, aligning one edge with the edge of the hearth and the adjoining edge with the wall. Using spacers to maintain the correct gap between tiles, install the rest of the course the same way (above). Using a carpenter's level, check that the tiles are level; use a rubber mallet to gently tap and level out any tiles that sit too high.

3 SPREADING ADHESIVE ON THE HEARTH Wearing rubber gloves, mix thinset mortar following the manufacturer's instructions and apply it to the hearth with a notched trowel. Angle the trowel at 45 degrees and sweep it across the surface (above); the notches will produce ridges of mortar the correct height and thickness.

5 PLOTTING THE WALL TILES Holding a carpenter's level against the wall so one edge is flush with the outside edge of the hearth tiles, mark a guideline on the wall (above). Repeat on the other side of the fireplace. Mark a level line on the wall across the top of the fireplace so all three guidelines are the same distance from the fireplace opening. Use your story stick to lay out the wall tiles within the guidelines, allowing for a grout joint along the tiles' outside edges.

Continued on next page >

6 ADDING MOLDING FOR THE WALL TILES Measure the vertical guidelines on the wall and then cut two pieces of quarter-round shoe molding to this length, mitering one end of each piece at 45 degrees in a miter box. With the bottom of the molding on the hearth and the inside edges flush with the vertical guidelines, fasten the molding to the wall, driving a 1-inch finishing nail every 12 inches. Cut a third length to fit between the vertical pieces, mitering both ends at 45 degrees, and nail it in place. Sink the nail heads using a nail set.

7 SETTING THE WALL TILES Cut tiles to fit on the wall as described in step 2. Since the wall surfaces to be tiled are relatively narrow, use the notched trowel to apply adhesive directly to the back of the tiles, a technique known as "backbuttering." Starting with the space to one side of the fireplace, lay any short tile first, then set the next tile (above). Be sure to use tile spacers to maintain the correct distance between tiles.

8 LEVELING THE WALL TILES After laying the second tile, set a torpedo level across the top (above). Gently tap the top end with a rubber mallet, as necessary, to level the tile. Continue laying and leveling tiles until they are all in place. Then use the carpenter's level to check that the tiles are plumb and that none projects from the wall more than the others. To plumb a tile, press on it by hand or, if that doesn't work, lay a 2-by-4 wrapped in a piece of carpet on the tile and gently tap the board with the mallet. Let the mortar set following the manufacturer's directions.

9 GROUTING THE JOINTS Prepare grout following the manufacturer's directions. With a grout float, spread grout across the tiles, holding the float diagonally to compact the grout into the joints (above). Scrape excess grout off the tiles with the edge of the float, then let the grout harden for about 15 minutes.

10 CLEANING THE TILES Wipe the tiles clean with a damp sponge (above). Let the grout set overnight and clean off any remaining grout haze with a clean, damp cloth.

decorative painting on ceramic tiles

Painting ceramic tiles can breathe life onto a plain wall or kitchen backsplash. Tiles with a matte finish are the easiest to decorate because paint adheres best to them, but glossy tiles can be painted as well. Either way, start by thoroughly cleaning the tiles with a household cleaner to remove dirt, dust, and fingerprints—any of which can result in a poor bond between the paint and tiles. Dry the tiles before painting them. Once the painting is done, cover the tiles with glaze to protect the paint from wear.

One of the attractions of this project is its flexibility. Although creating your own pattern will provide a more personal touch, you can also rely on an existing design. It's best to choose a simple design that is proportional to the size of the individual tiles. The design pictured here, for example, was outlined from a cardboard stencil created by photocopying a decorative painting stamp available at Lowe's and scaling it down to fit the 4-by-4-inch tiles.

MATERIALS

❖ Pébéo Ceramic Tile Paint, brilliant gloss
❖ Pébéo Ceramic Tile Clear Glaze
❖ Cardboard
❖ Kraft paper

TOOLS

❖ Masking tape
❖ Hobby knife
❖ Artist's paintbrush
❖ Foam applicator

1 TRACING THE DESIGN ONTO THE TILES Cut a thick piece of cardboard to the same size as the tiles and trace your design onto it. Cut out the design with a hobby knife. Before painting any tiles, test your stencil on paper and revise as necessary. Once you are satisfied with the result, align the edges of the stencil with those of a tile and tape the stencil in place. Outline the design on the tile with a pencil (above). Remove the stencil.

2 PAINTING THE TILES Spread a sheet of kraft paper on the countertop to protect the surface from stray paint. Carefully fill in the outline with ceramic tile paint. Tape the stencil to another tile and repeat the process (above).

3 APPLYING THE GLAZE Once you have painted all the tiles, let the paint dry following the manufacturer's directions. Then, using a wide foam applicator, carefully apply a thin coat of ceramic tile glaze to each painted tile (above). Avoid touching the tiles for a few days while the glaze dries completely.

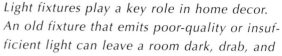

changing a light fixture

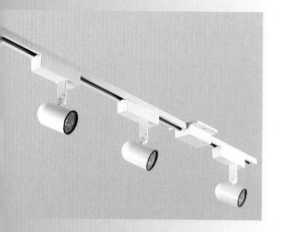

Light fixtures play a key role in home decor. An old fixture that emits poor-quality or insufficient light can leave a room dark, drab, and uninviting. If the fixture itself is unattractive, it can detract from the effect you are trying to create.

Lowe's stocks a wide variety of light fixtures that can serve double-duty in your decorating scheme. An attractive fixture can become the focal point of a room. And by producing the quality and quantity of light you need, a light fixture makes a room brighter and more inviting.

Track lighting has a lot going for it. Compact and inexpensive, track lighting lends a room a contemporary look. A fixture with several lights on a single track can direct light in different directions to highlight various details or provide special-task lighting. And track lighting is easy to install.

The following steps demonstrate how to wire track lighting to an existing electrical box where an old fixture has been removed. Although most units feature the parts shown here, the sequence of steps may be different for the lighting you buy. Always follow the manufacturer's instructions. Shut off electrical power to the circuit before starting to work.

MATERIALS

❖ Emerald Track Lighting Kit: low-voltage halogen, 4-foot track

TOOLS

❖ Voltage tester
❖ Tape measure
❖ Screwdriver
❖ Straightedge
❖ Electric drill

The orientation of the bracket determines the direction in which the track will run. Track lights are typically installed so the track is parallel to the nearest wall.

❖

Drill a hole large enough for the toggles, not just the bolts. In most cases, you'll need a 5/8-inch bit.

1 WIRING THE BOX BRACKET Shut off power to the circuit at the service panel. Unscrew the old fixture from the electrical box, then, without touching any bare wires, undo the wire nuts. Use a voltage tester to confirm the power is off, touching one probe to the box and the other probe to the black wire ends. Repeat with the white wires and the ground wires. The tester should not glow during any test. If it does, return to the service panel and turn off the correct circuit, then retest. Once you're sure the power is off, disconnect the fixture's wires. Twist the wire ends of the track lighting box bracket to the cable wires: black to black, white to white, and green or bare copper ground to ground. Twist a wire nut onto each connection (left).

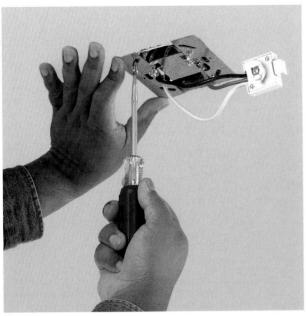

2 FASTENING THE BOX BRACKET With the screws supplied, attach the box bracket to the electrical box so it rests flat against the ceiling, making sure the bracket is oriented in the appropriate direction (above).

3 MARKING THE TRACK TOGGLE BOLT HOLES Position the track in the desired location on the ceiling and hold it in place temporarily by tightening the setscrews on either it or the box bracket. Mark the track screw holes on the ceiling with a pencil (above).

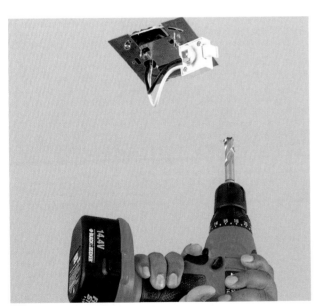

4 DRILLING HOLES FOR THE TOGGLE BOLTS Remove the track from the box and set it aside. Drill a hole at each mark for the toggle bolts supplied (above).

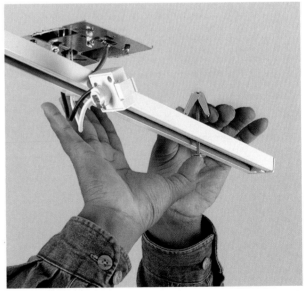

5 INSERTING THE TOGGLE BOLTS Slip a bolt through each hole in the track, then thread a toggle onto each bolt. Holding the track near the ceiling, collapse one of the toggles and push it into a hole in the ceiling (above). Insert the remaining toggles in the same way.

Continued on next page >

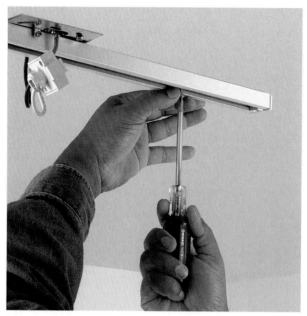

6 SECURING THE TRACK Tugging down gently on the track, tighten one of the toggle bolts until the track sits snugly on the ceiling. Finish tightening the other toggle bolts (above). Next, tighten the setscrews on the edges of the box bracket.

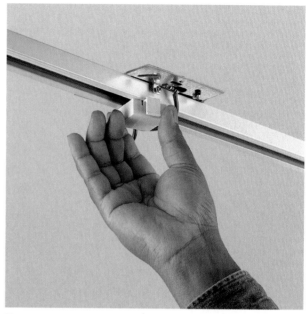

7 INSTALLING THE ADAPTER Slide the adapter into its groove in the track, making sure that its double contacts line up against the side of the track's two conductors. Gently twist the adapter until its spring-loaded locking plate snaps into place on the track (above).

8 INSTALLING THE CANOPY The final step in wiring the track lights is to install the canopy that conceals the wires, adapter, and box bracket. Center the canopy over the adapter and screw it to the bracket (above).

9 CONNECTING THE LIGHTS Fit each bulb housing with a halogen bulb following the manufacturer's instructions. Insert each housing into the track, then pull down on the grooved tab and twist the housing until it locks in place (right), making sure the light's double contacts align with the track's double copper conductors. Restore power to the circuit.

GUIDE TO LOWE'S COLOR PALETTES

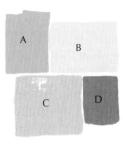

PAGE 239
A. 91-39C Belle Grove Moss (AT)
   310-4 Bahia Grass (UC)
B. 260 Vanilla Cream (E)
   212-3 Butterfly Bush (UC)
C. 320-2 Aloof (E)
   414-4 Dusty Trail (UC)
D. 126-7 Copper Penny (UC)
   235-A5 California Poppy (E)

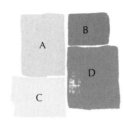

PAGE 249
A. 145-4 Lavender Sachet (UC)
   215-3 Evening Sky (E)
B. 143-6 Vintage Violet (UC)
   214-4 Clear Amethyst (E)
C. 214-3 Dusty Yellow (UC)
   92-A Oatlands Yellow (AT)
D. 145-6 Frosted Grape (UC)
   215-5 Paradise (E)

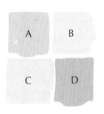

PAGE 241
A. 311-3 Canary Grass (UC)
   92-40A Seacrest Green (AT)
B. 210-5 Golden Cricket (UC)
   229A-3 Dewy Green (E)
C. 454-3 Scandinavian Sky (UC)
   94-23B Air Castle Blue (AT)
D. 312-4 Nettle (UC)
   91-1B Balsam Beige (AT)

PAGE 251
A. 336-2 Pink Pail (UC)
   272-1 Pearl Blush (E)
B. 436-6 Cabernet (UC)
   412 Burgundy 6 (LA)
C. 513-4 Whiskers (UC)
   AJ807 Powdered Snows (AJ)
D. 411-3 French Gray Linen (UC)
   343-2 Soft Moss (E)
E. 274B-6 Plum Velvet (E)
   91-20A Oatlands Violet (AT)
F. 542-7 Blackberry (UC)
   95-19B Midnight Purple (AT)

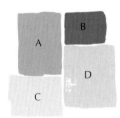

PAGE 243
A. 310-5 Dill (UC)
   316-4 Green Pastures (E)
B. 338-6 Wild Strawberry (UC)
   240-5 Wineberry (E)
C. 238-3 Candytuft (UC)
   240-1 Pink Chablis (E)
D. 310-3 Pickling Spice (UC)
   316-2 Martinique Morn (E)

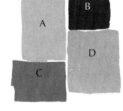

PAGE 253
A. 409-4 Light Sage (UC)
   94-33A Garden Herb (AT)
B. 442-7 Purple Coneflower (UC)
   242-6 King's Robe (E)
C. 443-6 Purple Rain (UC)
   243-4 Alpine Violet (E)
D. 94-14A Del Coronado
   Dusty Rose (AT)
   301A-3 Santa Fe Smoke (E)

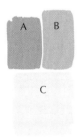

PAGE 245
A. 310-5 Dill (UC)
   289A-4 Vegetable Garden (E)
B. 454-4 Mountain Stream (UC)
   282-2 Noonday (E)
C. 356-2 Mountain Dew (UC)
   282A-1 Azure Skies (E)

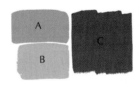

PAGE 255
A. 311-5 Pea Soup (UC)
   318-4 Green Sulphur (E)
B. 122-5 Orange Marmalade (UC)
   205A-4 Horizon Orange (E)
C. 331-7 Autumn Ridge (UC)
   95-6C Retro Rust (AT)

PAGE 247
A. AJ709 Autumn Harvests (AJ)
   248-5 Remembrance (E)
B. 95-11A Crushed Strawberries (AT)
   233-7 Red Gumball (UC)
C. 95-23C Jack Black (AT)
   518-7 Black Magic (UC)
D. 92-30A Spring Fling (AT)
   222-3 Neptune (E)

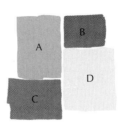

PAGE 257
A. 228-5 Opal Fire (UC)
   91-12C Woodlawn
   Marmalade (AT)
B. 401-6 Evening Emerald (UC)
   93-26B Juniper Green (AT)
C. 551-6 Prussian Blue (UC)
   93-22B Colonial Blue (AT)
D. 114-4 Golden Slumber (UC)
   202-2 Pale Daffodil (E)

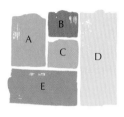

PAGE 259
A. 233-4 River Rouge (UC)
    237-4 Sandy Rose (E)
B. 233-5 Red Cedar (UC)
    237-5 Rosebud (E)
C. 353-4 Crystal Lake (UC)
    250-3 Blue Dream (E)
D. 122-4 Shrimp Toast (UC)
    235-3 Peach Shadow (E)
E. 143-6 Vintage Violet (UC)
    242-5 Royal Pageant (E)

PAGE 261
A. 345-7 Roman Violet (UC)
    244-6 Gloxinia (E)
B. 130-6 Candy Corn (UC)
    95-5B Monarch Orange (AT)
C. 144-6 Berry Jam (UC)
    214-5 Grape Slush (E)
D. 116-5 Honey Toast (UC)
    232-4 Waxberry (E)

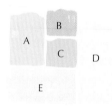

PAGE 266 TOP
A. 123-1 Peach Statice (UC)
    206-1 Peach Opal (E)
B. 209-4 Lettuce Alone (UC)
    258A-3 Paloverde (E)
C. 123-3 Perfect Peach (UC)
    206-2 Peaches 'N Cream (E)
D. 518-1 Delicate White (UC)
    93-42B White Peony (AT)
E. 209-2 Honeydew Melon (UC)
    258A-2 Palm Frond (E)

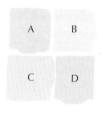

PAGE 266 BOTTOM
A. 510-4 Balsam (UC)
    94-31B Belle Grove Valley
        Fog (AT)
B. 410-2 White Sage (UC)
    94-2C Cliveden Mist (AT)
C. 142-3 Syrian Violet (UC)
    92-19C Floss Flower (AT)
D. 348-3 Blue Thistle (UC)
    92-22B Iceland Mist (AT)

PAGE 267 TOP
A. 356-2 Mountain Dew (UC)
    252B-1 Jade Reflection (E)
B. 214-2 Sausalito (UC)
    262A-1 Luminary Yellow (E)
C. 226-2 Ceramic Glaze (UC)
    236-1 Bee's Nectar (E)
D. 307-2 Sweetbriar (UC)
    284A-1 Misty Meadow (E)

PAGE 267 BOTTOM
A. 436-1 Silk Sheets (UC)
    271A-1 Spring Iris (E)
B. 286A-4 Succulent Green (E)
C. 437-4 Sweetheart Rose (UC)
    271-A3 Irish Rose (E)
D. 308-2 Mint Wafer (UC)
    286A-2 Desert Willow (E)
E. 115-3 Shiny Silk (UC)
    231-1 Kira Caramel (E)

PAGE 268 TOP
A. 316-5 Applesauce Cake (UC)
B. 408-6 Hidden Meadow (UC)
    312-6 Tortoise Shell (E)
C. 334-7 Apple-A-Day (UC)
    239A-6 Berry Red (E)
D. 116-3 Vanilla Wafer (UC)
    292-1 Tea Biscuit (E)
E. 450-5 Stormy Ridge (UC)
    278-5 Smoky Blue (E)

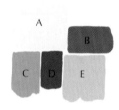

PAGE 268 BOTTOM
A. 213-2 Crescent Moon (UC)
    92-5C Woodlawn Misty Morn (AT)
B. 355-7 Caribbean Holiday (UC)
    95-31C St.Croix Blue (AT)
C. 413-5 Saddle Soap (UC)
    93-2C East Side Gold (AT)
D. 334-7 Apple-A-Day (UC)
E. 312-3 Safari (UC)
    94-2A Husk Gold (AT)

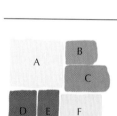

PAGE 269 TOP
A. 117-2 Mesa Beige (UC)
    262-1 Honeysweet (E)
B. 216-5 Lion's Mane (UC)
    262-4 Ale (E)
C. 517-4 Gray Stone (UC)
D. 512-5 Olive Gray (UC)
    348-4 Moth (E)
E. 216-7 Cider Toddy (UC)
    262-6 Document (E)
F. 117-4 Winter Wheat (UC)
    262-2 Sheepskin (E)

PAGE 269 BOTTOM
A. 229-6 Freckles (UC)
    268-4 Red Earth (E)
B. 243-7 Byzantine Purple (UC)
    242-6 King's Robe (E)
C. 216-4 Toffee Crunch (UC)
    204-2 Canyon Haze (E)
D. 313-4 Earthy Cane (UC)
    292-3 Crouton (E)
E. 316-6 Deep Jungle (E)
F. 441-7 Pansy Petal (UC)
    302-6 Very Grape (E)

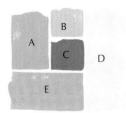

PAGE 270 TOP
A. 449-3 Rendezvous (UC)
   277-2 Nouveau Blue (E)
B. 243-3 Grape Lavender (UC)
   243-2 Quartz Moon (E)
C. 347-5 Kimono (UC)
   276-A5 Image Blue (E)
D. 554-1 Evening Mist (UC)
   308-1 Moby Dick (E)
E. 456-3 Julep Green (UC)
   283-2 Foamy Sea (E)

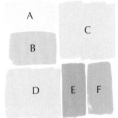

PAGE 270 BOTTOM
A. 112-3 Sunbeam (UC)
   200A-2 Sunbathed (E)
B. 353-2 Embellishment (UC)
   282-1 Whispy (E)
C. 209-3 Aloe Vera (UC)
   259A-2 Lime Sparkle (E)
D. 309-2 Lime Spritz (UC)
   312-1 Tinted Spearmint (E)
E. 309-5 Guacamole (UC)
   288-4 Denver Grass (E)
F. 349-3 Everlasting (UC)
   247-3 Lake of Lucerne (E)

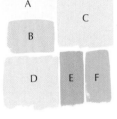

PAGE 271 TOP
A. 521-4 Silver Dollar (UC)
   334A-3 Rocky Slope (E)
B. 448-2 Memory Lane (UC)
   277-1 Blue Moon (E)
C. 517-2 Tear Drop (UC)
   343D-1 Lighthouse Beam (E)
D. 518-2 Aria (UC)
   337-1 Touch of Gray (E)
E. 419-4 Taupe Trivia (UC)
   343D-3 Bayou Sand (E)
F. 448-4 Sterling Silver (UC)
   277-2 Nouveau Blue (E)

PAGE 271 BOTTOM
A. 309-2 Lime Spritz (UC)
   288-2 Sky Green (E)
B. 405-2 Venetian Dew (UC)
   284-1 Dinner Mint (E)
C. 405-4 Bonsai (UC)
   284-4 Surrey Green (E)
D. 301-2 Big Sky (UC)
   283-1 Aquanot (E)
E. 301-4 Pitter Patter (UC)
   283-3 High Tide (E)
F. 311-3 Canary Grass (UC)
   289B-2 Trailing Vine (E)

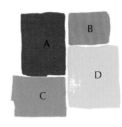

PAGE 272 TOP
A. 139-7 Wild Mulberry (UC)
   211-6 Magenta Mist (E)
B. 201-5 Artesian Well (UC)
   253-4 Michigan (E)
C. 246-5 Blue Hyacinth (UC)
   244-3 Blue Iris (E)
D. 114-7 Del Sol (UC)
   02A-4 Gold Finch (E)

PAGE 272 BOTTOM
A. 226-5 Copper Kettle (UC)
   268-2 Mayan Sun (E)
B. 320-6 Cowboy Hat (UC)
   265A-6 Ablaze (E)
C. 214-3 Dusty Yellow (UC)
   233A-3 Southern Exposure (E)
D. 213-5 Gold Buttercup (UC)
   232-5 Harvest Moon (E)
E. 218-5 Caramel Apple (UC)
   234A-4 Fresh Melon (E)
F. 330-6 Cinnabar (UC)
   269-4 Aztec Rouge (E)

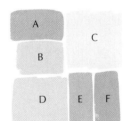

PAGE 273 TOP
A. 355-4 Alpine Valley (UC)
   91-29C Lyndhurst Duchess
   Blue (AT)
B. 234-5 Mexican Chile (UC)
   91-15B Cliveden Colonial Rose (AT)
C. 120-6 Goldfish (UC)
   91-8B La Fonda Sombrero (AT)
D. 309-4 Quaking Grass (UC)
   91-39C Belle Grove Moss (AT)
E. 215-4 Gold Buff (UC)
   91-6C Georgian Yellow (AT)

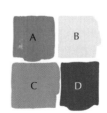

PAGE 273 BOTTOM
A. 130-6 Candy Corn (UC)
   95-4B Pomegranate (AT)
B. 412-3 Tabu (UC)
   94-2B Bamboo Stalk (AT)
C. 310-5 Dill (UC)
   93-35C La Fonda Cactus (AT)
D. 244-7 Eggplant (UC)
   95-20B Victoria Blue (AT)

AJ = Alexander Julian
AT = American Tradition
E = Enterprise
LA = Laura Ashley

O = Olympic Paint
UC = Ultimate Colors
V = Valspar Paint

design

FRONT MATTER

1 *INTERIOR DESIGN:* Tres McKinney/Laura Ashley **5** *DESIGN:* Dovetail Design **6–7**
INTERIOR DESIGN: Kathryne Designs **8–9** *INTERIOR DESIGN:* Kit Parmentier/Allison Rose
11 (TOP) *INTERIOR DESIGN:* Gigi Rogers Designs, www.gigirogersdesigns.com **(BOTTOM)**
INTERIOR DESIGN: Alexandra Owen Interiors **12 (TOP)** *INTERIOR
DESIGN:* City Studios **(BOTTOM)** *INTERIOR DESIGN:* Kathleen
Navarra/Navarra Design Consultants **13** *INTERIOR DESIGN:* Sasha
Emerson Design Studio

ROOM-BY-ROOM DESIGN

14–15 *INTERIOR DESIGN:* Molly McGowan Interiors; *CABINETRY:* Rutt of Lafayette, www.
ruttoflafayette.com **16–17** *INTERIOR DESIGN:* Shirley Jensen/Forget-Me-Nots Designs;
CONSTRUCTION: Dru Jensen **18 (TOP)** *INTERIOR DESIGN:* Gail Lesley Diehl Interiors **(BOTTOM)**
INTERIOR DESIGN: Kimberly Lamer Interiors and Sandra Lamer Interiors **19** *INTERIOR
DESIGN:* McWhorter/Ross Design Group, www.mcwhorterdesign.com **20 (LEFT)** *INTERIOR
DESIGN:* Shirley Jensen/Forget-Me-Nots Designs; *CONSTRUCTION:* Dru Jensen **20–21** *PAINT:*
Sydney Harbour Paint Company, www.sydneyharbourpaintco.com **21 (RIGHT)** *INTERIOR
DESIGN:* Claudia Fleury/Claudia's Designs, www.claudiafleury.com **22–23** *INTERIOR
DESIGN:* Joel Hendler and Christopher Pollock/Hendler Design, www.hendler.com
24–25 *INTERIOR DESIGN:* Tobeler Design, www.tobelerdesign.com **26–27** *INTERIOR
DESIGN:* Kendall Wilkinson Design **28–29** *INTERIOR DESIGN:* David Dalton Associates Inc.,
www.daviddaltoninc.com **30–33** *INTERIOR DESIGN:* Elizabeth Hill/Selby House Ltd.
34–35 *DESIGN:* Dovetail Design **36 (LEFT)** *ARCHITECT:* Backen, Arragoni & Ross **36–37**
INTERIOR DESIGN: Gordon Phaby/Sechrist Design Associates Inc., www.sechristdesign.
com **38–39** *DESIGN:* Sue Kalm; *WALL UPHOLSTERY:* Cri-Cri Morelle **40 (LEFT)** *INTERIOR
DESIGN:* Jane Langmuir Interior Design **40–41** *INTERIOR DESIGN:* Roberta Brown Root
41 (RIGHT) *INTERIOR DESIGN:* David Dalton Associates Inc., www.daviddaltoninc.com
42–43 *INTERIOR DESIGN:* Elizabeth Hill/Selby House Ltd. **44–45** *INTERIOR DESIGN:* Molly
McGowan Interiors; *CABINETRY:* Rutt of Lafayette, www.ruttoflafayette.com **46** *INTERIOR
DESIGN:* Leczinski Design Associates; *ARCHITECTURAL DESIGN:* Doug Walter Architects
47 *DESIGN:* Summer House at One Ford Road, Newport Beach, by Pacific Bay Homes
48–49 *INTERIOR DESIGN:* Kathryne Designs **50–53** *INTERIOR DESIGN:* Tucker & Marks Inc.,
www.tuckerandmarks.com **54–55** *INTERIOR DESIGN:* Kathryne Designs **56–57** *INTERIOR
DESIGN:* Joan Osburn/Osburn Design, www.osburndesign.com **58–59** *INTERIOR DESIGN:*
D. Kimberly Smith/Deer Creek Design **60–61** *INTERIOR DESIGN:* Claudia Fleury/Claudia's
Designs, www.claudiafleury.com **62–63** *INTERIOR DESIGN:* Jan Kavale for Sunset's North-
west Idea House **64–67** *INTERIOR DESIGN:* David Ramey/David Ramey Interior Design
68–69 *INTERIOR DESIGN:* Kremer Design Group **70–71** *INTERIOR DESIGN:* Molly McGowan
Interiors; *CABINETRY:* Rutt of Lafayette, www.ruttoflafayette.com **72–73** *INTERIOR DESIGN:*
Shirley Jensen/Forget-Me-Nots Designs; *CONSTRUCTION:* Dru Jensen **74–77** *INTERIOR
DESIGN:* Eugenia Erskine Jesberg/EJ Interior Design, www.ejinteriordesign.com **78–79**
INTERIOR DESIGN: Amy Devault, assisted by Kira Taylor and Lynn Klopfenstein/Amy Devault
Interior Design **80 (TOP)** *INTERIOR DESIGN:* Roberta Brown Root **(BOTTOM)** *INTERIOR
DESIGN:* D. Kimberly Smith/Deer Creek Design **81** *INTERIOR DESIGN:* Gail LeVine/Pierre
Deux, www.pierredeux.com **82** *INTERIOR DESIGN:* J. van Doorn Design **83 (TOP)** *INTERIOR*

DESIGN: Wendi Anton and Susan Sawasy/Anton Foster Interior Design **(BOTTOM)** *INTERIOR DESIGN*: Elizabeth Hill/Selby House Ltd. **84–85** *INTERIOR DESIGN*: David Dalton Associates Inc., www.daviddaltoninc.com **86–89** *INTERIOR DESIGN*: Gigi Rogers Designs, www. gigirogersdesigns.com **90–91** *INTERIOR DESIGN*: Jeanese Rowell Design, www.jrdesign.com **92 (TOP)** *INTERIOR DESIGN*: City Studios **93** *INTERIOR DESIGN*: Carolyn E. Oliver-Broder/ Oliver's Interiors and Antiques, www.oliversinteriors.com **94–95** *INTERIOR DESIGN*: Jean Horn Interiors **96–97** *INTERIOR DESIGN*: Amoroso/Holman Design Group **98–99** *INTERIOR DESIGN*: Joan Osburn/Osburn Design, www.osburndesign.com **100–101** *INTERIOR DESIGN*: Norm Claybaugh/Juvenile Lifestyles Inc., www.juvenilelifestyles. com **102–103** *INTERIOR DESIGN*: Mary Engelbreit's Studio **104–105** *INTERIOR DESIGN*: Norm Claybaugh/Juvenile Lifestyles Inc., www.juvenilelifestyles.com **106–107** *INTERIOR DESIGN*: Norm Claybaugh/Juvenile Lifestyles Inc., juvenilelifestyles.com **108–109** *INTERIOR DESIGN*: Kathleen Navarra/Navarra Design Consultants **110–111** *INTERIOR DESIGN*: Molly McGowan Interiors; *CABINETRY*: Rutt of Lafayette, www.ruttoflafayette.com **112–113** *INTERIOR DESIGN*: Hilary Thatz; *ARCHITECTURAL DESIGN AND CONSTRUCTION*: Dennis J. O'Connor, Design/Build; *GARDEN DESIGN*: Marilee A. Gaffney **116–117** *INTERIOR DESIGN*: Kit Parmentier/Allison Rose **118–119** *INTERIOR DESIGN*: Molly McGowan Interiors; *CABINETRY*: Rutt of Lafayette, www.ruttoflafayette **120** *INTERIOR DESIGN*: Kit Parmentier/Allison Rose **121** *DESIGN*: Cameron Polmanteer **122 (TOP)** *ARCHITECTURAL DESIGN*: Jarvis Architects **(BOTTOM)** *INTERIOR DESIGN*: Debi Cekosh/Cekosh Design Studio; *ARCHITECTURAL DESIGN*: Michael Gibson **123** *DESIGN*: Janine Liddle/A Room with a View **126 (TOP)** *INTERIOR DESIGN*: Jennie Gisslow **(BOTTOM)** *INTERIOR DESIGN*: Melissa Griggs; *ARCHITECTURAL DESIGN*: Bill Galli, www.wdgalli.com **127** *INTERIOR DESIGN*: Jan Kavale for Sunset's Northwest Idea House **128–129** *DESIGN*: Rosmari Agostini; *STYLING*: Mary Jane Ryburn **130–131** *INTERIOR DESIGN*: Kathryne Dahlman and Meg Carper/ Kathryne Designs **132 (TOP)** *ARCHITECTURAL DESIGN*: Bokal & Sneed Architects **(BOTTOM)** *DESIGN*: Jenny and Peter Venegas **133** *LANDSCAPE DESIGN*: The Berger Partnership **134 (TOP)** *DESIGN*: Artistic Botanical Creations **(BOTTOM)** *DESIGN*: John Copeland **135** *INTERIOR DESIGN*: Claudia Fleury/Claudia's Designs, www.claudiafleury.com **136–137** *INTERIOR DESIGN*: Michaela Scherer Interior Design and RozaLynn Woods Interior Design **138–141** *INTERIOR DESIGN*: Linda Applewhite **142–143** *DESIGN*: Sandra C. Watkins; *PAINT COLOR AND FABRICS*: Joan Osburn/Osburn Design, www.osburndesign. com; *PAINT*: Mark McMahon and Mark Dillon/Chameleon Fine Painting; *OFFICE UNIT AND SHELVING*: Thomas Wold Furniture Design and Fabrication **144–145** *INTERIOR DESIGN*: Roberta Brown Root **146–147** *INTERIOR DESIGN*: Trish Dietze; *FLORAL DESIGN*: Tom Stokey; *GARDEN DESIGN*: Trish Dietze, Randy Bommarito, and Joye Long **148–149** *DESIGN*: Sarah Kaplan/Great Jones Home; *FLORAL DESIGN*: Nisha Kelen/Fleurish **150–151** *INTERIOR DESIGN*: Gigi Rogers Designs, www.gigirogersdesigns.com **152–153** *INTERIOR DESIGN*: Shirley Jensen/Forget-Me-Nots Designs; *ARCHITECTURAL DESIGN*: Michael Bolton; *CONSTRUCTION*: Dru Jensen; *DECORATIVE PAINTING*: Jolene Howell **154–155** *DESIGN*: Freddy Moran **156–157** *INTERIOR DESIGN*: Sasha Emerson Design Studio **158–159** *INTERIOR DESIGN*: Monty Collins Interior Design **160–163** *ARCHITECTURAL DESIGN*: David Stark Wilson, www.dswdesign.com **164–167** *INTERIOR DESIGN*: Joan Osburn/Osburn Design, www.osburndesign.com

PRACTICAL DESIGN

169 *INTERIOR DESIGN*: Kathleen Navarra/Navarra Design Consultants **170** *INTERIOR DESIGN*: Melissa Griggs Interior Design; *ARCHITECTURAL DESIGN*: Bill Galli, www.wdgalli. com **171 (BOTTOM)** *INTERIOR DESIGN*: Camille Fanucci/Interior Design Concepts, www.fanucciinteriordesign.com, and Patricia Whitt Designs **173 (TOP)** *INTERIOR DESIGN*: Paulette Trainor/Trainor and Associates Design **(BOTTOM)** *INTERIOR DESIGN*: Carol S. Shawn **176–177** *INTERIOR DESIGN*: Joan Osburn/Osburn Design, www.osburndesign.com

178–179 *INTERIOR DESIGN:* Frank Van Duerm Design Associates **182** *INTERIOR DESIGN:* Tres McKinney/ Laura Ashley **183 (TOP)** *INTERIOR DESIGN:* Kathleen Navarra/Navarra Design Consultants **(BOTTOM)** *DESIGN:* "idea house" at San Francisco Design Center **184** *DESIGN:* "idea house" at San Francisco Design Center **185 (TOP)** *INTERIOR DESIGN:* Jeff Shuller **(BOTTOM)** *INTERIOR DESIGN:* David Ramey/David Ramey Interior Design **186–187** *INTERIOR DESIGN:* Tres McKinney/Laura Ashley **192** *INTERIOR DESIGN:* Tobeler Design, www.tobelerdesign.com **193 (TOP)** *INTERIOR DESIGN:* Victoria Lohse/Korb Interiors, www.design4thepassionate.com **194 (TOP)** *INTERIOR DESIGN:* Marc Reusser and Debra Bergstrom/Reusser Bergstrom Associates, www.rbadesign.com **(BOTTOM)** *INTERIOR DESIGN:* David Dalton Associates Inc., www.daviddaltoninc.com **195** *INTERIOR DESIGN:* Richard Witzel & Associates **196 (BOTTOM)** *DESIGN:* Summer House at One Ford Road, Newport Beach, by Pacific Bay Homes **197** *INTERIOR DESIGN:* Jeff Shuller **198 (TOP)** *INTERIOR DESIGN:* Kimberly Lamer Interiors and Sandra Lamer Interiors **(BOTTOM)** *ARCHITECTURAL DESIGN:* J. Allen Sayles **199** *DESIGN AND DECORATIVE PAINTING:* Peggy Del Rosario **200** *INTERIOR DESIGN:* Kimberly Lamer Interiors; *CONSTRUCTION:* KNK Builders; *DECORATIVE PAINTING:* Jean-Pierre Berthy **201 (TOP)** *ARCHITECTURAL DESIGN:* Steven Goldstein **203** *INTERIOR DESIGN:* Kimberly Lamer Interiors and Sandra Lamer Interiors **204** *INTERIOR DESIGN:* Richard Witzel & Associates **206** *INTERIOR DESIGN:* Peter R. Baty **207 (TOP LEFT)** *INTERIOR DESIGN:* Mark Sommerfield/Derapage Design, www.derapage.com **(TOP RIGHT)** *INTERIOR DESIGN:* Paulette Trainor/Trainor and Associates Design **(BOTTOM LEFT)** *INTERIOR DESIGN:* David Dalton Associates Inc., www.daviddaltoninc.com **(BOTTOM RIGHT)** *DECORATIVE PAINTING:* Studio Christo Braun, www.christobraun.com **208** *ARCHITECTURAL DESIGN:* James Shay; *FURNITURE DESIGN:* Jeff Benedetto **209 (TOP)** *DESIGN:* David Stark Wilson, www.dswdesign.com **(BOTTOM)** *ARCHITECTURAL DESIGN:* Steven Foote/Perry Dean Rogers & Partners **210 (TOP)** *INTERIOR DESIGN:* Agins Interiors **(BOTTOM)** *PAINT:* Sydney Harbour Paint Company, www.sydneyharbourpaintco.com **211 (BOTTOM)** *INTERIOR DESIGN:* Lisa DeLong/DeLong Designs & Interiors **212 (TOP)** *DESIGN:* Michael Walters **(BOTTOM)** *INTERIOR DESIGN:* Jeff Shuller **213** *DESIGN:* Michael Walters **214** *INTERIOR DESIGN:* Tucker & Marks Inc., www.tuckerandmarks.com **215 (TOP)** *INTERIOR DESIGN:* Roberta Kuri/Classic Interior Designs **(BOTTOM)** *INTERIOR DESIGN:* Carolyn E. Oliver-Broder/Oliver's Interiors and Antiques, www.oliversinteriors.com; *DECORATIVE PAINTING:* Loretta Weeks **216 (TOP)** *INTERIOR DESIGN:* Denise Foley Design and David Brewster **(BOTTOM)** *INTERIOR DESIGN:* Trish Dietze; *FLORAL DESIGN:* Tom Stokey **217** *DESIGN:* Loretta Gargan Landscape + Design **218 (TOP)** *INTERIOR DESIGN:* Shirley Jensen/Forget-Me-Nots Designs; *ARCHITECTURAL DESIGN:* Michael Bolton; *CONSTRUCTION:* Dru Jensen; *DECORATIVE PAINTING:* Jolene Howell **(BOTTOM)** *DESIGN AND DECORATIVE PAINTING:* Peggy Del Rosario **219 (BOTTOM)** *DESIGN:* Sarah Kaplan/Great Jones Home; *FLORAL DESIGN:* Nisha Kelen/Fleurish **220 (TOP)** *DESIGN:* "idea house" at San Francisco Design Center **(BOTTOM)** *INTERIOR DESIGN:* Robert Salazar and Richard McNulty **221** *ARCHITECTURAL DESIGN:* James Shay; *IRON FABRICATOR:* John O'Hare **222** *INTERIOR DESIGN:* Denise Foley Design and David Brewster **223 (LEFT)** *DESIGN:* Freddy Moran **(RIGHT)** *DESIGN:* Sue Kalm

GETTING COLOR RIGHT

224–225 *INTERIOR DESIGN:* Joan Osburn/Osburn Design, www.osburndesign.com **226** *INTERIOR DESIGN:* Eugenia Erskine Jesberg/EJ Interior Design, www.ejinteriordesign.com **227 (TOP)** *INTERIOR DESIGN:* Nestor D. Matthews/Matthews Studio **(BOTTOM)** *INTERIOR DESIGN:* LouAnn Bauer, Bauer Design, www.bauerdesign.com **232** *ARCHITEC-*

TURAL DESIGN: Alla Kazovsky/Kids' Studio **233 (TOP LEFT)** *INTERIOR DESIGN:* LouAnn Bauer, Bauer Design, www.bauerdesign.com **(TOP RIGHT)** *INTERIOR DESIGN:* Sasha Emerson Design Studio **(BOTTOM)** *ARCHITECTURAL DESIGN:* Steven Goldstein **234** *DESIGN:* David and Vicki Ritter; *CONSTRUCTION:* David Ritter Construction **235** *INTERIOR DESIGN:* Joan Osburn/Osburn Design, www.osburndesign.com **237** *INTERIOR DESIGN:* City Studios **238 (BOTTOM)** *ARCHITECTURAL DESIGN:* Andre Rothblatt **239 (TOP)** *INTERIOR DESIGN:* Colienne Brennan/Brenco Design; *DESIGN:* Urban Development Group of Denver, adapted by Pacific Peninsula Architecture **(BOTTOM)** *INTERIOR DESIGN:* City Studios **241 (TOP)** Eugenia Erskine Jesberg/EJ Interior Design, www.ejinteriordesign.com **242 (TOP)** *INTERIOR DESIGN:* Joan Osburn/Osburn Design, www.osburndesign.com **(BOTTOM)** *ARCHITECTURAL DESIGN:* Tim Andreas **243 (TOP)** *INTERIOR DESIGN:* Alison Lufkin/Sullivan & Company **244 (TOP)** *INTERIOR DESIGN:* Kimberly Lamer Interiors **(BOTTOM)** *DESIGN:* Brad Polvorosa **245 (TOP)** *INTERIOR DESIGN:* Susan Federman & Marie Johnston Interior Design **246 (TOP)** *INTERIOR DESIGN:* City Studios **(BOTTOM)** *INTERIOR DESIGN:* Elizabeth Hill, Selby House Ltd.; *WINDOW TREATMENT:* Rosetti & Corriea Draperies **247 (TOP)** *DESIGN:* Freddy Moran **(BOTTOM)** *INTERIOR DESIGN:* Lisa DeLong/DeLong Designs & Interiors **248 (BOTTOM)** *DECORATIVE PAINTING AND FURNITURE:* Debra Disman/The Artifactory; *ANGEL:* Christina Spartano; *WINDOW TREATMENT:* Colleen Bailey **249 (TOP)** *INTERIOR DESIGN:* Joan Osburn/Osburn Design, www.osburndesign.com **(BOTTOM)** *DESIGN AND ARCHITECTURAL DESIGN:* Carlos Jimenez **250 (TOP)** *INTERIOR DESIGN:* Kathy Coomer/Art Pie, Daniel Daniloff/Design Changes, and Kay Kimpton/K Kimpton Contemporary Art **(BOTTOM)** *PAINT:* Sydney Harbour Paint Company, www.sydneyharbourpaintco.com **251 (TOP)** *DESIGN:* "idea house" at San Francisco Design Center **(BOTTOM)** *PAINT:* Sydney Harbour Paint Company, www.sydneyharbourpaintco.com **252 (BOTTOM)** *LIGHTING DESIGN:* Epifanio Juarez/Juarez Design; *INTERIOR AND ARCHITECTURAL DESIGN:* Scott Design **253 (BOTTOM)** *INTERIOR DESIGN:* Joan Osburn/Osburn Design, www.osburndesign.com **254 (TOP)** *INTERIOR DESIGN:* Joan Osburn/Osburn Design, www.osburndesign.com **(BOTTOM)** *INTERIOR DESIGN:* Penelope Rozis Interior Design, www.pennyrozis.com **255 (TOP)** *INTERIOR DESIGN:* Kendall Wilkinson Design **(BOTTOM)** *INTERIOR DESIGN:* Tucker & Marks Inc., www.tuckerandmarks.com; *ARCHITECTURAL DESIGN:* Hunt, Hale & Associates; *CONSTRUCTION:* Kelly Pacific; *DECORATIVE PAINTING:* Page Kelleher **256 (BOTTOM)** *INTERIOR DESIGN:* David Dalton Associates Inc., www.daviddaltoninc.com **257 (TOP)** *INTERIOR DESIGN:* Joan Osburn/Osburn Design, www.osburndesign.com **(BOTTOM)** *DESIGN:* Donghia **259 (TOP)** *INTERIOR DESIGN:* Joan Osburn/Osburn Design, www.osburndesign. com **261 (LEFT)** *DESIGN:* Sandra C. Watkins; *PAINT COLOR AND FABRICS:* Joan Osburn/ Osburn Design, www.osburndesign.com **262** *DESIGN AND DECORATIVE PAINTING:* Adele Crawford Painted Finishes **263 (TOP)** *DESIGN AND CONSTRUCTION:* Lamperti Associates **(BOTTOM)** *INTERIOR DESIGN:* David Dalton Associates Inc., www.daviddaltoninc.com **264** *INTERIOR DESIGN:* Jeff Shuller **265 (TOP)** *INTERIOR DESIGN:* Kathy Coomer/Art Pie, Daniel Daniloff/Design Changes, and Kay Kimpton/K Kimpton Contemporary Art **(BOTTOM)** *DESIGN:* "idea house" at San Francisco Design Center

ELEMENTS OF A ROOM

274–275 *INTERIOR DESIGN:* Jeff Shuller **278** *DESIGN:* David Barrett and Peter Rosson **279** *DESIGN:* Freddy Moran **280** *DECORATIVE PAINTING:* Deborah Disman/The Artifactory Studio **281** *INTERIOR DESIGN:* Melissa Griggs Interior Design **283 (TOP)** *INTERIOR DESIGN:* LouAnn Bauer, Bauer Design, www.bauerdesign.com; *DECORATIVE PAINTING:* Jennifer LaPierre **(BOTTOM)** Laura Ashley **284** *INTERIOR DESIGN:* Neos Design **285** *DECORATIVE PAINTING:* Lynne Rutter, www.lynnerutter.com **286 (3)** *DECORATIVE PAINTING:* Robert O'Conner Designs **(4)** *INTERIOR DESIGN:* Threadneedle Street of Montclair; *DECORATIVE PAINTING:* Lillian Bingham and Katie Scott Rosenshein/Paintrix **(5)** *INTERIOR DESIGN:* Stephanie Stokes **(6)** *DECORATIVE PAINTING:* Erik Seniska **288 (1)** *INTERIOR DESIGN:* Susan Hunter; *ARCHITECTURAL DESIGN:* Daniel Hunter **(2)** *DESIGN:* Debbie Weiss

(4) *INTERIOR DESIGN:* D. Kimberly Smith/Deer Creek Design (5) *INTERIOR DESIGN:* Tobeler Design, www.tobelerdesign.com (6) *INTERIOR DESIGN:* Douglas Boggs/Boggs Design **290** (1) *INTERIOR DESIGN:* Eugenia Erskine Jesberg/EJ Interior Design, www.ejinteriordesign.com (2) *ARCHITECTURAL DESIGN:* Chuck Peterson (3) *INTERIOR DESIGN:* Kimberly Lamer Interiors; *CONSTRUCTION:* KNK Builders; *DECORATIVE PAINTING:* Jean-Pierre Berthy (5) *DESIGN:* Paul Wiseman (6) *ARCHITECTURAL DESIGN:* Reiter & Reiter **292–293** *INTERIOR DESIGN:* Joan Osburn/Osburn Design, www.osburndesign.com **294** *INTERIOR DESIGN:* Jeanese Rowell Design, www.jrdesign.com **295** *DESIGN:* Woodis Demayo **296** (1) *ARCHITECTURAL DESIGN:* Philip Mathews, www.mathewsarchitect.com (2) *INTERIOR DESIGN:* Arabesque (3) *DESIGN:* Brian Murphy (4) *INTERIOR DESIGN:* Drysdale Associates Interior Design (5) *INTERIOR DESIGN:* Gordon Phaby/Sechrist Design, www.sechristdesign.com (7) *INTERIOR DESIGN:* Ann Jones Interiors (8) Timbergrass, www.timbergrass.com **298** (3) *INTERIOR DESIGN:* Kathleen Navarra/Navarra Design Consultants (6) *INTERIOR DESIGN:* Roberta Brown Root (7) *ARCHITECTURAL DESIGN:* Morimoto Architects, www.morimotoarchitects.com (8) Alexander's Decorative Rugs, www.alexandersrugs.com **300** (1) *INTERIOR DESIGN:* Debi Cekosh, Cekosh Design Studio (2) *INTERIOR DESIGN:* Barbara Magee and Ann Johnson/Custom House Furniture (4) *DESIGN:* Lynne Barry Roe (5) *INTERIOR DESIGN:* Arabesque **302** (1) *ARCHITECTURAL DESIGN:* Morimoto Architects, www.morimotoarchitects.com (2) *DESIGN:* Taylor Woodrow (3) *DESIGN:* Taylor Woodrow (4) *INTERIOR DESIGN:* Kimberly Lamer Interiors; *CONSTRUCTION:* KNK Builders; *DECORATIVE PAINTING:* Jean-Pierre Berthy (5) Galleria Tile (6) *ARCHITECTURAL DESIGN:* Remick Associates Architects-Builders Inc.; *TILE:* Stone Light Tile Company **305 (TOP)** *INTERIOR DESIGN:* Beatrice Krell; *LIGHTING DESIGN:* Linda Ferry **(BOTTOM)** Jill Smith/Insatiable Studios **306** *ARCHITECT:* Cliff May **307** *INTERIOR DESIGN:* Michelle Pheasant Design; *LIGHTING DESIGN:* Linda Ferry; *ARCHITECTURAL DESIGN:* Charles Rose **308** *ARCHITECTURAL DESIGN:* Olson/Sundberg Architects **309 (TOP)** *INTERIOR AND LIGHTING DESIGN:* Kenton Knapp **(BOTTOM)** *ARCHITECTURAL DESIGN:* Backen, Arragoni & Ross **310** (1) *ARCHITECTURAL DESIGN:* Marc Randall Robinson; *LIGHTING DESIGN:* Epifanio Juarez/Juarez Design; *INTERIOR AND ARCHITECTURAL DESIGN:* Scott Design (2) *INTERIOR DESIGN:* Lawrence Masnada; *LIGHTING DESIGN:* Randall Whitehead/Lightsource (3) *INTERIOR DESIGN:* Joan Osburn/Osburn Design, www.osburndesign.com (4) *INTERIOR DESIGN:* Kathy Coomer/Art Pie and Daniel Daniloff/Design Changes (5) *INTERIOR DESIGN:* Gigi Rogers Designs, www.gigirogersdesigns.com (6) *INTERIOR DESIGN:* Tucker & Marks Inc., www.tuckerandmarks.com (7) Jill Smith/Insatiable Studios **312–313** *LIGHTING DESIGN:* Melinda Morrison Lighting Design; *ARCHITECTURAL DESIGN:* Byron Kuth, Liz Ranieri, and Doug Thornley of Kuth/Ranieri **314** *INTERIOR DESIGN:* Joan Osburn/Osburn Design, www.osburndesign.com **315 (LEFT)** *INTERIOR DESIGN:* J. van Doorn Design **(RIGHT)** *INTERIOR DESIGN:* Susan Federman & Marie Johnston Interior Design **316** (1) *INTERIOR DESIGN:* Paulette Trainor/Trainor and Associates Design (2) *INTERIOR DESIGN:* Lindsay Steenblock/County Clare Design (3) *INTERIOR DESIGN:* Janice L. McCabe/McCabe & Sommers Interiors (4) *INTERIOR DESIGN:* Kathryne Designs (5) *INTERIOR DESIGN:* Joel Hendler and Christopher Pollack/Hendler Design, www.hendlerdesign.com (6) *INTERIOR DESIGN:* Claire L. Sommers/McCabe & Sommers Interiors (7) *INTERIOR DESIGN:* Lisa DeLong/DeLong Designs & Interiors **318** (1) *INTERIOR DESIGN:* Dominique Sanchot Stenzel/La Belle France (2) smith+noble windoware, Maxwell Window Shades, and The Roman Shade Co. (3) *INTERIOR DESIGN:* Dianna V. (4) *INTERIOR DESIGN:* George Davis Interiors (5) *INTERIOR DESIGN:* Elizabeth Benefield (6) smith+noble windoware (7) *INTERIOR*

DESIGN: Frank Van Duerm Design Associates **320** (**1**) INTERIOR DESIGN: Lynz Designs & Associates (**2**) INTERIOR DESIGN: Colienne Brennan (**3**) smith+noble windoware (**4**) INTERIOR DESIGN: Kathryn Hill Interiors (**5**) DESIGN: Summer House at One Ford Road, Newport Beach, by Pacific Bay Homes (**6**) DESIGN: Japan Woodworking and Design **322** (**1**) INTERIOR DESIGN: Monty Collins Interior Design (**3**) INTERIOR DESIGN: Tres McKinney/Laura Ashley (**4**) INTERIOR DESIGN: Kathryne Designs (**5**) INTERIOR DESIGN: Elizabeth Hill/Selby House Ltd. (**6**) INTERIOR DESIGN: Janice L. McCabe/McCabe & Sommers Interiors **324** (**1**) Cassidy West, Creative Expressions, Kirsch, and Springs Window Fashion (**2**) INTERIOR DESIGN: Kit Parmentier/Allison Rose (**3**) INTERIOR DESIGN: LouAnn Bauer, Bauer Design, www.bauerdesign.com (**4**) DESIGN AND DECORATIVE PAINTING: Peggy Del Rosario (**5**) Creative Expressions and Kirsch (**6**) INTERIOR DESIGN: Joan Osburn/Osburn Design, www.osburndesign.com **326** INTERIOR DESIGN: Gigi Rogers Designs, www.gigirogersdesigns.com **327** INTERIOR DESIGN: Richard Witzel & Associates **328** INTERIOR DESIGN: Drysdale Associates Interior Design **329** INTERIOR DESIGN: Judith Swenson and Kathy Bloodworth/Interior Concepts **330** INTERIOR DESIGN: Traci Larsen, assisted by Dawn Busalacchi **332** INTERIOR DESIGN: Norm Claybaugh/ Juvenile Lifestyles Inc., www.juvenilelifestylesinc.com **333** INTERIOR DESIGN: Roberta Brown Root **334** DESIGN: "idea house" at San Francisco Design Center **335** INTERIOR DESIGN: Gigi Rogers Designs, www.gigirogersdesigns.com **336** (**2**) DESIGN: Sarah Kaplan/ Great Jones Home (**3**) INTERIOR DESIGN: Gigi Rogers Designs, www.gigirogersdesigns.com (**4**) INTERIOR DESIGN: Kathryn Hill Interiors (**5**) INTERIOR DESIGN: Camille Fanucci/Interior Design Concepts, www.fanucciinteriordesign.com, and Patricia Whitt Designs (**6**) DCS Décor (**7**) INTERIOR DESIGN: Janine Liddle/A Room with a View (**8**) DCS Décor **338** (**1**) INTERIOR DESIGN: D. Kimberly Smith/Deer Creek Design (**2**) INTERIOR DESIGN: Barbara McQueen Interior Design (**3**) Donghia (**4**) INTERIOR DESIGN: Molly McGowan Interiors (**5**) DCS Décor (**6**) DESIGN: Sarah Kaplan/Great Jones Home (**7**) DCS Décor (**8**) DESIGN: "idea house" at San Francisco Design Center **340** INTERIOR DESIGN: Jay Jeffers/Richard Witzel & Associates **341** DESIGN: Charles Riley **342** DESIGN: David Barrett and Peter Rosson **343** INTERIOR DESIGN: Kendall Wilkinson Design **345** INTERIOR DESIGN: Barbara McQueen Interior Design **346** (**1**) INTERIOR DESIGN: Kathleen Navarra/Navarra Design Consultants (**2**) INTERIOR DESIGN: Sasha Emerson Design Studio (**3**) Calico Corners (**4**) INTERIOR DESIGN: de sousa hughes, www.desousahughes.com (**5**) DESIGN: Geoffrey De Sousa/de sousa hughes, www.desousahughes.com (**6**) INTERIOR DESIGN: David Dalton Associates Inc., www.daviddaltoninc.com (**7**) INTERIOR DESIGN: Gordon Phaby/Sechrist Design, www.sechristdesign.com (**8**) INTERIOR DESIGN: Sasha Emerson Design Studio **348** (**1**) INTERIOR DESIGN: Joan Osburn/Osburn Design, www.osburndesign.com (**2**) INTERIOR DESIGN: Kathleen Navarra/Navarra Design Consultants (**3**) smith+noble windoware (**4**) INTERIOR DESIGN: Alla Kazovsky/Kids' Studio (**5**) Broadstreet Furnishings (**6**) Hedman Furniture (**7**) INTERIOR DESIGN: Norm Claybaugh/Juvenile Lifestyles Inc., www.juvenilelifestylesinc.com **349** INTERIOR DESIGN: Drysdale Associates Interior Design **350** (**1**) INTERIOR DESIGN: Bob and Isabel Higgins; DESIGN: Holden & Dupuy (**2**) INTERIOR DESIGN: Kathleen Navarra/Navarra Design Consultants (**3**) ARCHITECTURAL DESIGN: Scholz & Barclay Architects (**5**) INTERIOR DESIGN: Judith Swenson and Kathy Bloodworth/Interior Concepts (**6**) INTERIOR DESIGN: Kathleen Navarra/Navarra Design Consultants **352** (**8**) DESIGN: Eurodesign (**9**) INTERIOR DESIGN: Elizabeth Hill/Selby House Ltd. (**10**) INTERIOR DESIGN: Joan Osburn/Osburn Design, www.osburndesign.com (**11**) INTERIOR DESIGN: Laurie McCartney, www.babystyle.com **353** INTERIOR DESIGN: Jeanese Rowell Design, www.jrdesign.com **354** (**1**) CONSTRUCTION: Tom Hampson (**2**) INTERIOR DESIGN: Bauer Design, www.bauerdesign.com (**3**) INTERIOR DESIGN: Norm Claybaugh, Juvenile Lifestyles Inc., www.juvenilelifestylesinc.com (**4**) INTERIOR DESIGN: Tobeler Design, www.tobelerdesign.com (**5**) ARCHITECTURAL DESIGN: Sam Wells/Sam Wells & Associates; STYLING: Julie Atwood (**6**) INTERIOR DESIGN: Melissa Griggs Interior Design

photography

Jean Allsopp: 171 top, 201 bottom, 248 top; **Caroline Bureau, Robert Chartier, Michel Thibault:** 356–420; **James Carrier:** 168, 236, 283 bottom, 301, 324 (1, 5); **Jared Chandler:** 126 top; **J. Curtis:** 46 both; **Mark Darley/Esto:** 257 top; **Eurodesign:** 352 (8); **James Scott Geras:** 82, 185 top, 197 both, 212 bottom, 264, 274–275; Tria Giovan: 259 bottom; **Ken Gutmaker:** 21 right, 22, 24–25 all, 50–51 all, 56, 60–61 all, 74 bottom, 104–105 all, 112, 113, 122 top, 126 bottom, 135, 138–141 all, 152–153 all, 170, 180, 192, 201 top, 208, 214, 218 top, 233 bottom, 238 bottom, 243 top, 250 top, 257 bottom, 258 bottom, 265 top, 281 bottom, 283 top, 288 (1, 5), 294, 296 (1, 7), 298 (8), 304, 310 (4, 6), 322 (2), 324 (3), 338 (3), 348 (1), 350 (6), 354 (2, 4, 6); **Jamie Hadley:** 6, 7 both, 8, 9 both, 13, 18 top, 19, 65 top right, 94 both, 108–109 all, 116–117, 120 both, 137 bottom right, 142–143 all, 146–147 all, 150–151 all, 156–157 all, 183 top, 185 bottom, 193 top, 200, 207 top left, 216 bottom, 219 top, 233 top right, 244 top, 261 left, 284, 288 (6), 290 (3), 300 (2), 302 (4), 310 (5), 316 (4), 324 (2), 326, 335, 336 (5), 346 (4); **John M. Hall:** 286 (5); **Philip Harvey:** 36 left, 68, 69, 98 both, 132 top, 133, 134 top, 173 bottom, 199, 206, 212 top, 213 both, 218 bottom, 227 top, 237 bottom, 239 top, 242 top, 244 bottom, 249 top, 252 bottom, 253 bottom, 254 top, 259 top, 263 top, 292 left and bottom right, 293, 302 (1, 2, 3, 5, 6), 305 top, 307–309 all, 310 (1, 2), 312–313 all, 316 (3), 320 (2), 324 (4, 6), 352 (10); **Richard Horn:** 95 both; **Muffy Kibbey:** 240 bottom, 260 bottom; **Dennis Krukowski:** 286 (4); **Barry Lewis:** 128–129 both; **David Duncan Livingston:** 64–65 all, 99, 124, 125, 171 bottom, 245 bottom, 261 right, 276, 327, 352 (7); **Stephen Marley:** 306; **Barbara Elliot Martin:** 102–103 all; **Sylvia Martin:** 11 bottom, 193 bottom, 211 top, 277, 341; **Steven Mays:** 288 (3); **E. Andrew McKinney:** 1, 5, 11 top, 12 both, 14–17 all, 18 bottom, 20 both, 23, 26–27 all, 30–32 all, 34, 35, 38–39 all, 42–45 all, 47, 50 top left and bottom, 52, 57–59 all, 66, 70–72 all, 74 top, 74–75, 76, 78, 79, 80 bottom, 81, 83 both, 86–88 all, 90, 91, 92 top, 93, 96–97 all, 100, 101, 106–107 all, 110–111 all, 118, 119, 121, 123, 130–131 all, 132 bottom, 154–155 all, 158–159 all, 169, 173 top, 174–179 all, 181 both, 182, 183 bottom, 184, 186–189 all, 194 top, 195, 196 bottom, 198 both, 203 both, 204, 207 top right and bottom right, 210 both, 211 bottom, 215 bottom, 216 top, 220 both, 221, 222–223 all, 224, 226, 227 bottom, 232, 233 top left, 234, 235 both, 237 top, 238 top, 239 bottom, 241 top, 245 top, 246–247 all, 248 bottom, 250 bottom, 251 both, 252 top, 254 bottom, 255 both, 256 top, 258 top, 260 top, 265 bottom, 274, 278–280 all, 281 top, 282, 286 (3, 6), 288 (2, 4), 290 (1), 295, 296 (2, 6), 298 (1, 2, 3, 4, 7), 300 (5), 305 bottom, 310 (3), 314–315 all, 316 (1, 2, 5, 6, 7), 318 (1, 2, 3, 4, 5, 7), 320 (1, 4, 5, 6), 322 (1, 3, 5, 6), 324 (7), 330, 332, 334, 336 (1, 3, 4, 6, 7, 8), 338 (1, 3, 4, 5, 7, 8), 339, 340, 342, 343, 346 (1, 3), 348 (1, 2, 3, 5, 6, 7), 350 (2), 352 (9, 11), 353, 354; **Emily Minton:** 10; **David Papas:** 285; **J.D. Peterson:** 240 top; **David Phelps:** 136–137, 137 top; **Tom Rider:** 191 bottom, 196 top, 290 (2), 329, 350 (5), 354 (5); **Ogden Robertson:** 241 bottom, 331; **Sibila Savage:** 217; **Meg McKinney Simle:** 172; **Michael Skott:** 28–29 all, 37 all, 40–41, 41 right, 48–49 all, 54, 55, 80 top, 84–85 all, 114–115 all, 122 bottom, 144–145 all, 148–149 all, 191 top, 194 bottom, 207 bottom left, 215 top, 219 bottom, 256 bottom, 263 bottom, 296 (1, 5, 8), 298 (5, 6), 300 (1, 4), 310 (7), 322 (4), 333, 336 (2), 338 (2, 6), 345, 346 (2, 6, 7, 8), 350 (4); **Tim Street-Porter:** 2–3, 134 bottom, 190, 243 bottom, 249 bottom, 253 top, 290 (4, 5), 296 (3), 350 (1); **Sue Tallon:** 346 (5); **Brian Vanden Brink:** 40 left, 209 bottom, 286 (1, 2), 290 (6), 296 (4), 328, 344, 349, 350 (3), 354 (1); **John M. Vaughan:** 292 top right; **Dominique Vorillon:** 242 bottom; **David Wakely:** 62–63 all, 92 bottom, 127; **David Weigle:** 164–167 all, 224-225; **David Stark Wilson:** 160–163 all, 209 top; **Tom Wyatt:** 262, 300 (3); **Ed Young:** 73

INDEX